Hugh Fraser

Letters from Japan

A record of modern life in the island empire

Hugh Fraser

Letters from Japan
A record of modern life in the island empire

ISBN/EAN: 9783744722698

Printed in Europe, USA, Canada, Australia, Japan

Cover: Foto ©ninafisch / pixelio.de

More available books at **www.hansebooks.com**

LETTERS FROM JAPAN

AN OUTDOOR GREETING. *Frontispiece*

LETTERS FROM JAPAN

A RECORD OF MODERN LIFE IN
THE ISLAND EMPIRE

BY

MRS. HUGH FRASER

AUTHOR OF "PALLADIA," "THE LOOMS OF TIME," "A CHAPTER
OF ACCIDENTS," ETC.

WITH TWO HUNDRED AND FIFTY ILLUSTRATIONS

VOL. II

New York
THE MACMILLAN COMPANY
LONDON: MACMILLAN & CO., Ltd.
1899

All rights reserved

COPYRIGHT, 1899,
BY THE MACMILLAN COMPANY.

CONTENTS TO VOL. II

CHAPTER XXI

Enoshima, the Island of the Tortoise — The Sea-goddess's City — The Home of the Shells — "A Bath in the Wine of Life" — Kings and Queens of the Deep — Benten Sama's Temple — The Cave of the Dragon 1

CHAPTER XXII

A Sensational Journey — Ikao and the Great Hills — Kindly Showers — A Walk up the Gorge — Buddha among the Teacups — The Colour of Ikao — Pictures in the Village Street — Fishing for Goldfish 21

CHAPTER XXIII

From Ikao to Karuizawa — The Silk Harvest — A Rest at Iizuka — Climbing up the Pass — A Sea of Peaks — The Palace of Peace — Our own Policeman 41

CHAPTER XXIV

"In the Dawn of Time" — The Star Lovers and their Story — The Pitiful History of O Sho Kung 55

CHAPTER XXV

The Approach of the Storm — At the Heart of the Typhoon — A Funny Sight — The Usui Toge — The Story of a Hero, and a Heroine — Yamato's Repentance — "In the Sweet Open Fields" 73

CHAPTER XXVI

The Charcoal-burner loses his Way — "A Mistake no Crime" — Invasion! — Pilgrims and their Ways — Pilgrim Clubs — An Enterprising Old Lady 93

CHAPTER XXVII

The Autumn Typhoon — The Loss of the *Ertogroul* — Legends of Fuji — The Great Upheaval — Chinese Tradition and the Sacred Mountain — The Story of Jofuku — The Lotus Peak . . . 108

CHAPTER XXVIII

The Opening of the Diet — The Attack on the Russian Legation — *Soshi* at our own Gates — Prince Komatsu and the Grand Cross of the Bath — The Imperial Chrysanthemums 125

CHAPTER XXIX

Nikko at last! — The Bridge of Beauty and the Bridge of Use — In the Temple Courts — The Story of Iyeyasu — His Friend, Will Adams, the Rochester Pilot — A Piece of Imprisoned Sunshine — Maples and Waterfalls — Chuzenji 148

CHAPTER XXX

Another Christmas Tree — Babies, European and Japanese — Ideals of Home and School — A Day at Meguro — A Little *Samurai* Girl — A Visitation of Influenza — Miyanoshita as a Sanatorium — Burning of the Houses of Parliament 168

CHAPTER XXXI

A Reading Society — Stories for the Japanese Ladies — The Empress's Verses — The Exaggeration of a Virtue — Marriage, Eastern and Western — Motherhood and Fatherhood — Parental Ties — New Laws of Inheritance 188

CHAPTER XXXII

The Death of Prince Sanjo — A State Funeral — A Brave Daughter — Ogita's Farewell — The Shiba Temples — A Feast of Beauty   210

CHAPTER XXXIII

In the Empress's own Garden — A White Sail set Square to the Wind — The Boys' Festival, its Origin and Meaning — Hideyoshi and his Battle Standard — The Mongolian Invasion 231

CHAPTER XXXIV

The Attack on the Cesarévitch — Loyal Women — Tsuda Sanzo and his Life History — A Nation in Mourning — Courageous Judges — A *Samurai* Maiden 253

CHAPTER XXXV

The Cottage at Horiuchi — The Dear Dead — Gifts for the Spirits — The Bottom of the Sea — Fishing in the Empress's Sea Garden . 272

CHAPTER XXXVI

Karuizawa again — Furihata is restored to us — Our own Volcano — The Mountain's Outer Court — The Iriyama Toge and the Cathedral Rocks — Sunset Lilies — A Forgotten Monastery and a Dying Man 285

CHAPTER XXXVII

Death of Father Testevuide — Holy Poverty — Unsuspected Philanthropists — The Leper Hospital again — A Leper's Death — Mère Sainte-Mathilde 303

CHAPTER XXXVIII

The Definition of a *Samurai* — *Samurai* Men and Women — *Samurai* Ideals — The Red Cross Society — Sword-damascening — Clan Government — Sayonara, Toki ! 312

CHAPTER XXXIX

A Terrible Earthquake — Destruction of a Province — *Kakke*, a Strange Disease — Japanese Trained Nurses . . . 326

CHAPTER XL

The Marriage of Prince Kanin and Princess Chiye Sanjo — The Wedding Dinner and the Wedding Cake — The Story of the Sun-goddess — Buddhist and Shinto Nuns — An Imperial Abbess 340

CHAPTER XLI

A Visit to the Museum — An Ancient Car — My Guide — Christian Relics — Persecutors and Persecuted — An Hour in the Art School among the Lacquer-workers 357

CHAPTER XLII

The Emperor's Silver Wedding — A Typical Gathering — *Nō* Dancing — The Curtain Falls 373

LIST OF ILLUSTRATIONS

VOL. II

	PAGE
An Outdoor Greeting .. *Frontispiece*	
Benten Sama	5
"Water, wind-dimpled, sun-kissed"	9
A Stone Lantern . . .	12
A Street in Enoshima .	15
Enoshima . . .	17
The Lights of the Chaya .	24
Moon and Lantern	27
Washing the Hands before praying in the Temple .	31
A China Shop	35
Silk Reeling	42
Our Summer Home Awake .	51
And Asleep . .	51
How the Rice grows	53
The Gentle Birds	59
Left Alone	60
Shadow Games	62
Shadow Games	63
A Daimyo's Daughter	67
The Departure of O Sho Kung . .	71
Pines in our Mountain Garden . .	74
A Rain Storm	77
In Miyadzu's Palace	80
Dhàrmi, a Sage who floated to Japan through the Water	97
Pilgrims	99
An Old Woman Pilgrim . .	104
Pleasure-boats on the Lake	111
In the Land of Reeds and Shadows	114

LIST OF ILLUSTRATIONS

	PAGE
Fujiyama from Hakone Lake	116
Fujiyama from Iwabuchi	121
H. I. H. Prince Fushimi No Miya	127
H. I. H. Princess Fushimi No Miya	127
Portrait and Autograph of H. I. H. Prince Arisugawa Taruhito	131
Portrait and Autograph of H. I. H. Princess Arisugawa Tada	135
H. I. H. Prince Kita Shirakawa	139
H. I. H. Prince Komatsu	141
H. I. H. Princess Komatsu	141
Chrysanthemums	145
The Bridge of Beauty, Nikko	151
A Temple Gate at Nikko	157
One of the Nikko Temples	159
The Long, Long Row of Buddhas	163
Chuzenji Lake	166
One of our Guests	170
One of the Children	178
Carrying Dolly	181
Yorkshire Margaret and her Brothers	184
A Japanese Professor and his Family	190
Tying on the Obi	193
A Japanese Lady	196
Coming from the Bath	205
Prince Sanjo	213
The Sacred Lotus	216
The Shiba Cemetery	224
Gate of the Shiba Temple	227
The Hall of the Books	229
A Very Old Cherry Tree in Bloom	233
The Fish Festival	237
A Pleasure-boat on the Canal	241
A Toy Standard	244
Kublai Khan	250
Kyoto	257
The Daughter of Viscount Aoki	266
A Bronze Incense-burner	268
Incense-burner in the Shape of a Junk	269
By the Summer Sea	274

LIST OF ILLUSTRATIONS

	PAGE
A Greeting	277
Great Fish and Little Fish	280
A Shoal of Fish	283
Asama Yama	292
Crows in Japan	295
The Running Postman	297
A Brown-winged Falcon	301
A Blind Masseur	305
"A Woman's Spirit is her Mirror"	317
"The Fencing has begun!"	318
A Samurai Lady imploring her Son not to commit Suicide	319
Results of the Earthquake	329
A Relief Camp	332
A Trained Nurse	337
Prince Kotohito Kanin	342
Moon Panel (in Gold Lacquer)	345
Moon and Mist (Gold Lacquer)	346
Prayer Beads among the Sacred Treasures of Isé	347
The God who is called the Thinker	350
Cherry Trees on the Sumida River	358
"The Empress . . . stands in the midst of them"	361
A Daimyo's Medicine-box in Lacquer (Back)	365
A Medicine-box (Front)	365
A Gold-lacquered Casket of the Earliest Period	367
A Happy Family	370
The Grand Master of Ceremonies	375
Count Inouye	377
Marquis Saigo	377
Silver Wedding Medal	379
Count Okuma	380
Baron Ito	381
My Silver Crane	385

LETTERS FROM JAPAN

CHAPTER XXI

ENOSHIMA, THE ISLAND OF THE TORTOISE. — THE SEA-GODDESS'S CITY. — THE HOME OF THE SHELLS. — "A BATH IN THE WINE OF LIFE." — KINGS AND QUEENS OF THE DEEP. — BENTEN SAMA'S TEMPLE. — THE CAVE OF THE DRAGON

ENOSHIMA, *May*, 1890.

THE name is so beautiful that I must write it at the top of my paper, although I am sitting in the hotel at Kamakura, and I cannot catch a glimpse of the dream island where I spent my yesterday.

Enoshima! On a lovely morning of sunshine and showers we left Kamakura, and passed through the low screen of hills which shuts it in to the right. The rain had laid the dust, and the air was keen and saltly sweet; for the night had been a somewhat stormy one. As we rounded down from the hills through deep-cut paths to the shore, we could hear the slow rollers thundering in before we caught a glimpse of the sea itself. Then, as we climbed the crest of a sand-dune, it lay wide and near, laughing in the sunshine, moving in lazy billows as if tired with its rough play.

of the night. A wide stretch of sand, dun in the shade, gold in the sun, and smooth as the cheek of a little child, swept away in a perfect curve that broke once under the climbing waves, and then rose high in a dusky embowered mass, floating in haze and sunshine out at sea, the island of the tortoise, Enoshima. "How can we reach it?" I asked of Ogita; "there is no boat there!" "Boat not in, but honourably walking," Ogita replied; and pointed to a light wooden causeway, which seemed to dance on the water, more like a toy bridge in a lady's garden than a serious link between island and mainland. But Ogita explained: the water was only a foot or two deep beneath the woodwork; and this would not be needed at all, were it not that, when the wind blew violently from the south, the waves washed up far beyond their usual limit. There was no danger; to-night we could probably return on the sands.

So leaving our jinrikshas, we started on foot towards the mystic island, so full of strange gods and strange presences, so wrapped in the web of story, so little a part of the life of to-day, that one almost expects to see it float out to sea and melt into cloud on the horizon. But not to-day, not until I have passed over the swaying bridge, where the water breaks up lightly, splashing my feet, and even throwing a little spray in my eyes, so that the splendid bronze gate of the sea-goddess's city towers and sways for a moment in my dazzled vision. Then the drops clear away, and I see the *torii* in all its grandeur. Its beautiful shape seems, as it were, to square the circle, to give all that is strong in angles, all that is lovely in curves; and through its dragon-wrought, wave-swept portal I see the long street of a climbing town, climbing high up to the sunshine on wings of fluttering blue that feather its sides above, on feet of mother-of-pearl, where the shells lie heaped on doorstep and window and wall — shells white and lustrous as bridal moons; shells dazzling and whorled as the snow-queen's crown; shells rosy, thick, thousands upon thousands, like shed petals piled together, as if all the cherry blossoms of the spring had been blown out to Enoshima on one saving breeze, and touched to immortality as they fell on the brown strand of Benten's magic island.

Enoshima is the home of all the shells in Japan, and those which the sea does not give it are brought there by the gatherers from far and near. My little friends on the Kamakura beaches have doubtless added their store to the rosy heaps which lie in open baskets on either hand as I climb the steep street. The flutter of blue wings overhead is made by hundreds of shop signs, strange white letters on blue cotton for the most part, hanging close together, and serving as a sign to the passer-by, and a shade to the indwellers of the little houses. To these people the sea is their one treasure-house, the gracious provider for all their simple needs; and they take it and its wonders for granted. To us, outsiders, who go to Enoshima once in a lifetime, the visit is a revelation of the riches and beauties of the world of water that laps round our world of earth. How can I put before you any picture of the white and rosy wonders piled on either side of the rough, poor little street? In Europe we never see these things in their glory; occasionally one poor specimen, brought home in a seaman's chest, finds its way to a dull shop, grey and mournful as the northern winter, and arrests us as with a dazzle of tropical sunshine, a flushing of rose, and a call of the southern sea. In my wanderings about Vienna, of all unlikely places, I came once on a naturalist's den, where, in a dusty corner, lay one of these incurled cups of the sea, warm ivory on the fluted verge, sunset colour nearer the heart, its curves as free and fine as the soft blown draperies on young limbs which some Greek sculptor saw in the laurel groves of Hellas and reproduced with tears in his slavery in Rome. I knelt down, there in Vienna, and put my ear to the great shell's mouth; and deep in its heart it was singing still, a song of morning seas and velvet sands and fisher-lads, the song that I heard again to-day on the sacred steps of Enoshima. For Enoshima is sacred, from the caves at its foot to the temples on its summit; consecrated at first to Benten, the goddess of love and good fortune, always gracious and helpful to the lads who must make their living at sea. But Benten was a Buddhist goddess, and at the so-called "Purification of Shinto" in the early part of the present reign, she was banished from her temples in Enoshima with other Buddhist divinities, and her island kingdom was given over to the care of Shinto priests. But the people in Enoshima have not concurred in the Imperial condemnation, and Benten Sama still reigns there, none the less supreme because she is invisible. The first

BENTEN SAMA

fisher-lad on the shore will offer to guide you to her temple, and in the little silent curious crowd which follows you from place to place deprecatory glances and pitying smiles will be exchanged if you say that you do not mean to climb so far.

And at first, in truth, I did not say I would; for I thought the hours of daylight would hardly see me past the street of shells. The sun was mounting high, and shot down hotly between the flutterings of the flags; inside the low shops were a thousand strange things, to be bought for such tiny sums that all my following had both hands full in half an hour; a breeze from the sea, warm and cool at once, and wholly salt and refreshing, lifted the cotton screens and caused them to rustle and snap joyously; and I stayed on, turning from one thing to another in the luminous low shops. The light has a strange quality in Enoshima. All through Japan it is admirably strong and pure; but here it almost has a colour of its own — a colour made of the sheen of mother-of-pearl and the gem-gleams under the sea, and morning haze, and the shadow of the rock on the waves; a million vibrations reaching the eye at once, all dancing, alive, iridescent, melted in one copious wash of sunshine, to me like a bath in the wine of life. Against it all shadows are transparent, cool, just light of another colour, light asleep, no darkness anywhere. The low-roofed treasure-house of shells has no dusky corners; every detail is absolutely clear, every beauty stands out to be praised and catalogued. Here at my feet are the kings and queens of the deep, — huge nautilus shells like hollow pearls filled with moonlight, open shells where Benten (or Venus or Freya, it is but a change of name) must have rested and slept one summer's night, for they are warm and rosy still, and reach out their curved lips laughingly for something to kiss; there are solemn conch shells, that have slept under brown seaweed in autumn starlight, and have caught the rhymed chant of the waves on the shore; open shells of green and grey mother-of-pearl, with shifting crimson gleams on the vigorous edge turned in like an ear strained and alert, where five round holes pierce through in mystic symmetry, as if the sea-king's daughter had been trying her earrings there; and there are little shells in myriads as I have said, thick as the Empress's cherry blossoms in spring; there are showers of spun glass, as sharp and silvery as moonbeams on ice, and these are the glass ropes of the beautiful Hyalonema sponges; there are huge tortoise shields, measuring four and five feet across, but these we would not look at, having been promised a sight of a mythical tortoise whose home is supposed to be somewhere in the Enoshima caves, and who is said to measure twenty-three feet across his old back; there are sprays of shells like lilies-of-the-valley dipped in milk, sea-foam lilies — they are born of a kiss, where the sun met the wave: and besides all these, hundreds of ornaments cut out of mother-of-pearl — big fish and little fish (I bought strings of these all hung together, of the softest pink, and rarely carved), hairpins with moons and rabbits and roses and branches of plum and cherry blossom; and tiny glass cups blown double, with a shell or two and a wisp of seaweed and a gleam of gold-dust loose inside the glass, running down to your lip as you drink, but never passing from the crystal prison unless you break it, when you will lose the value of three-quarters of a farthing, and destroy a thing of fairy beauty which would have told you stories of sea and sunshine to the day of your death!

At last I tore myself away from the shells, and climbed a path that led up by grey stone steps under solemn trees to an inn, which hangs like a gull's nest high on the face of the cliff, staring out to sea. And what a sea! The breadth and the blue of it! From that high place the horizon is so distant that it almost ceases to be; the world is a sapphire globe endomed in sun-shot crystal; earth seems an accident, Enoshima here a seaweed freak that has come up to breathe; and it may pass away, but sea and sunshine seem eternal in their white empire of noon.

The little inn is fresh and white, and open to the bay as an empty shell. On the side to the sea all the screens have been removed, and the wooden verandah runs past three rooms as open as itself, and then drops suddenly, as it were, down a very steep staircase, shining as lacquer and innocent of a handrail. Also the steps have no connecting planks; and as one goes up or down one sees between them the laughing brown faces of coolies or pilgrims resting in the space below, and much amused to see how high-heeled foreign shoes catch and slip on the polished wood. As I look down through the openings, I see the maid of the inn making my tea with care under Ogita's directions, and Rinzo is toasting bread on his chopsticks over a *hibachi;* so I turn back, and wait for the simple meal, feeling rather ashamed to need food at all in the face of such a view on such a morning! But one is only human after all, and emotions are distinctly exhausting; so I am very glad when the *musumë* comes in, on her knees, and pushes towards me a carved tray in the

"WATER, WIND-DIMPLED, SUN-KISSED"

form of a lotus leaf, with a teapot shaped like a shell, and cups painted with little goldfish swimming round the base of Fuji San.

My companions have gone away, and for a moment I am alone in Japan — that much of Japan which surrounds me here. On the floor are cool wheat-coloured mats, and thin silk cushions in bright silks lie about for seats. The inner screens of the rooms have much white wood about them; and what paper there is, is pale blue, with a sprinkling of silver pine needles on it. The alcove of honour, the *tokonoma*, is framed in by a tree, a beautiful ash trunk, still wearing its fine bark; and a branch reaching out is embedded in the ceiling, and marks the arch of the alcove. Here the paper is very rich, a running melon design in crusted silver, and against it hangs a scroll, with a poem written on it in bold grass characters. Below, on the step, stands a tall bronze vase, holding some sea-grasses and a branch of pine; and on the side of the frame opposite the tree trunk a bamboo stand for fans is hung, and holds two or three of the hotel fans, which are presented to the guests as keepsakes. They are rather violent in colour — on one side scarlet, with the name of the inn printed in white, but the back is softer, with a picture of an enormous turtle with a fringed tail creeping up on a very small rock; the rock represents Enoshima, and the turtle the inn, for it is called "The House of the Golden Turtle."

The *musumë* creeps in to know if I will have some more tea, and I keep her to tell me something about herself. Her name is Ko, she says, and she is seventeen, and very glad that I admire her bright-green sash, which was a present from her brother at New Year. Her brother is a waiter at Atami; and she too goes to Atami in the winter, for then no one visits Enoshima, and the mistress here keeps no maid. Wages? No, she has no wages, but her food and a summer dress; and the visitors are honourably kind. Two English ladies stayed here ten days a little while ago, and they also made pictures — ah! but this Okusama's picture is prettier; and she comes and laughs over the drawing of herself in my sketch-book, and then some one calls for her, and she bows and glides away; and I hear her drop softly down the polished stairs, and slip on her straw *zori* with a little click at the bottom.

And now the time for rest is over, and I must climb the hill and see Benten Sama's Temple, and go down to the caves on the other side, and do many things for which the day seems short. The sun has passed over to the other side of the island ridge, and all the path on this side is in shadow. A light moisture seems hanging in the air, and fern fronds are uncurling, and pine branches seem to be stretching in the cool relief of the afternoon. As we leave the inn and turn up the ascending road, a party of pilgrims pass us, an old, old man with his sons and grandsons, all carrying staves, with the little blue towels which they will take as offerings to the shrine tied to them, done up in gay printed papers. They look at us curiously, and go on, in single file, saying some prayers, I think, for they exchange no remarks on our appearance as they go by. We are taking it slowly, enjoying the delicious freshness of the sea, and in no hurry to face the sun, still hot on the other slope. And so we pass from terrace to terrace of the island stair; for the sides of Enoshima are steep, and rise from the sea in huge steps like the vine terraces of Amalfi. But here there are stone balustrades at the edge, and behind them stone lanterns, and here and there a *torii*, and here and there a shrine, decayed and empty, but not quite forgotten, as the rough bamboo vases filled with still fresh wild flowers testify; and more than once an incense-stick just lighted sends up its close-curling spiral of smoke, blue-grey against the weather-worn stone, and everywhere the background is deep-green foliage growing straight and thick against the cliff.

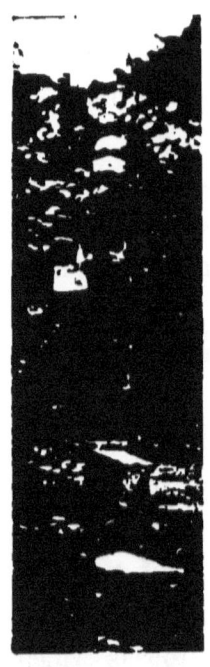

A STONE LANTERN

The three temples of Benten Sama stand one above the other, separated by a wave of dark trees, each sadder and more deserted than the last, till the third crowns the ridge with something of stately desolation. The Shinto reform, whatever it was, seems, like some other so-called reforms, to have been a thing sour and unlovely, strong only for destruction, and incapable of filling up the shrines emptied by its iconoclastic rage. Where it reigns alone, "purified," as its adherents call it, it strikes one with dull depression. There is nothing in the dusty mirror and the torn *gohei* to inspire hope in the future or courage in the present. The face of Buddha is as the face of a friend, serene, merciful, gracious to poor humanity; but in the mirror of Shinto man finds only his own travel-stained reflection — the picture of that self which must be left behind before he can enter into peace.

Round the entrance of the chief Temple is an enclosing fence, called, I think, the "Jewel Hedge" in Shinto phraseology, but enclosing no jewels here, or at least only the mystic ones which would have no value for mankind at large. The Temple is empty and dusty like the others; but Ogita, with superb contempt for the "purification of Shinto," persuades me to sit down on a mossy stone, and listen to his stories of Benten Sama and all her goodness and greatness and beauty. I think she must be Ogita's patron goddess, for he rarely waxes eloquent about any other, and smiles rather pityingly at many a strange idol that I want stories about. But when he speaks of Benten Sama his eyes light up, his delicate aquiline face takes on a flush of colour, and there is quite a ring in his queerly constructed phrases. He is a *samurai*, a great swordsman still, and a favourite instructor in the noble art; so I am a little surprised at this devotion to the lady of love and luck. As for explanations, ask them not of a Japanese! The springs of action for him and you are separated by an almost impassable gulf. After years of intercourse, he might understand the real drift of your question; more years would have to elapse before you could understand his answer.

But while we were philosophising on the portal of Benten's desecrated home, the sun had passed away from us to the western slope of the island, and we must follow, or night would fall long before we could reach the mainland again, for there is much to see on the western side. Unfortunately, I suppose, I am a very slow sight-seer. That which pleases me must be seen to the uttermost before I want to move on to the next object of interest, even if it be incomparably more important. On the very crest of Benten's island I found some little tea-houses, open to the sea, empty for the breeze to riot through, airy sun-dried nests, where one could sit in the shade of a thin awning, and look out on the blue world of water — water wind-dimpled, sun-kissed, deepest sapphire in the shadow of a rock a thousand feet below me, but fading into tender haze far off on the horizon, where, away to the south, the island volcano of Oshima sent up the thin spiral of smoke which I used to watch for hours from the Atami shore. That light cloud, never changing shape, white by night and grey by day, has a kind of symbolic importance in this coast landscape. It is like the gentle regret of a faithful soul, a shred of mist on the background of life, the sound of a sigh in every pause of its brave music!

Here on the hill a very, very old woman gave me tea, and bowed her poor grey head to the ground when I praised the view. She said her house was poor and mean, and I made Ogita tell her that it was rich in beauty, and her tea most refreshing; whereupon she made me a present of a fairy teacup, of the thinnest china, with the ghost of Fuji San dreamed into it — if you will forgive the barbaric phrase. English is a clumsy, square-toed vehicle of expression, and stumbles along, crushing a thousand beauties of my Japanese thought garden, which a more delicate language (or a

more skilful writer!) might have preserved for you.
The little old woman was such a personality, the only
soul in sight, for the other houses seemed empty; her
grey hair was cut almost short, and gathered in with
a comb at the back of her head; her hands were like
knotty twigs on old pine trees, and her brown body

A STREET IN ENOSHIMA

was so withered and sea-dried that it was more like a
weather-beaten shell than anything which still has to
consume and decay; her eyes were bright still, even
through the tears of old age, and her coarse blue
garments were clean and faded, as if they had often
been washed in salt water. One son was a soldier,
she said, one a fisherman, who had been drowned at
sea; her granddaughter had gone down the cliff to
wash her clothes, and—august thanks—would the lady
return some day—return soon? Sayonara, Sayonara!

We left her standing before the square opening which she called her house, behind her the farther sea, the awning over her head flapping like a dazzling white wing against its blueness, at her feet the first of a long flight of steps cut in yellowish stone, which led down the steep cliff to the famous cave of the Dragon, whose opening is hardly above high-water level. If the Dragon ever lived here, he went long ago — went perhaps with Benten Sama to the under-world; Ogita tells me that the cave only holds its name on account of its shape, like a dragon's tail, twisting and curving and diminishing as it runs into the island's heart, where it is lost in blackness. At the foot of the rude steps (far ruder and steeper than I cared for) one or two natural terraces are formed by rocks jutting out and then shelving down to the water. They are connected with planks, forming rather crazy bridges, much shaken by the thud of the water breaking below. We have to scramble over these to get round to the entrance of the cave; the water has receded now, and left a few pools, where boys are diving for crabs, the little Enoshima crabs which are much prized in Tokyo. Then we find a girl, who must be the granddaughter of our old hostess on the cliff, kneeling on bare knees by a pool, her sleeves all bound back, her skirts kilted up, washing some poor blue wisps of clothing which seem hardly worth the toil. We pass a stone lantern, pass the boys, who want to sell us crabs, and then suddenly our swaying bridge with its broken handrail turns where the sea rushes with a roar into the cleft

heart of the rocks, and we follow it dizzily, deafened with the thundering echoes of the cave, and more than once blinded by a drift of spray, breaking high on its wet black sides.

Some little way within the entrance we come to solid ground, marked by a shrine, where a soft gleam of light makes a ring of gold on the gloom — a little wooden shrine, which must, I think, be the one of which Rein says that it has to be removed every spring, and put back several feet from where it can stand in the winter, because, while the south-west monsoon blows, the water piles higher on all the south coast, and then falls again when the monsoon changes. As I approach I find the golden ring growing larger, and can distinguish a number of candles burning behind the shrine; they have been carried into the cave by pilgrims, and are left here as an offering when the exploration is over. A shadowy guardian sells some of them again to us, and we creep into the damp twisting passage, from which other passages branch off blackly. We pass rough gods hewn in the rock, grey and solemn, buried in this eternal darkness near the springs of things, feeling the earthquake rive its way to the light through the heart of the world, hearing the thud of breakers on the outer wall of their island castle; visited day after day in the kindly summer by poor pilgrims, rich in faith and devotion to the only gods their twilight has revealed, left alone in the long months of winter while the salt creeps over their faces like a veil, and the crawling sea things have it all to themselves in the empty passages. What! I must stoop and creep through that black hole to reach the last and most holy shrine? No, Ogita, the daylight is sweet, and holy too; and here there is a drip of dead water, the air is thick and grave-bound. Out to the world again, please; I have no mind to be buried before my time, and I fear to faint in this choking darkness. Ah! there it is, beyond the damp rock walls and the smoking candles, beyond the cave's mouth is my world — a world of sunlit breakers, and scudding clouds, and fresh salt breeze stinging every sense to triumphant life again.

An hour later I look back from the sandy pass over the dune. Enoshima seems to have swum out to sea, and lies a misty mass, its face turned away from me to the dull-red line which shows where the sun dropped but a few moments ago. The night is upon us, quick and cold; we must draw our wraps closely, as we speed along the darkened road. Sayonara, Enoshima!

CHAPTER XXII

A SENSATIONAL JOURNEY. — IKAO AND THE GREAT HILLS. — KINDLY SHOWERS. — A WALK UP THE GORGE. — BUDDHA AMONG THE TEACUPS. — THE COLOUR OF IKAO. — PICTURES IN THE VILLAGE STREET. — FISHING FOR GOLDFISH

IKAO, *July*, 1890.

THE summer quarters in Karuizawa were not quite ready, so we came up here for a fortnight, since Tokyo had become unbearably warm and damp. The dampness is here too; for it rains much, and between the rains a soft cool mist hangs on the hillsides and clings to one's garments, and even creeps into the rooms of Murumatsu's hotel, where we are staying. H—— could not leave Tokyo at once, so I came on first with a friend; and a rather adventurous time we two women had of it before we reached this nest in the clouds. There are many things which are still vague, uncatalogued as it were, in Japan, and the measurement of distance is one of them. You ask a weary foot-traveller with a pack on his back how far it is to the next town, and he replies, "A long way — at least five ri" (just about twelve miles). Then you meet a fresh, well-set-up youth coming out of a tea-house, where he has had a rest and a meal. "Is it really five ri to Ikao?" you ask, in a despairing voice; and he laughs as he replies, "Five ri! No, indeed; perhaps one and a half — not more!" All of which is very puzzling and misleading to us prosaic foreigners, who do not measure distances (as of course they should be measured) by our sensations in regard to them. And so it happened that my friend and I left Tokyo very comfortably towards noon, having four hours of railway journey, and, after that, four hours (as we were told) of easy hill-travelling, which would bring us to Ikao in time for sunset clouds, dinner, and twilight on the verandah and a full moon afterwards. The railway journey was new to me, for I have never travelled on this northern line before. The carriages are much more comfortable than those on the other lines, and by a kind attention of the English superintendent we found a charming little tea-table laid out in the carriage, and amused ourselves with making tea at least three times in the course of the short journey. The scenery is rather flat until Mayebashi is reached; but everything was still in its summer freshness, the little stations along the line are pictures of neatness, and at each one there is always a group of peasants and children and coolies, leaning over the great gates and gazing at the amazing toy, which seems to be no less interesting to them now than when it first ploughed its smoky way past their quiet villages.

At Mayebashi we left the train, and took refuge from the blazing heat in a cool tea-house, where we lingered willingly while Ogita, who had been sent on by an earlier train, organised the usual procession of jinrikshas and chair-coolies; these last took a great deal of finding and bribing, as chairs are quite unknown in this part of the world. My chair had come on in Ogita's train; but before I had been in it ten minutes, I regretted that I had not chosen the humble jinriksha instead, for the men had, of course, not learnt to keep step, and changed shoulder to the poles every few minutes, so that I felt somewhat as Mazeppa might have done between the four wild horses. I noticed O'Matsu and Ogita having a rather serious talk with the innkeeper, and found afterwards that they had been making inquiries as to the distance to Ikao, neither of them having been in this part of the country before. The answers had been disconcerting, and they concluded that the innkeeper was dishonestly exaggerating the length of the journey so as to keep us at Mayebashi for the night, so they decided that nothing need be said to me on the matter. So we started off, by white dusty roads across the burning plain; the day wore on and on, and the Ikao Mountains looked as far off as ever. We were very tired, and also hungry, for by some mistake Ogita had allowed the luncheon-basket to be sent on in the morning with the heavy luggage, and we could get nothing but Japanese tea and peppermint cakes at the teahouses on the road.

At last, to our intense relief, a light rain began to fall; but before we had ceased to be thankful for it, it became a deluge. Then the night fell unmistakably, and at last we pulled up at a *chaya*, whose yellow lanterns and leaping fire stood out pleasantly against the blackness of the great hills looming up behind it. The men were spent, and we and they quite drenched; so we stopped for a short rest. The poor coolies pulled off their straw sandals, caked with mud, and threw them

THE LIGHTS OF THE CHAYA

away; then crept round the big fire blazing in the lower part of the inn, the open kitchen where travellers of the lower class are welcome to rest and warm themselves. The *nesan* (or elder sister, as they call the maid) brought them steaming bowls of macaroni, of which we also would gladly have eaten but for the impossible flavouring of *daikon* which seemed to accompany it. *Daikon* is a giant horse-radish, having a naturally rank and corrupt odour; this the Japanese improve upon by various methods of pickling and long keeping, till, when it is ready for use, it is so pungent and horrible that, as somebody observed of Limburger cheese, it might be employed as a danger signal at sea. I once (perhaps rather unkindly) asked a Japanese gentleman how his people could enjoy such horrors; and he replied, "It is our Stilton cheese, you see!" The truth is, that the staples of food here — rice, macaroni, and a kind of pulse — are all quite tasteless, and must also be eaten in great quantities to sustain existence; so a strong cheap pickle is an absolute necessity to the masses.

Perhaps the *daikon* spurred me on. It seemed too all-pervading to escape from inside the house; and when Ogita, with a very long face, came to tell me that, according to local authorities, it would take us three hours of night-travelling through the pouring rain to reach Ikao, I decided to face that rather than remain where we were, without baggage or European food of any kind, and — with the *daikon*. So, slowly and unwillingly, we set off, hoping against hope that there might be some mistake about the distance. As we climbed into the hills, the darkness was so thick that often only the wet gleam of the coolies' lanterns showed me where my companions were. I had by this time taken to a jinriksha for the more speed; and the last glimpse I had of my chair showed it to me standing out in the village street, while one of the coolies, having got into it, was trying to copy my usual attitude, leaning back with a hand on either arm, and to smoke a pipe at the same time. He must have been dreadfully uncomfortable, for the rain was coming down on him in sheets; but he evidently felt quite repaid for that by sitting in the seat of honour which had sat so heavily on his shoulders all day.

We had a very weird night ride, through the mist and rain, over solitary moors, where we could only see a few yards of the track at a time. The men came along bravely, never grumbling at the awful state of the path — one cannot call it a road — and even making little jokes at the worst places. The cheery dauntlessness of these poor fellows makes one feel ashamed of growling over any of our much more bearable discomforts. But I was too much interested in the queer experience to feel the fatigue or even the chill of the night rain; there was just enough light to show enormous sweeps of rain-swept mountains, deep valleys full of white cloud armies that rose like awakened ghosts and crept up the hill behind us, pushing us on into the darkness beyond. Suddenly, in a lull of the rain, I saw a great white star moving slowly down towards me out of the sky. Only when it floated close to my eyes did I discover that it was the very patriarch of all the fireflies, though what he was doing abroad on such a night I cannot imagine. Now and then the men would stop to rest, and draw all our jinrikshas together against a bank, where the lanterns hung on the shafts made a faint circle of light in the ghostly air, and · showed visibly the hopeless wetness of all near objects. The coolies would get to the lee of our little wooden carriages, and try to light a pipe; and the whiff of their coarse tobacco floated comfortingly for a moment through the mist. Then they would start off again; and in a few minutes the first ones in the long line loomed huge and threatening on a rise before us against a pale patch of sky, behind which the full moon should have been shining.

At last we saw lights in the distance, and in a few minutes a whole tribe of little gnomes, carrying big round lanterns and huge oil-paper umbrellas, were bowing and bobbing beside us, and saying, "Murumatsu, Murumatsu," over and over again, to show that they came from the hotel. One last effort of our poor coolies dragged us up through an avenue of dripping firs, so steep that the trees might have been growing up the side of a house; and then we stopped for good under a hospitable porch full of red lanterns and smiling faces. Slowly we unpacked our drenched coverings, and crawled out, stiff and sore, and mighty glad to be under shelter at last. Oh the comfort of the sweet-smelling matted rooms, with their closed shutters, against which the rain beat in vain! In less time than it takes to tell it, our good Ogita and the servants had dry things unpacked, the wet wraps carried away, a pretty dinner-table laid out,

MOON AND LANTERN

with a bright lamp and fresh flowers to cheer us, and food and wine to make us forget the long hungry day. I felt rather like the forlorn little girl in the fairy tale, when the black hillside opened and the kind gnomes took care of her in their warm earth-home.

The view from those particular rooms is rather a celebrated one; so I rose and looked out the next morning as soon as the maid had crept round the balconies to remove the *amados*, the friendly outer shutters, which had kept out the rain of the night. Alas! it was the rain of the morning too; and the wide valley below us and the great mountains of Nikko beyond were only visible in shadowy gradations through the wet grey veil of rain. Not for this were they less beautiful; for the very greyness gives the outlines more grandeur, and the moving film of rain, now lighter, now heavier, now falling straight and sharp, now driven slanting up the valleys by a rush of the breeze, imparts a constant play of expression to the tear-stained face of Nature which it can never wear in the equalising gold of the sunshine. And when the worst is over, and the rain is sucked up into that wonderful mist of Japan, which makes and unmakes a hundred sky-pictures in an hour, each more weird and ethereal than the last, then one cannot quarrel with the rain. As I stand on the covered balcony, and smell the dear wetness of the earth and catch a stray drop on my cheek, my mind goes back to the thirsty lands of earth,— to our Roman campagna, burnt purple-brown in August, and too scorching to touch with the bare hand; to Chile, where every tree is sere by midsummer, and the gasping country is buried in its own dust before its ten months' drought is quenched in icy rain; to that "land of sand and ruin and gold," Pechili, where a child may be a year old before the rain has christened it; where I used to go and sit on the baked hillside by our temple home and look across the quivering plain to Peking and—down into the face of an English baby dying of the heat. And I remember there came a day when I said to its mother, "Take courage; if it only rains to-night, he will live! Surely that is a cloud in the south!" And the rain came that night, and the little one lived — to die of another year's heat. Ah, dear rain, it is not I that will be quarrelling with you this day! In the outer life, thank God for the kindly showers that temper the breeze of the sunshine; in the inner, thank Him still more for the grey clouds of anxiety and the wholesome tears of pain, which keep us from being burnt dry and hard in the noonday of our prosperity.

And as I finished these reflections my friend came and stood by my side, and said, "Come, it is lighter now; let us go and have a look at things." Then we went out into the queer terraced town, clinging so closely to the wall of the hill that the main-street is a staircase, and a steep one too. From it the side-streets branch off, herringbone-wise, full of little inns where the bathers stay; for Ikao has hot springs (115° F.), which have been used for the cure of many diseases since very early times, and which still attract great numbers of Japanese to the place. The town is built around and over the springs, which seem to bubble up so freely in this volcanic land, sometimes hot and strong, sometimes weak and tepid, but everywhere within the reach of the sick poor, who are able for very small sums to get cures which in Europe are costly in the extreme. Here, some two thousand five hundred feet above sea-level, the hot jets burst out of the green mountain-side, and the little town has had to accommodate itself to them. The long street of stairs, full of quaint shops and fluttering signs, ends in a tall shaft of still steeper steps above the town; and these are crowned by a little temple, with stone benches before it, where one can sit and gaze at the enormous hills across the sweep of the upland valley. The temple has stone lanterns, which are votive offerings, and many fluttering banners, which are also offerings, though of a more perishable kind. At the foot of its grey steps is a little terrace, which is all one iris garden in full bloom; the sun suddenly shone down on it as I looked, and a hundred flowers, white and blue and royal purple, shook out flags in the mountain breeze which came fresh and sweet round the spur of the hill from the woods beyond.

The breeze seemed to be showing us the way; so when we had rested a little, we left the temple, and followed a road leading towards a deep ravine on the right. Here a noisy river tears down over boulders the colour of rust, for the water is rich in iron, and coats everything exposed to it with a heavy yellow layer; but the level walk on the side of the ravine is

WASHING THE HANDS BEFORE PRAYING IN THE TEMPLE

so thickly wooded that the stream is hidden half the time, and only its everlasting song comes up to say it is there. Slowly we went on into the green heart of the hills, the path overhung by deepest woods above, and below, plunging down in sudden precipices to where the torrent literally boils over the yellow stones with clouds of steam and hot spray, and rushes on to turn a huge mill-wheel in the gorge, just as any common cold stream could do! But up on the path all is solitude and quiet, and it seems quite fitting to come unawares on a little shrine with a smiling Buddha sitting on his mat, amid countless offerings of cups and vases, and smaller Buddhas to keep him company. But Buddha took my breath away by smiling benignantly right into my eyes, and rocking forward on his base in friendly salutation. Then I saw that the shrine is only a little china shop, as clean and silent as the heart of a flower, and apparently about as distantly connected with money-making; for without even moving from his place, Buddha let me carry off an exquisite blue cup, for which he received seven cents, and seemed as satisfied as if I had spent seven pounds at his dainty shrine. Beyond him the road became suddenly steeper, and we stood for a moment gazing up its green murmuring arches, broken where a glorious white hydrangea hung out a dancing tent of blossom over the sun-flecked path.

At the end of the path is an inn, with baths and many patients; and one can buy strange specimens of petrified woods, and stone cups beautifully polished.

Here there is a beautiful network of bamboo pipes, supported on tree branches or wistaria roots, or anything else that comes handy; and they run all the way down the valley to supply the different hotels with the mineral water; and in the stream itself lie strips of cotton, which are left there until they have absorbed enough iron to turn them yellow, and are then used as strength-giving belts, much prized by the people.

On our return I think we must have entered every shop on the way. In one we bought whole pieces of Ikao cotton crape, a rough heavy fabric, with a brilliant reddish-yellow ground, exactly the colour of the iron-coated stones in the stream where the sun touches them; and the maker had the stream in his mind, I know, for up the lengths of yellow crape against the stream swim hundreds of vigorous carp, the symbol of persevering fortitude, amid waves and clouds dashed on in the sharp white and blue of a winter morning. The whole mass takes one's breath away with its rattling bravura of colour, and the eye rests gratefully on a pile of grey-green basket-work, made out of wistaria tendrils, the very tint of the twilight woods imprisoned in the meshes. Then there is pottery of every kind, for every use, but almost uniform in colour —the colour of Ikao, the colour of rust in the sun. There is a delight which I cannot name in finding these subtle harmonies, taken for granted by these people who are still close to the knee of Nature, but only touched by chance among us, who have forgotten

A CHINA SHOP

our nursery lessons in the dreary board-school of life. I see that in Japanese eyes I am a barbarian even in my buyings; for I take a dozen things which have nought to do with each other, and Ogita and O'Matsu look gravely disapproving when the fairings are all tumbled out together on the mats of my little sitting-room.

There is another walk in Ikao, and this one goes down instead of up the hill, and is quite full of excitements. As we turned down it, I saw a quaint group. A small child was standing stock still in the middle of the road, with her back towards us; her hair, shaven away in a neat tonsure on the top of her head, fell from there in a straight black curtain to her shoulders; her fat little body was wrapped in a pale-blue *kimono;* and in one hand she carried a teapot, pale blue also, and swinging by its wicker handle. Evidently she had been sent to fetch saké or hot water; but her little bare feet seemed rooted to the ground, and she was gazing with silent terror into the face of a terrible beast who had set himself down directly in front of her. The beast was a yellow mongrel (Ikao colour, of course), who, by cocking his ears and stretching his fore-legs out as long as possible, had brought his head just to the level of the little maid's, and was looking at her with an expression which said far more clearly than words: "Yes, my dear, I *am* a very terrible dog, and all this road belongs to me, and you have no business here whatever; but *perhaps* I won't eat you quite up this time — oh! oh!

who are these awful creatures?" One sight of us was enough; with a long howl, the terrible dog fled down the street, and the little girl clutched her teapot, and shrank to one side as far as the road would allow, and looked up at us pitifully, as if she would say: "You see, the dog didn't eat me; I hope you won't, either!"

So we went on quickly to set her mind at rest, and came on a still funnier sight. A little bath-house, with no door, close to the road, was sending out fumes of steam mixed with talk; inside, in a space not more than a yard square, three dames of the village, with only their heads above water, were having a good gossip. On the edge, among the discarded clothing, lay a baby, trying hard to wriggle into the water too. Of course all the heads turned to have a look at us; two of the ladies hopped out of the water like frogs, and sat on the edge of the bath discussing our appearance, absolutely untroubled by their own, and then hopped in again for another dip. I saw one of them walking home later, with most of her clothes under one arm and the baby on the other. There is so much desinvoltura about Japanese manners!

Farther on we came to a bow-and-arrow booth, where the owner was very anxious that we should have a shot at the painted target; but we were much more interested in a queer grey monkey, tailless as a Japanese cat, who was jumping about as far as his tether would let him, against grey-green rocks the very colour of himself. He too saw that we were foreign monsters of some kind, and showed off all his tricks

and then flashed his fiery red face and human eyes
round at us to see if we had been impressed by them,
and he was visibly chagrined when we moved on. At
the foot of the hill lives a knotty little old man, who
looks as if he had been made out of dried twigs. His
hair stands up in bristles all over his head, his eyes
dance with good humour, and at every word he says,
whether he means it or not, down goes his head to
his poor old knees in the most engaging bow. This
is because he keeps a tea-house with two splendid fish-
ponds; and his business is to come out into the road
and stop the travellers, and beg them to come into his
" dirty house," as he humbly puts it, for a little tea
and some good fishing; and that is why he has got
into such a habit of bowing that he could not stop if
he would. There is a little old woman too; but she
sits inside on the mats, and invitingly pushes cushions
and trays of tea towards you, if you will only come
near enough. I suppose she had legs once, but she
must have sat them off by this time, for she never gets
up, and there are no particular signs of them anywhere.
The ponds are too delightful to be passed by. There
are neat benches and planked footways beside them;
and by one you can sit, and catch gold and silver
fish, like any princess in a fairy tale, for a few cents
an hour; by the other you may also sit, and watch
how the great fat old goldfish, almost as big as carp,
come and fight for the cakes that are thrown in, how
they shove out the younger ones, and kick and splash
and struggle till the water is all churned up and the

biscuit they are fighting for is thrown high and dry on the bank. Then the fish go off in a rage, and the little old man laughs indulgently, and creeps warily down the bank and throws the pink biscuit out to sea, and the comedy begins all over again. We were not the only guests at the inn of the gold and silver fish; on the bench by the pond sat a middle-aged Japanese, in European dress. He was gravely catching goldfish with a thread and a bit of bamboo; he looked intensely solemn, and frowned visibly when we laughed and chattered on the other side of the pond; and he dropped the "take" with great care into his best top hat, turned upside down for the purpose.

CHAPTER XXIII

FROM IKAO TO KARUIZAWA. — THE SILK HARVEST. — A REST AT IIZUKA. — CLIMBING UP THE PASS. — A SEA OF PEAKS. — THE PALACE OF PEACE. — OUR OWN POLICEMAN

KARUIZAWA, *July*, 1890.

WE left Ikao rather regretfully, and, mindful of past experiences, very early in the morning. The road, all shining in the early sunshine, did not seem to be the same one up which we had toiled in rain and darkness two weeks ago. The valleys were green and wet below us, and the hills beyond towered against a brilliantly blue sky just flecked with little clouds of dazzling white. The banks of the road were beautiful with blue lilies, and the air was full of song-birds. The Japanese are early risers, and all the little cottage homes were open to the day; in almost all, the business of silk-spinning was going forward, for this is the time when the cocoons are ripe, and the precious threads must be saved ere the moth feels his wings and bites his way through to freedom.

It is a pretty sight, when the little brown cottages are full of piles of the delicate cocoons, light as puff-balls, and generally a snowy white, or soft flaxen colour, but mingled here and there with large cocoons of a pale yellowish green, the production of a silkworm who lives on a certain species of wild oak. As far as I could gather, these cocoons are collected in the woods, and the worm, if reared in captivity, takes to mulberry leaves, and becomes small and tame like any other silkworm. But this may be only a peasant tradition. The silk reeled from these greenish cocoons is of a

SILK REELING

coarse and heavy kind, and cannot be used with other varieties. The work of reeling off the thread seems to be done in this part of the world by old people, who can no longer do rough work in the fields. I passed one cottage after another where an old man or woman, sometimes an aged couple, sat on the ground among piles of the soft white balls, reeling off the silk on the roughest kind of hand-wheel, to which it passes from a little trough filled with hot water, constantly renewed.

The knotty old fingers manipulate the strands very delicately; but the reeled thread is full of knots and inequalities, and could only, I should think, be used for inferior silks. Even in that form it is valuable, and the old people's little crop will probably go far towards maintaining them for the rest of the year.

As we descended into the plain, the cottages were scattered more thickly along the road, and we passed through village streets where every house was full of cocoon piles, making the effect of snowdrifts swept back from the road into the houses. We were making for Iizuka, a station a little farther up the line than Takaski, from which we could do an hour or so of railway-travelling in the direction of Karuizawa before taking to chairs and jinrikshas again. We had found some firstrate chair-coolies in Ikao, and they carried me down the hilly roads at a swinging trot, and with none of the misery which had attended the upward journey. But the heat was intense as soon as we reached the plain, and no words can describe how grateful and refreshing was the hospitality of the pretty tea-house at Iizuka, where we had an hour's rest before our train could pass. The little upper rooms, cool, matted, open on every side to the air under the wide verandah roof, seemed luxuriously spacious and quiet; from the eaves hung fern-wreaths grown in quaint shapes on wistaria roots, each one having a small glass bell fastened to it, and a bit of paper with a word or two of poetry dangling from the bell. The lightest puff of breeze sets the paper moving, and then the bell speaks in a little musical tinkle like the sound of running water. Our hostess brought up a fairy meal of strawberries and scraped ice and lemonade; and O'Matsu brought a fan, and kept the air cool while we tasted it. By the time the train steamed up, we had forgotten the heat and weariness of the morning, and started out refreshed for the second part of our journey. This stage brought us as far as Yokukawa, a town nestling close in at the foot of the Usui Pass, which leads up into the great dividing range, the central Alps of Japan.

Yokukawa is demoralised by the railway and tram traffic, and has very little that is picturesque about it. The railway stops here,[1] and the traveller is carried on into the hills by a crazy tram service, composed of tiny carriages drawn by broken-down horses, up a road which is washed away by rain or whelmed in landslips at least once a week. When the cars are not thrown off the line, they jump about so alarmingly that the unfortunate passengers are black and blue by the time they reach Karuizawa; altogether, the journey was considered too sensational for me, and the Ikao coolies had been brought on to carry me up the pass. Some of the party were in jinrikshas, which can follow the tramway line; but for me there was the delightful luxury of a long chair ride through shady paths up wooded steeps, where the tendrils of the creepers brushed my face, and the delicate woodsy smell of

[1] The railway is now (1898) completed, and connects Yokukawa with Shin-Karuizawa.

fern and pine, wistaria and hydrangea, came in waves out of the solemn greennesses of the forest. Now and then we stopped, that the men might rest at one of those tiny brown dwellings scattered like empty chestnut burrs along the path; always planted near a stream or a trickling waterfall, with perhaps the virgin rock for a background, they consist of one tiny room open to the woods, with a bench for the pilgrim to rest on, a low-burning fire to make his tea over, and a few scrupulously clean blue cups and bowls to serve it in. And how refreshing the Japanese tea is! One of our party had followed me on foot, and was glad enough of the pale gold-coloured liquid steaming in its tiny cups. It quenches thirst far better than any of our luxurious iced drinks, and gives just the amount of nerve stimulant needed during long walks in the heat. The perfume is faint and fine, and has become so connected with our roamings in Japan that, no matter how many years had passed, it would instantly bring back to me the house in the forest or by the roadside, the kind brown faces, the balmy air, the luminous whiteness of the Eastern day.

The woods were left behind at last, and from their cloistered depths we came out on the ridges where not a landscape but a universe seemed to sink away from below our feet, in a wash of warm silver and green gold, filmed with a network of rivers that flowed on from our mountains, in ribbons of level light, towards the hazy glories of the plain. One knew not which way to look; that one supreme moment of a summer day had come, when every tint is purified to a jewel-like perfection, every dell is mantled in living velvet, every rock leaps into amethyst flame, every pool is a piece of heaven, and the sunshine is over all, a swimming haze of gold, tender and radiant and warm as the very tears of happiness.

I cannot name the sea of peaks which rose behind and before us. As the summer goes on, they will become individually familiar to me, no doubt; but on this first day their greatness and their multiplicity were too overwhelming for me to even ask their names. Thousands of feet above the dreaming plain, arrested in the cisterns of the hills, a sea of wildly tossing breakers, the white horses of the hurricane must have been caught and changed to stone at the stormiest moment of their splendid play. Empty as the ocean hollows, barren as the breaker's crest, sharp-edged as the north wind's bite — ah! what can ever put before you all that I saw that day, as I stood on the mountain's ridge between heaven and earth, watching the fires of the sunset kiss the cold crags they could never warm to life?

We dared not linger long, for the night would fall chill in the hills after such a burning day. We let our men rest for a little in the inn of the village which crowns the Usui Toge, a poor grey village, with a temple to keep watch over the pilgrims who pass through it in the summer-time. There are broad stone steps to the temple, and from there the view is glorious; if the contemplation of beauty conduces to holiness, then its priest should be a very holy man. His son, a lad of ten, who stood leaning against the gate, watching us with bold bright eyes, is the black sheep of the village; and we were told sad stories of his pranks by the innkeeper, at which the boy laughed defiantly. He will not go to school, and sometimes tears down the *gohei*, or white prayer papers, which pious souls hang up with straw ropes at the temple gate; he tears his clothes, and loses his father's books; but the worst of all his sins is that he plays practical jokes on that sacred person, his paternal grandmother! Once he killed her cat; another day he nailed a dead crow to the shutters of her house, and then called her out in a hurry, saying that a beautiful procession was going by. Altogether the village seems to have little hope of the young reprobate, and agree in thinking that it is "a sair dispensation for the meenister!"

From the top of the pass we descended quickly and easily for a little way, and then stood for a few minutes to gaze at Asama Yama, the great active volcano which dominates all this side of the hills, and has more than once filled the upland plain of Karuizawa with ashy desolation. It rises very grandly from beyond the green foothills, looking far nearer than it really is. Heavy clouds of smoke pour from the crater, which looks from Karuizawa towards the south-west, and takes the form of a horizontal tunnel into the mountain, as I am told. From that point on the pass there is a wonderful evening effect, as the sun sinks almost behind the peak and rims its heavy clouds of smoke with crimson and gold. We lost it as we plunged into the deep-cut paths below; and when at last we reached our own boundaries, the grey twilight calm was hushing the hills to rest.

And now I am writing in the most lovely study in the world. Over my head the pine branches meet in arches of kindly green; the pillars of my hall are warm brown trunks, roughened in mystic runes by the sun and the wind, and full of sweet gums that catch and cling to my hand if I lay it against the bark; underfoot a hundred layers of pine needles have been weaving a carpet so elastic that the weariest foot must press it lightly; and, lest I should want for music, a stream, deep-running between hedges of wild clematis and white hydrangea and crowding wistaria tangle, sings a cool tune near by, while the hum of happy insects in the air sounds the high note of noon, the hot Eastern noon, when every bird is still.

Very, very early this morning I crept to the verandah of my bedroom, and pushed aside the *amado* and looked out, down the green depths of my woodsy garden, across the foothills below us to the plain beyond, dreaming and blue still in the virginal lights of the dawn. Near by, on either side, the forest spread from our little clearing, up and up to the summits of the hills that guard us on the left. On the right it rolled more gradually to the foot of a green wall, up whose sides some rocky steps lead to what must be a shrine; I can see figures cut in the rock, and a seat below, and a green bough waving far out from some crevice above. All was still and silent, as if just created and waiting for the breath of life to be infused by the Creator. Then, as the silence became too intense to be borne, one liquid rippling note rang out of the sleeping woods in a burst of joy, so breathless, so triumphant that it might have come from the gates of paradise. When it ceased, the clear vibrations still went ringing up through the hills; and in a moment the answer thrilled back from the distant groves below the lonely shrine. I do not know how long I stood listening; it was one of those moments in life which mark an epoch, when time has no value and identity is forgotten. I know that all the other birds listened as silently as I until my Lord and Lady Nightingale had finished their golden matins, and that when other songs broke forth, and the sun touched the hilltops to life, I turned away satisfied with beauty, one more hour of perfect happiness added to that rich inheritance of which no future grief or privation can ever rob me.

We have named our summer home the Palace of Peace; for though it is close to the only track leading up the pass, it is wrapped in green seclusion. The village — there is a village — is not seen till you have passed out at the foot of our garden, between the pine trees that guard the gate, across two streams bridged somewhat shakily, and down a bit of road that turns with the turning hillside. Then, indeed, a few houses are seen; and if you go on, a long poor street winds away before you, reaches another bridge, and passes thence among the wild flowers of the plain, which stretches its level for many miles, bordered on either hand by beautiful green mountains, itself more than three thousand feet above the sea. The plain we see from our windows; but not a single roof-tree breaks the enchanting sense of solitude. Our house is a Japanese one, two-storied, built of wood, with deep galleries running round both floors, the upper one protected by wide eaves, and also by glazed screens instead of the usual paper slides; so that even in very bad weather we need not shut out the light by closing the wooden shutters, as people have to do usually in Japanese houses.

The inner walls are also of glass, where they look on the verandah. The dividing ones between the rooms are papered, and can be removed at will; so that we can have one very huge apartment or several small ones, according to taste and fancy. All the glass walls have in their turn curtains of heavy mosquito netting, which fall from ceiling to floor, with a slit here and there to allow of passing through; and they both keep out the insects, and ensure a certain amount of privacy. There is just room for ourselves and two of the staff, they occupying one verandah and we the other; while servants' quarters and offices go meandering back somewhere into the heart of the hill, whence an ingenious system of bamboo-tubing supplies all the bathrooms (one to every room in the delightfully civilized Eastern fashion), as well as the dinner-table, with the purest, freshest water I have ever tasted. It wells right out of the rock, and the servants bring the bottles down all misty and impearled with the coldness of it.

OUR SUMMER HOUSE AWAKE . . .

AND ASLEEP

Of course all the rooms are matted, and a recess under the lowest stair holds our house-slippers. When we come in from a walk, everybody sits down on the outer step of the verandah, the servants run out with our clean slippers in hand, and not until they are donned do we tread on the delicate mats. These are so fine and soft that I constantly 'sit on them instead of in my chair; and in warm weather they are delightful to sleep on, cool, resisting, and yet elastic. There are chairs of all sorts of pretty rustic patterns; the whole furniture of my bedroom is made in matting set in soft grey bark, the original untouched tree; the mirror frame is a lovely setting of twigs, the table legs the slender boughs of saplings, — all this being the idea of the Japanese carpenter who made the furniture, and who thought I would like to have something in harmony with the woods around.

HOW THE RICE GROWS

Everywhere is the smell of sweet new planks and fresh grass blinds and the murmur of streams and pine woods, and — it is heavenly cool! We can use a blanket at night, and I am wearing light flannel dresses in the afternoon.

As we sat on the verandah in delightful repose on the evening of our arrival, a dancing light appeared at the far end of the garden, and came slowly nearer until it resolved itself into a bobbing lantern, which roused our five dogs to one defiant howl. The lantern-bearer paused, then found courage to approach, and a gorgeous person in white uniform, white gloves, and a good deal of gold about him, slowly loomed on our astonished sight, and stopped at the verandah-step with a military bow. This was our special policeman, under whose charge we are to be for the summer. He held out a piece of paper towards us, exclaiming, "My card!" Then he looked at H——. "You — Minister?" he inquired; and when H—— nodded, he proceeded to explain that he had been sent up from Nagano to look after us, and that he should carry out his orders with vigilance and zeal. The English was very queer, and ground out a word at a time; but he would not be helped, and was rather offended when Mr. G—— addressed him in fluent Japanese. His parting salutation was original: "Please! Receive! Sleep!" Then he left us, and he and his lantern bobbed off into the darkness again. He is quartered in the village, and I hear takes advantage of his special mission to swagger fearfully among his colleagues and compatriots.

CHAPTER XXIV

"IN THE DAWN OF TIME." — THE STAR LOVERS AND THEIR
STORY. — THE PITIFUL HISTORY OF O SHO KUNG

KARUIZAWA, *July*, 1890.

THE evenings are almost as enchanting as the mornings in this July weather. We sit out till very late, watching the stars shining through the clear air as they never shine for us when we are on the plain. Our green lawnlet (the turf was brought bit by bit from a great distance, and is growing beautifully now) slopes down to a pond where the stars all find their doubles on these still nights; and that reminds me that this is the month of the Star Lovers, and that I must tell you their story — a story so old that it came to Japan two thousand five hundred years ago, when Cyrus reigned in Persia, when Rome was a collection of huts in a wolf-haunted swamp, when the family of the kings reigned in purple and gold among the vines and poppies of Etruria. Japan was then standing, as it were, at the knees of China; and this is the tale which the teacher told her in some July twilight — the tale of the seventh night of the seventh moon, the story of the festival called *Tana-Bata*.

In the dawn of time, before the immortal gods had

descended to earth, the Sky Father, the Emperor of Heaven, had one daughter, so beautiful that even Amaterasu, the sun-goddess, seemed dark beside her, and so skilful that she wove all the garments for the Court of Heaven — garments of mist all dew-impearled, State robes of sunshine dazzling as the light, veils of rosy film, and mantles of night-black velvet showered with diamond stars. There was no other weaver who could spin such threads or weave such webs in all the heavenly family, and she sat always at her golden loom, glad and content with her fair task, and asking no more than to sit there always, because she knew not love; and they called her Shokucho, the weaver of the skies, but we call her Vega.

Now seeing how fair and wise she was, many of the gods came asking for Shokucho to wife; but she loved none of them, and the Emperor of Heaven was glad to keep her, and sent them all away, saying, "My daughter is wedded to her golden loom! No other husband does her heart desire." And the other gods laughed and jeered, saying, "Truly the Princess Shokucho is a slave, and not a goddess! Except she marry, will she not grow old? Except she love, how can she keep her immortality? A cruel father art thou to her!" For it is well known that even a goddess will not gain eternity except she have loved, since the birth of love is the birth of her spirit, which may not die. And the Sky Father, Tiû, Tenshu Sama, Dyaus Piter, pondered as he sat on his throne in the sunrising; and he drew his fingers through his beard, which was long and white as the autumn moonbeams, and he said, "The gods speak truth, young and turbulent though they be. Shokucho must love, or she will pass with the warp of the sunshine and decay with the woof of the dawn. Now where shall we find a husband so fair that she may love him, so obscure that he dare not carry her away?"

Then his eyes fell on a goodly herdsman, driving his cattle in the heavenly plain. His countenance was lordly, but his raiment was poor, and he followed his white oxen with slow contented feet in the starry meadows; and in our earth he is known as a child of Aquila.

The Emperor of Heaven said to his daughter, "Princess, seest thou yon herdsman, tall and straight as the reed that groweth in water?"

"Yea, father," said the Princess, "I have looked on him once; and lest my eyes should be blinded by his beauty and my heart burnt with vain desire, I have looked no more. My golden loom and my jewel-weaving seem dark to me now."

"That is well," said the Sky Father, "for Kenkyo shall be thy husband."

Then Shokucho was so happy that she laid her head on her golden work and wept for joy, and her tears fell through its sunshine and made the first rainbow; and that very day she wed the herdsman Kenkyo, who had loved her so long that he could say but one word, her name.

And there was rejoicing in the Courts of Heaven, because Shokucho had earned her immortality; and she herself cared little for immortality while Kenkyo sat by her side, and said her name again and again, and found other words to tell her how he loved her. Neither did she care for her weaving any more; still stood the golden shuttles of the loom, and still stood Kenkyo's white steers, not knowing their way to pasture, and wondering that their master led them thither no more. The herdsman forgot his herding, the weaver Princess forgot her weaving, and each could think only of the other in the July starlight.

Then the Sky Father was exceedingly angry, and he said to Kenkyo, "Presumptuous herdsman, had I known thou wouldst stop my daughter's weaving, never would I have given her to thee to wife! Begone to the other bank of the heavenly river, the Ama no gawa, the milky stream! Not till a year has passed shalt thou embrace Shokucho again!"

Then a great eagle came and lifted Kenkyo in his claws, and set him down on the farther side of the river that runs so wide and white through the blue meadows of Heaven, and his kine swam after him across the stream; but Shokucho was left wringing her hands, as she knelt on the bank, and weeping bitter tears.

"Back to thy weaving, daughter," said Tenshu Sama, "and still thy foolish grief! In a year from to-day thou shalt have one night by thy herdsman's side."

So slowly and sadly Shokucho went back to her loom, and sat there working silently till twelve moons had waxed and waned; and every beating of her heart was a cry of love for Kenkyo. And poor Kenkyo

THE GENTLE BIRDS

looked across the river from where his kine stood knee deep in celestial pasturage — looked to where Shokucho sat in the heart of the light that glowed from the loom, white or crimson or green as she flung in threads of jewels. And at last the seventh night of the seventh moon came round, and the shuttle stopped of itself, and the Milky Way began to part that the lovers might meet dryshod. But there came a strong rustling of wings in the air, and it was suddenly darkened with myriads of gentle birds, magpies who had grieved for the poor lovers; and they hung in air, wing to wing and beak to beak, till they made a bridge from side to side of the Milky River; and Kenkyo rushed across, and met Shokucho and clasped her in his arms, and for one short summer night the Star Lovers were united. But at the next dawn Kenkyo had to leave his beloved, and wait through twelve months more before he might speak to her again. She comes to the white river's bank night after night, and stretches out her arms to him, and calls his name; and he, seeing her also, stretches out longing arms towards her; but because of the wide impetuous torrent neither can hear the

LEFT ALONE

other speak, — till this magic night. The magpies never forget them; the bridge of Kasa-saji, built of gleaming wings, always spans the flood; and their great love makes them forget in this one night of happiness all the weary waiting of the year.

So Shokucho and Kenkyo are the patrons of all separated lovers, of all faithful husbands and wives to whom absence teaches a higher love, a harder constancy. On this night a hungry heart may pray for the sweet food of love, in certain hope of receiving an answer to its prayer; happy lovers invoke the lovers in the sky to protect them from change or bereavement, and offer tender sympathy to those for whom this night's meeting means a year of separation; the widow commends to them the soul of her dead husband; the woman left alone in the little home entreats protection for the dear one who is forced to take a lonely journey; the maidens pray for skill in rare embroidery, and put their work under the weaver's patronage. All pray that it may not rain on this night; for if it rains, the river overflows, and the heavenly lovers may not meet. The poets make many a poem on love, and their sonnets are written on beautiful poem-papers, painted with flowers and powdered with gold, which the young people tie on the branches of two leafy bamboos, such as are set up in every garden on this night. The light breeze makes the poems flutter airily among the leaves, and then it passes on to where in the open room a large party of young people sit together on the mats, feasting on flowery sweets, and drinking their perfumed tea, while one after another repeats some verse of a poem, or sings it to the humming accompaniment of the *samisen*; then games are played, shadow games behind the screens, or hide-and-seek in and out of the simple home, and the elaborate garden, with its trees and stepping-stones and bridges, its fairy dells and toy mountains, till the air is full of the laughter of young

SHADOW GAMES

voices, the flutter of flying draperies, the joyous life-measure marked by young feet as the boys and girls chase one another down the dusky paths.

There is a story of another Sho, who is called in Japan O Sho Kung, the remaining syllables, whether in this name or that of the Star Weaver, being mere

SHADOW GAMES

affixes denoting rank or age; in Japan, Ko or Cho is usually added to a girl's name in her own family as long as she is very young. The story of O Sho Kung properly belongs to September; but I will tell it to you here since it is in my mind. I learnt it from a strange little picture that I have, and whose meaning, though touching some distant point in my memory, remained unexplained till a Japanese friend told me that it referred to a Chinese story, and as he told it I began to remember. The picture is a delicately coloured print representing a young girl, slender and pale and richly dressed, wearing an expression of horror and despair. She is seated on a horse, which ambles on amid a group of fierce and hairy Mongols, whose faces are of a deep reddish brown; hands and faces are covered with bristles, and they wear the unmistakable look of the rough dirty Tartar of to-day. One of them walks beside the horse, and holds the poor shrinking girl in her place; the captain, recognisable by his richer dress, stands at one side, with his arms crossed and a hideous scowl on his countenance; his underlings are evidently rejoicing at the beautiful prize so roughly carried away.

That, said my friend, is a picture of the lady O Sho Kung, and her story is a very sad one. Many centuries ago, when the Han dynasty was ruling in China, the Emperor was obliged to give many rich presents to the Khan of Mongolia, who, instead of returning them, would constantly break across the frontier and take far more than the Emperor cared to give him. However, he was just then so much the stronger that it was useless to think of resistance. The Khan had heard that the Chinese Court was full of beautiful ladies, and he thought it would be a fine thing to have a wife from hence; so he sent a great embassy to the Emperor, asking for a beautiful Princess to be the Khan's wife. The Emperor was very angry at the presumption of the barbarian, and could not reconcile himself to the idea that a Princess of his family should fill such a position. However, he seems to have answered the envoys politely, and only begged for a little time, so that he might indeed select the most beautiful Princess in China to be the consort of the Khan. Then the messengers were feasted, and had many presents given to them, and managed to pass the time very pleasantly while the Emperor in the seclusion of the Palace pondered as to what should be done.

Seeing his trouble, the Empress-Mother came to him, and said, "Let not the Son of Heaven be cast down! No Imperial Princess shall be sent to this barbarian. Let us now choose a Court lady, skilled and beautiful, and let us send her to the Mongol!"

And the Emperor saw that it was good counsel, and very quickly the news spread, and great was the consternation among the Emperor's three hundred concubines, the beautiful girls who had been brought up in the Palace under the Empress-Mother's eyes, and who were skilled in every art to please and cheer. The young Empress comforted them, saying, "Nay, my sisters, fear not! You who are the happy slaves of the Son of Heaven may never leave the Palace or look in the face of any Chinese prince, much less of any common man. The Khan's bride will be sought elsewhere."

And so it happened; for the Emperor said to himself, "What does this barbarian know of beauty? Verily a peasant-woman would be fine and fair enough for him. However, since he is very powerful, we will cause a fair woman to be sought out, and we will tell these moles of envoys that she is a Princess, and no one will be the wiser." For of course no man ever looked on the faces of the Court ladies, except the Emperor and their own attendants.

So the order went out that all the fair women in any way connected with the Court should have their portraits painted, so that the Emperor should look at them and decide who should be sent to the barbarian's country; and the Emperor's own painter was sent to all the pavilions of the Summer Palace, and the Hunting Palace, and the Golden Palace in Peking, where dwelt many beautiful girls in attendance on the Empress-Mother and the Princesses, and also the daughters of great mandarins who were Court officials. But the true object of the search was kept a secret. And when the women found out by teasing and coaxing, that it was the Son of Heaven himself who had sent for their portraits, each one implored and bribed the painter to make her the most beautiful, so that she might find favour in the Emperor's eyes.

Each one — except O Sho Kung. I do not for a moment think that that was her name. She was probably called Shung-Ma; and the thread through the labyrinth of transposition will lead us back to the Star Weaver who was separated from her love, even as was this poor little lady of Pechili, on whom the Japanese poets have written endless elegies. However, she is O Sho Kung in the land where I heard her sad story; so I will call her by her Japanese name. She was the daughter of a great mandarin, and was brought up in the women's pavilion in his beautiful house by the Pali-Chuang Pagoda. There was a great garden and a lotus lake, where she and her friends pushed about their little boats among the dreamy pink

A DAIMYO'S DAUGHTER

flowers, and halted under white marble bridges to write little love poems on scented paper; and O Sho Kung was very happy. When she was fourteen, she was betrothed to a young noble, who, she was told, was everything that was brave and handsome. She would not be allowed to see him or he her until after the wedding, when he could raise the scarlet veil from her face; but the old go-between woman told wonderful tales of O Sho Kung to Tsêng Shi, and of Tsêng Shi to O Sho Kung; and one day, when he was riding by, the girl hid behind a lattice in the garden wall and saw him clearly, and he carried away her poor little heart dangling on his huge peaked saddle-bow. And she debated within herself whether she really must weep for three days before her wedding, and make resistance when taken to her husband's house, as every well-brought-up girl was expected to do. For though she loved her parents, she thought there would be nothing to cry over when the time came for her to be married to that kind-looking handsome youth who was to be her husband.

The preparations for the wedding were nearly completed, when the Emperor's messenger with the Emperor's painter appeared at the gates, and requested to have an interview with O Sho Kung's father. The mandarin was not greatly pleased that two strange men should be allowed to look on his child's face; but the Emperor's command carried all before it, and the world already knew of the existence of the mandarin's beautiful daughter. She was covered with confusion in the presence of the envoy, who kindly explained that the Son of Heaven had particular reasons for wishing to have her portrait. "Why mine?" cried the modest girl; "I am but a roadside weed, and his august Palace is full of beautiful jessamine flowers!" And then, with the cunning of love, she managed to bribe the painter with a handful of jewels to say that she was ugly and deformed, and her face unworthy to be portrayed for the Emperor to see, that so he might never wish to have her brought to the Palace. The painter laughed, and took the jewels, and did even as she begged him to do. All the other women had given him jewels to make their portraits as lovely as possible, each hoping that the choice would fall on her, and never dreaming of the dreadful fate that would follow the choice.

And so it happened that, when the messengers returned to their master, they brought a collection of portraits of such beautiful women that the Son of Heaven was glad and angry at the same time. "What!" he cried, "is my empire so rich in fair women that the gods might envy it, and yet so weak that I must send one of these pomegranate blossoms to mate with a filthy barbarian? Not one shall go — not one!"

Then the wily messenger told him of the lady O Sho Kung, and said that she had a dark skin and round eyes and big mouth, even as she had begged him to do; and the Emperor laughed, and said, "You did well to tell me of her ugly face! It will match with the countenance of the Khan! Let O Sho Kung be sent to Mongolia to be the bride of the churl."

So the message was carried back that O Sho Kung was wanted as a bride for the Khan, and the commands were very precise that she was to come to the Palace at once. And she who had wondered if indeed she must weep when she left her father's house wept most bitter tears when she was torn away from it, and her father and mother went with her, and their hearts were heavy as lead. When they reached the Palace, O Sho Kung was taken to the Empress-Mother, who told her that which lay in store for her; and O Sho Kung became white and dumb because of the anguish of her heart, she being young and new to pain. And the Empress-Mother's handmaids dressed her in the robes of a Princess with royal jewels and great pomp, and on her head they put the diadem of the golden phœnix which only the royal ladies might wear. At last it was all done, and as the Empress-Mother looked at the girl in her shining robes she said to herself, "Verily the messenger lied to my son! This maiden is a white pomegranate blossom, fairer than all the Princesses! Would I could keep her here!"

But it was too late for that. The command came that the envoys were ready to depart, and that they were even now having their last audience with the Emperor, and O Sho Kung was commanded to go and make obeisance to the Son of Heaven before starting on her journey. And her heart was like marble, but her courage was high, and not a tear was on her cheek as she was led to the Emperor's presence. And as she entered the throne-room he said carelessly to the envoys, "Behold the Princess whom we have chosen for the honour of sharing your master's throne!" And only when he had spoken did he look up, and there before him stood O Sho Kung, beautiful as a full moon when no stars are in the sky, proud and graceful as the young willow by a peaceful stream. And the Emperor's heart leapt up in his bosom, and red anger took him that this fairest of women must go from his Court, to set like a setting moon in the sandy desert. And for one moment he wavered; then he thought of his royal word already given to the rough messengers, who gazed open-mouthed on the lovely vision; and the Emperor covered his face with his sleeve, and O Sho Kung prostrated herself before him, and passed from his sight for ever.

THE DEPARTURE OF O SHO KUNG

And when her mother saw her set on a horse and led out of the city by rude men who laughed at her tears and handled her roughly, while O Sho Kung held out her arms for help which neither father nor mother could give since the Emperor had spoken —

then her mother cut her own throat, entreating that at least her spirit might follow her daughter to watch over her; and her father cursed the Emperor in his heart, and began to plot to deliver him and his city into the hands of the Khan, who greatly coveted it. But Tsêng Shi married another girl, and lived happy, forgetting O Sho Kung.

I know what became of her at last, after she had ridden for twenty days through the grass-lands to the north; but I must not tell you all my stories in these letters, or there will be none left to bring home. How do I know, are you saying, how is it possible that I should know, when it all happened so long ago, in those strange climes? Well, some of the story was told me here, and some, I think, one summer's day by the lotus ponds of Pali-Chuang, and some was whispered in the grass-lands through which I, too, did ride. Who shall limit that which is breathed in the hearing ear?

CHAPTER XXV

THE APPROACH OF THE STORM.— AT THE HEART OF THE TYPHOON. — A FUNNY SIGHT. — THE USUI TOGE. — THE STORY OF A HERO, AND A HEROINE. — YAMATO'S REPENTANCE. — "IN THE SWEET OPEN FIELDS ".

KARUIZAWA, August, 1890.

I BROUGHT a whole library of instructive books up here; but reading is sheer waste of time in these surroundings, and one's eyes are too filled with new and lovely sights to go back contentedly to printed books and other people's thoughts. What book that ever was published brings the sense of strength and peace that the sight of pine branches waving across the morning sky can give? God's books are not all written in printer's ink. On this wind-swept upstairs gallery where I write I am on a level with the second story of the pines, and they are reaching out their green and gold towards me with generous hands. I have just come back from a long walk over the plain; we have had a fearful typhoon; and the first *Lilium auratum* has been brought in: of which shall I tell you first? The typhoon, of course? Ah, well, there is no accounting for tastes.

The typhoon burst upon us last week, happily not

quite without warning. When it rains ramrods for twenty-four hours, and the barometer behaves as if it had St. Vitus's dance, we know what to expect in this part of the world, and look to chimneys and shutters, see that the animals are under cover, and, up here,

PINES IN OUR MOUNTAIN GARDEN

shovel away the dam which turns a part of the mountain stream through the washhouse, and see that the auxiliary streamlet is returned with thanks before the worst floods rush by. But all the precautions in the world cannot make the visitation anything but a very dreadful one; and when it is over, one is more inclined to thank Heaven for that which has not happened than to grumble at damage done. I think I told you that our cottage is built on a three-cornered piece of land, bounded on the two lower sides by converging streams, and rising into the hills at the back. The whole is on a rather sharp slope, a fortunate circumstance, for floods and freshets drain off quickly without doing much damage to the house or garden, but wreaking their fury on our communications with the outer world beyond. All through that memorable day the heat was intense, the rain fell with mechanical regularity in straight bars which rattled like iron on all our roofs, made the lawn and paths one moving sheet of water, and churned our toy pond into sputtering froth. All the galleries were safely enclosed with the glass screens; but on two sides the heavy night-shutters had to be put up to keep the rooms from being flooded. Whatever there was of insect life in the garden and woods seemed to be taking refuge in the house. Mosquitoes, moths, huge armed cockchafers heavy as stones — all flung themselves against the glass; and for the thousandth time I was glad that we had not windowed our house with paper in real Japanese fashion — we should have had to sit all day with candles behind closed shutters, as many of our friends did through this very storm.

The poor servants were much alarmed, for they knew as well as we did what was coming. The cook was seen climbing the roof of the kitchen off the shoulders of "Chisai Cook San" (Little Cook Mr.) to inspect an extra long iron chimney, which he had induced me in a moment of foolhardiness to have put up for his benefit. The servants live so much out of doors, that there are numberless little properties in their own yard to be got under cover, if a very bad storm is coming. Even the dogs lay wise and silent, asking no questions and expecting no walks; not even nosing about under the front doorsteps, where they bury their best bones. Our good policeman (his name is Furihata) came up several times instead of only twice in the course of the day to see if all was right with us; and Mr. G—— visited the waterworks anxiously, fearing either that we should be swamped or else have all our bamboo pipes carried away down the main stream.

The intense oppression and excitement that I have felt in other typhoons was upon us all; we seemed to be fighting the air, hot, choking, evil air, full of enemies to soul and body. Our great volcano neighbour, Asama Yama, had sent out more than one long roar, and the earth had heaved once and twice under our feet, when at last the storm reached us, swept over and round and through us in a concentrated fury of attack. Every moment it seemed as if the house must go, and we and it be hurled down to the drowning plain. The night came down black as wet pitch, and our poor little home, with its flickering lamps and quivering walls, seemed the only point left in the inky darkness. The wooden shutters had all been run into place and tightly bolted when the hurricane broke, for a wooden house of this kind could rise up and sail down the wind like an open umbrella if one lifting gust got under the roof. So all

A RAIN STORM

night long we sat, or lay down for a little, with everything prepared for flight should the storm prove the stronger; and again and again it seemed impossible that our wooden pillars resting on shallow stones should be able to withstand the force of the wind, which shrieked and beat and thundered against them all in turn. The whole safety of a Japanese house depends on the wooden pillars which support it (the walls are mere veils of plank stretched between), and an ingenious arrangement is resorted to in order that the pillars may have literally fair play. Each square pillar stands in a socket of stone, the only foundation used at all, and not placed more than two feet below the floor of the house. The pillar is square, and is rounded off at the base; and the socket is also round, and is slightly too large for the post which rests in it, thus allowing the post a chance of moving a very little in earthquake or storm, and righting itself again at once. In slight or medium shocks a house built in this way suffers hardly at all, its elasticity preventing the resistance which would wreck a hard and fast edifice; in the mad destruction of a violent earthquake, I doubt if the house has yet been built which would not suffer, and suffer greatly. Twice in that awful night I felt as if the house must really go, when two great lifting gusts seemed to have got under it; but the long hours passed, and again and again the whole fury of the storm hurled itself against us without doing any sensible damage. As we heard the thunder of the swollen torrents on either hand roll by, with many a crash of timber and cannonade of flying stones, and yet saw that our floors were dry and our roof whole, we took heart to sleep a little, hoping that the tempest would be over by the morning. It had raged for several hours, and all through the night I heard Mr. G—— tapping the barometer violently from time to time to see if it could not be induced to show signs of settling. One of the strangest portents of the storm was the wild excitement of the needle. It danced from side to side, and hardly stayed quiet for a moment till the gale was over; and then it settled to "Fair," and stayed there, in spite of black skies and a deluged world. I suppose it knew what it was about! I am told that this nervousness of the glass is an invariable feature of the true typhoon.

At last the fury of the storm passed away, and travelled up through the hills with long wails and half-heard shrieks so awful that they gave the impression of some agonised creature, invisible, close, being tortured to death before our eyes that saw nothing. Fainter and fainter it grew, and only when it passed away did we begin to hear clearly the angry roar of the torrents which had all night acted as an undernote to the tempestuous voices of the gale. As soon as daylight came — such wet grey daylight! — the more daring crept out to see what damage had been done. I was joyfully told that Cook San's dear chimney was none the worse, and I believe he must have made Chisai Cook San sit on the roof all night to hold it in place. But other things had not been so fortunate. The waterworks were badly damaged; several trees which had been planted symmetrically beside a fence had been bowled over like so many ninepins; the road over the pass was gone in many places, the one to the village was under water and torn to shreds; while our own bridge hung over the main torrent on one crazy beam, to be crept across with breathless care. As for the tramway and the telegraph lines, they had ceased to exist, and for five days after that visitation not a message of any kind reached us, and our supplies from Tokyo (on which we mainly depend for food) were entirely cut off. Our poor gardener, who sleeps in the village, struggled up here in the worst of the storm to see if he could do anything for us; and Furihata, our dear little policeman, behaved gallantly. At about three in the morning, when it was blowing great guns, I heard him going on his beat round the house, and, peeping out through a chink in the shutters, saw his faithful yellow lantern bobbing about, protected in some ingenious fashion by his oilskin cloak from the rain and wind. He came up again after daylight to tell us about the dangerous condition of the bridge, and to say that it should be mended immediately; but except that he and two of his colleagues have been seen staring at it with gravity, no steps have been taken as yet. We are in pleasing uncertainty as to where a large supply of wine, some new clothes, and a quantity of groceries have gone to, and I begin to understand the feelings of dear Ben Gunn when he longed for Christian diet on Treasure Island. But now the country is looking so perfect in its fresh beauty after the rain that I ought to be ashamed of repining at such small misfortunes. A harmless breeze is sweeping the soft white clouds into heaps and corners, the sky is sapphire blue between; our pond, composed again, is reflecting it all respectfully; and the air is full of the sound of the leaping streams, which are still having it all their own way for miles around. Through the forest I hear the woodcutter again at work; and farther off, below the stone shrine in the green hillside, a little thread of smoke rises dreamy blue above the pine-tops, showing that the charcoal-burner's family (I discovered them in one of my walks) are again at work.

We have been down through the village and out across the plain since the storm, and had a delightful sense of danger in picking our way over the dancing bridge. The wise dogs refused to trust themselves to it, and all except Bess, the old pointer, had to be carried across. The loose lava of the roads makes them like long ridges of rubble after the floods of last week; but the cool smell of everything and the whiff of vitality in the air make up for a little rough walking.

We had been out beyond the village, and were returning towards it, when a funny sight met our eyes. A bridge at the farther end had been a good deal knocked about by the storm, but still presented a respectable appearance. I saw two men riding towards it from the opposite side; they were smartly dressed in white European clothes and pith helmets such as our inspector wears in summer. As we know every soul in the place, I was curious to see who these strangers were, when the foremost horse stepped gaily on the bridge. Then — he went through it, at least his forefeet did, and he lay amazed, caught in the rotten wood, while the well-dressed stranger rolled over his head, scrambled to his feet, and turned out to be our cook in his new Sunday clothes, followed by Kané, the artistic pantry-boy, dressed exactly like him. Kané turned and fled — why, I know not, since there was no crime in hiring a horse and taking a ride, even if we were on foot at the time. The poor Cook San looked most uncomfortable, but pulled his steed up bravely, and led him aside while we passed. I only asked him if he had hurt himself, and denied myself the pleasure of looking back to see him scramble up again.

One other walk we have had since the storm, up the Usui Toge, to pay a visit to some friends who have taken a house for the summer in the hamlet which crowns the pass. The road was in many places a series of rifts, over which we had to scramble as we could; the loose tufa soil allows the rain to settle and sink through the surface cracks, and when the water has worked a yard or two down, the slightest shock detaches the whole piece, which goes rolling off into the torrent or the valley, leaving one more bare scar on the mountain-side. The clearest tramontana wind blew in our faces, and kept us cool, though it was four o'clock, quite the hottest hour of our August day. The brooks were rushing gloriously down the dells and gorges through which the path winds up, the flowers were full of wet sweetness in the sun, and the landscape was like one great washed jewel in the afternoon light. Our mountains, great volcanic crags, with their feet buried in soft green foothills, were all wreathed in golden haze. On the crest of the pass, we crept out on a dividing spur, a flying buttress of the mountains, whence all the plain stretches away on the left, and that mass of rocks called the Myogi San (the maiden pass) tosses its granite breakers off to the right. Here we sat long, and in silence, watching the rose creep into the gold, the purple into the rose, and some one said, "It will be dark in half an hour;" and we turned to hurry down the steep path while some daylight remained.

Like many another beautiful scene in Japan, the heights of the Usui Toge are connected with the history of one of the country's heroes. Yamato Take, or O-osu, was the son of the Emperor Keiko, who came to the throne, according to Japanese chronology, in the year 71 of our era. A whole edifice of stories has grown up round the figure of the heroic Yamato, and some of them are so picturesque that they are worth the telling. Like all Japanese heroes, he was born with a brave and reckless disposition; and his first exploit, performed when he was a mere boy, was the murder of his elder brother for some infringement of Palace etiquette which had displeased their father. The Emperor, instead of bewailing the death of his eldest son, seems to have regarded the circumstance as a welcome manifestation of the qualities of O-osu, as he was then called, and sent him, single-handed, to slay two fierce outlaws who were spreading terror through the district where they had their lair. O-osu undertook the matter gladly, and brought as much cunning as courage to the task. He was still so young and slight that he had no trouble in passing himself off as a girl. Dressed in the gorgeous robes of a courtesan, with his still long hair hanging down his back, he came smiling into their cave as the two robbers were feasting one autumn night. Surely they were glad to welcome the beautiful girl, who, gay as a maple in its crimson dress, passed under the overhanging boughs, to sing sweet songs and pledge them in wine in the October starlight. But where the heart should have been beating in the girl's gentle bosom a sharp short sword was hid; and as O-osu sat between the robbers, the lightning of his sword flashed in the air, and then was eclipsed in one man's life-blood. He fell dead; and his companion, terror-struck, rushed to the opening of the cave, with O-osu's clutch already on his garments, O-osu's sword already biting his back. "Pause, O Prince!" he gasped, as he fell under the boy's feet. "Prince thou art of a surety; but whence, why hast thou come?" And O-osu, standing above him in his gay dress, more crimson now, his sword dripping red streams down his upraised arm, told the robber that he was the avenger of evil, the Emperor's messenger of death to rebels. "A new name shalt thou have," said the dying robber. "Hitherto I and my dead brother there were called the bravest men of the west. To thee, august child, I bequeath our title. Let men call thee the bravest in Yamato!" Then he died.

And from that day the young Prince was called Yamato Take, and never did he wrong the name. The Emperor sent him to subdue rebellious tribes, to conquer barbarians, to bring the hairy Ainos under his father's rule; and since he was pious as well as brave, and always entreated the help of his ancestress, Amaterasu, the sun-goddess, before he undertook any task, all went well with him for a time. Then the Emperor gave him the command to go and subdue the savages of the east, who had never owned a master, and to overcome their gods. Yamato undertook the expedition; but his heart was heavy, and did not dance in his breast as it was wont to do at the thought of battle and carnage and victory. So he went to the shrine of the sun-goddess at Isé, where his aunt, the Princess Yamato, was high-priestess; and she offered prayers for him, and comforted him with a strange gift, a silken bag, richly embroidered, which he was not to open save in extreme peril. And after bidding her farewell, he went his way, with brave companions in arms, and one woman, his wife, who loved him so dearly that she counted labour and privation and danger as flowers and gold for his sake. But Yamato was cold and careless to her; and if she seemed grieved, he would say, "It is thine own fault, Oto Tachibana: on the battlefield, thoughts of war; on the mats, smiles and saké. Go back to thy home, Princess."

But she would not, saying to herself, "My august Lord has yet somewhat to learn; and that I, his poor servant, will have the honour of teaching him. A Princess of Yamato scorns the soft mats that are not pressed by her Lord's feet; she does not smile when he goes into danger; she drinks no wine while his sword drinks blood. I go with my Lord into the battle."

And so, leaving all her luxury and ease, dressed in her war garments, but keeping only her jewelled comb in her long hair, Oto Tachibana went with the Prince. And as they travelled, they came to the province called Owari, where lived the fairest woman in the world, the Princess Miyadzu. She had never worn the garments of war, and her robes were gay and dazzling, her face white as the jessamine in the inner room, and her hands that never had grasped bow or spear were delicate as the stamens of the lily. Her lotus feet knew not the rough road of duty, and her smile was like wine to the wanton in heart. Beside her Oto Tachibana, with her worn raiment and her sunburnt brow, seemed a peasant-girl, a thing of which the Prince was ashamed. So he said nothing of her being his wife, and she had to stand silent while he spoke aside with the Princess Miyadzu, while he walked in Miyadzu's garden and drank Miyadzu's wine; and she knew that he had made Miyadzu a promise that, when his work was done and the savages subdued, he would return the same way and marry her in state, and take her to rule over his home in Yamato. And even as he spoke, he felt Oto Tachibana's eyes upon him, and he turned and saw her looking sadly at him, and his heart became cold; but he did not repent. He said farewell to Miyadzu with much tenderness, and rode away with all his train, Oto Tachibana carrying his shield and making no sound, for she was a patient and noble lady.

I cannot stop to tell you all the strange adventures that he encountered, but they were many; and through all his wife followed him faithfully, and spoke not a word to sadden his heart or take away his courage. And at last he came to the place called Sagami, where the land runs out into the sea on both sides, and the village called the Door of the Bay lay within. And his followers sought for boats wherein he could cross the sea; and he scoffed, saying, "This is no sea, but a brook! I could jump across if I would!"

Then Riujin and the other sea-gods, hearing the insult, were angry, and caused a terrible storm; and Yamato Take was in danger of death, since the boat in which he was with his wife and his followers was tossed from wave to wave in the fierce tempest, and he rued bitterly his insult to the sea-gods. Then Oto Tachibana spoke, saying, "August husband, I will appease the deities; thy bright, honourable life shall be saved." And she caused the mats from the sleeping-place of the ship to be thrown on the waves, and she stood on the edge of the junk, and grief and the storm-wind had washed her brow white from sunburn and war stain, and the lightning played in her eyes so that she looked bright as the sun-goddess in the

IN MIYADZU'S PALACE

mirror of heaven; and she clasped her hands above her head, and cried, "In truth my place is on the soft mats, as thou didst say!" And she leapt from the boat into the sea, and the mats received her; and all her garments folded decorously around her as she sat, and the lightning showed her to the Prince as the waves carried her quickly away; and then the storm ceased, and the sea was still, because its gods were appeased.

Then Yamato Take was also still, and in silence he and his followers landed on the farther shore; and he fought as he had never fought before, penetrating into the lands of the Yemishi, the hairy barbarians, and subduing all their gods. And as he returned towards Sagami, he stopped on the top of the pass called the Usui Toge, and gazed long and sadly towards the sea where Oto Tachibana had given her life for his sake. And, thinking of all her faithfulness which he had betrayed, and all her love which he had scorned, he cried out bitterly, "Azuma, Azuma, ya!" (Oh, my wife, my wife!). And ever after, all that province between the mountains and the sea was called Azuma, even as it is at this day.

As for Oto Tachibana, the storm took her, and she never was seen again; but her jewelled comb was brought to shore by the sea-king's daughter, and Yamato Take built a great mausoleum over it to her memory.

And what became of Yamato Take? you say, as you read my letter aloud under the Barberini pines, looking across another plain to another sea. Well, he was a mân, you know; so he went back to the Princess Miyadzu afterwards. But she seemed less beautiful to him now, and soon he went off to fight more barbarians, being born a fighter, who breathed best in carnage. But he died at thirty-two, as he was struggling back to the Temple of Isé, to beg Yamato Kime, his aunt, to pray that he might be cured of a grievous sickness which had come upon him. He reached it not, and the death-agony found him under a lonely pine tree at Otsu, near Owari. And as he lay dying he made a poem, and called the single pine tree his elder brother, to whom he would gladly leave his sword of honour and his warrior's dress. And he seemed to gain strength from the kindly pine, and crept on farther, but died in the open fields, far from the shrine of Isé. But some of his friends were with him; for by one he sent his sword and bequeathed the spoils of his last conquest to the holy shrine of the sun-goddess, who was his ancestress. By another he sent a message to his father, to tell him that all his commands had been carried out, and that he grieved at not being able to bring the report himself, but that he "cared no longer for life, and lay dying in the sweet open fields."

CHAPTER XXVI

THE CHARCOAL-BURNER LOSES HIS WAY. — "A MISTAKE NO CRIME." — INVASION! — PILGRIMS AND THEIR WAYS. — PILGRIM CLUBS. — AN ENTERPRISING OLD LADY

KARUIZAWA, *September*, 1890.

EXACTLY eight days after our first typhoon, we had a second edition of it, which really worked fearful havoc among the hills, where the soil of the paths has been torn and rubble loosened by the first visitation. Our bridge went altogether this time; but fortunately we found that there is a little one where the stream is much smaller, through the deep hedge at the far end of our garden. The chief bridge is now being rebuilt; and meanwhile we have had to let people pass by the little one, which is intended as a short cut to the path leading off to the charcoal-burner's establishment. On a misty night or after an extra cup of saké it is difficult to distinguish the paths. One rather cloudy evening following on a rainy day, we were sitting on the verandah as usual after dinner, when a lantern, evidently in a state of extreme excitement, appeared far down the garden path. I never saw a lantern behave so curiously. First it waved about in the air, then it sank to the ground, then it swung from side to side. As it came nearer, it was carried low, and illuminated two extremely shaky brown legs, which staggered from side to side, tottered, recovered themselves, then began it all over again. We sat in amused silence while this strange creature appeared and disappeared among the shrubs, and at last came close to the verandah steps and revealed its whole identity. The light crept up from the round paper lantern over a sturdy body, very poorly dressed, and crowned by a sleepy face full of irresponsible smiles — a face which waggled joyfully from side to side, and was the colour of old wood; in fact, our neighbour the charcoal-burner, royally drunk.

"This is a very good house," he remarked; "better than the Bansho Kwan" (the village inn).

"What do you want?" Mr. G—— asked. "You have mistaken the road to your house."

"No," replied our visitor, shaking his head as gravely as he could, — "no mistake. House want, house find. Rain soon. Stay here."

He seemed about to sit down on the verandah, when some of the servants appeared; the man spoke in a loud excited way, and they had heard the strange voice.

"You have lost your way," Mr. G—— repeated; "this is not an inn. You shall be accompanied till you find the right path."

Then Rinzo and Uma, looking much amused, took each an arm of the stray lamb. Rinzo relieved him of his lantern, and they walked him down the path, he talking excitedly all the time about the Bansho Kwan, where he said there had been a wedding feast, and just a little — oh! very little — saké for everybody. And, indeed, he did not care to go away, although such honourable persons deigned to accompany him; for this was better than the Bansho Kwan — much better than the Bansho Kwan. His voice died off in the distance; and in about ten minutes our men came back, saying that they had put him in the right path, and he could make no mistakes now; besides, it was beginning to rain, and that would sober him, they thought.

The rain did not touch us under our broad verandah, so we sat on for some time, talking of everything under the sun, and unwilling to go and sit near the hot lamps in the drawing-room. The rain fell in soft splashes in our pond, and the trees began to talk, as they always do when there is rain enough to drop from branch to branch. The air was almost too sweet from the masses of *Lilium auratum*, which mark our real midsummer in the hills. The gardener stands them, in huge sheaves, in straight jars a yard high, in the doorways and verandahs; and we were telling wonderful tales of pink lilies, brown lilies, yellow lilies, when — that same crazy lantern appeared coming towards the house, still more erratically than before. As it approached, the sound of heavy steps dragging over the wet pebbles made itself heard between some indistinct remarks about the Bansho Kwan — our friend the charcoal-burner again! He was much tipsier than he had been an hour before, and came with something of a swagger up the wet, slippery path.

"Good house — much rain — very wet. This is a bright house, good for a man to stay in — much better than the Bansho Kwan!"

"Go home at once," said Mr. G——, who thought he was not so tipsy as he seemed. "You must have been drinking a great deal of saké not to know that you are making a mistake."

"A mistake no crime," replied the charcoal-burner. "No" (this to Rinzo, who took his arm), "I will not go away; why should a poor man be sent away? Why should a poor man be scolded because he loses his way? Is it a crime to lose one's way? Oh no! I will stay here — here!"

The servants were just about to remove him firmly, in spite of his violent protestations, when Furihata's highly official lantern marched quickly up the path; and at the sight of his cap and white gloves the poor tipsy intruder collapsed, and began to weep over his pitiful fate. He was carried off at last, still wailing about the nice house that was so very much better than the Bansho Kwan; and when the servants returned, they said that the stern Furihata had put the poor sinner comfortably to bed on the mats of the police station, where, as I was afterwards told, he woke up good and happy the next morning, and got home successfully by daylight.

Our garden entrance looks so like a piece of the road, that strangers and pilgrims constantly turn into it, and come wandering up to the house, which some of them take for a foreign hotel. One evening, when we returned very late from some expedition, we were told that two English gentlemen, riding down the pass, had entered the house, and ordered two bedrooms and dinner; they took Dinsmore for the proprietor, and were greatly overcome when they found that they had invaded a fellow-countryman's private castle. Some friends of ours, who have built a charming cottage at Chusenji, above Nikko, told me that last summer two hot and weary Englishmen burst into their house, and informed the astonished servant that breakfast for twelve people must be ready in half an hour; the rest of the party were on the road. They would have an omelette, beefsteaks, Kirin beer, and I know not how much more. But by the time they had gone into these details, the Japanese "boy" had remembered three words of English. He bowed politely, and then said, "This — European — house!" The unlucky intruders fled without saying another word, and probably found all they wanted at the excellent inn a few hundred yards farther up the path.

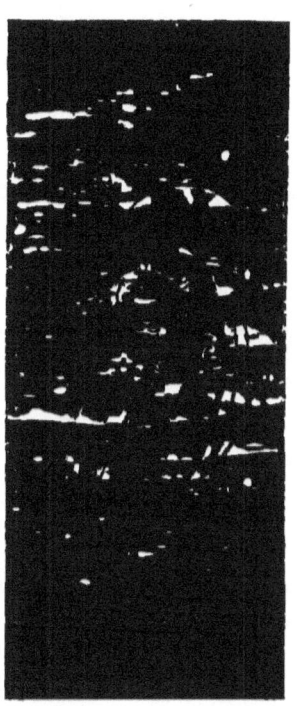

DHĀRMI, A SAGE WHO FLOATED TO JAPAN THROUGH THE WATER

Since I have spoken of the pilgrims, let me tell you something about them; for they go by us in great bands at this time of year, and are certainly the most picturesque and cheery devotees that ever walked. On the road that leads up the pass, there is a spot where an old tree has fallen, and makes a pleasant seat. Beyond, the path is steeper, and turns in to follow the trend of a gorge whose sides are all a tangle of wild forest. Sitting here to rest in the breathless afternoon, we hear the phantom of a sound, the tinkle of a bell so far off on the hillside that it sounds unreal, intermittent, and we strain our ears to catch it again. Yes, it is a little nearer now — now nearer still. A little farther up, the road is broken by the storms; and now passing feet are sending the loose rubble leaping down the slope in little showers. Now a chant is wafted to us, with the deep note of the bell; and in a moment a strange-looking train comes out of the green leafage and winds down the hill. There are nine of them to-day, and they are bound for Zenkogi, the great Temple at Nagano; their dress is that of pilgrims who ascend the holy mountains; and there are no women among them. The foremost is a tall handsome man, who carries a straight wooden standard, with strange characters painted black on its whiteness. He, like all those who follow him, is dressed in pure white, with sacred characters printed on the cotton. The close-fitting leggings are white too, and finish with *tabi* and straw sandals, *waraji*, which may be bought for next to nothing at every tea-house, and are seldom worn more than through one day's march. The pilgrim's robe is closely kilted up through his cotton girdle, which, tight

PILGRIMS

as it is, holds his money, his pipe, and any other valuables that he must carry. To the belt is attached that soft tinkling bell which gave us the signal of his coming; and on his head is a huge mushroom hat, made of lightest pith or shavings, and resting over, but not on, the head by means of a bamboo circle, from which spring light supports, so that the air passes in under the white umbrella. The hat is marked with the same ideograph that is stamped on his clothes, probably the name of the pilgrim club of his village or district; and on his shoulders he wears a piece of matting, which hangs round his neck by a string. This is his raincloak, his seat, his bed, and is called the *goza*. Then in his hand he carries a staff, with several names burnt into it — the names of the shrines he has visited; and a flask hangs at his side, in which he can bring home some of the water of a sacred lake or pond, such as many of the sanctuaries possess. His sleeves are as tightly tied up as his skirts; and although the costume may sound strange thus described in detail, yet nothing could look lighter or be more appropriate for the purpose of long walking in the heat.

I have described one man's dress, and have thus described the rest; for they are all alike, this being the prescribed uniform for climbing the high and holy peaks. The train looked wonderfully cool and picturesque coming out from the green foliage of the woods. The first man had a handsome face, very bronzed and healthy, with bright eyes, which glanced curiously at us, although he did not break off the chant in which he was leading the rest — a chant which is a constant repetition of one phrase: "Rokkon Shōjō, Oyama Kaisei" (May our six senses be pure, and honourable mountain weather fine). Behind him came a boy; then an old man, who must have made many pilgrimages, and is perhaps near the last of all; then a prosperous-looking tradesman; after him an ascetic, with pale face and immovable expression. The pilgrim club sends people from the counter and the factory, as well as from the farm and the rice-field, to tramp the holy roads together, and bring back blessings for the rest of the villagers or townsfolk, too busy or too old or too weak to perform the pilgrimage for themselves.

The pilgrim clubs are institutions existing all through the country, to enable even the very poor to visit holy places, and to get an immense amount of change and amusement and interest on the way. Hundreds of people (and often thousands) belong to a club, which can be started anywhere by anybody who chooses to obtain permission to do so from the authorities of his particular sect (and sects are numberless), and who has the energy or the necessary personality to get his friends to join him. A tiny entrance fee of a few cents is required, and the subscription varies from eight to fifteen cents a year. When all the expenses are paid, the remaining money is raffled for, and the winners (perhaps 2 or 3 per cent. of the whole number) spend their gains on the pilgrimage; but no one is debarred from going at his own expense if he pleases. The president of the club is always the leader, and his expenses are paid as a matter of course. He knows the road, he knows the shrines and the priests and the innkeepers; but he is not required to see to actual payments, a treasurer being elected, who has to give an account of all these. The inns take pilgrims at reduced prices, and the cost of even a very long expedition is so tiny that we Europeans in our stupid vulgar extravagance would hardly know that we had spent it at all. It is a matter of cents, and yet the Japanese manages to get weeks of travelling on it, to visit one holy or historical spot (it is the same thing very often in his country) after another, and to make acquaintance with endless numbers of his countrymen, all bound, during the few summer weeks of pilgrimage-time, on the same errand.

As the pilgrimages are really made on foot, of course the summer months are usually chosen, as the fine weather and long days add greatly to the pleasure of tramping through the country; indeed, the shrines on the peaks can only be visited between the middle of July and the beginning of September. Then the rest-houses are opened, the roads have been mended, the tea-houses are all ready to receive the guests, and the mountain is called "open." There are many holy peaks; but of all, Fuji is the greatest, and the ascent the most painful. Women belong to the pilgrim clubs, and have also clubs of their own; but they are not allowed (were not would be a better word) to mount to the summit. They were considered too common, made of too base a stuff, to tread the sacred ground of the mountain's crest, and were stopped at some distance from it; and in consequence they flocked to the lowland shrines, where they are welcomed and made to feel at home. They travel constantly to the great Temple of Zenkogi, which lies to our west in the town of Nagano; and to judge by their beaming faces and happy chatter, they must enjoy the expedition mightily, though most of them are old and grey, having handed over household cares to the useful daughter-in-law, and feeling now free to attend to their souls and their amusement. I once asked one of our servants about his mother — how she passed her time, what her occupations were. "No

AN OLD WOMAN PILGRIM

work; she not work now — too much old! Little temple go, little theatre go — very happy!"

The "O'Bassans" of the pilgrim parties are often accompanied by a grandchild, a bright little maid of twelve or thirteen, who waits on her grandmother, and stares amazed at barbarians like ourselves. It is surprising to find how far these old women and little girls can walk, carrying all their baggage in humble bundles — such tiny bundles! Some of them seem to be as little troubled with luggage as a migrating swallow.

So in the pleasant summer-time, through the length and breadth of the land, the roads are all alive with gay parties of people visiting the shrines of their own sect, and then those of any other sects which seem attractive or profitable. For in the curiously mixed condition of religious ideas, sect becomes confused with sect, not in principle, but in personality; for a person may belong to more than one at a time without prejudice to either. Some pious persons spend their whole time in making pilgrimages; but I must say that this kind of piety does not seem to interfere with their catching cheerfully at every straw of amusement that comes along. There is also, I fancy, much respect and consideration shown to pilgrims after they return to their own villages, and for all their lives they will rank higher in their townsmen's estimation than the people who have never performed them. A pilgrimage confers a kind of diploma of holiness, and is also a claim on the gratitude of the stayers at home, since it is hoped that the blessings prayed for by two or three at the distant shrine will descend individually and richly on the generous subscribers who enabled them to visit the sanctuary.

Very different are the laughing bands of the Japanese pilgrim clubs to the companies one meets just across the water, in China, where people never laugh. There is an eminently holy temple near Ningpo, where day after day, year after year, tottering painfully on the horrible swollen hoofs which are the inevitable evolution in age of the "golden lilies," the broken feet of childhood, bands of forlorn old women come with prayers and tears to entreat the merciful gods that in their next transmigration their crushed womanhood may be laid aside, and that they may return — as men.

We stood aside one day to let some pilgrims pass us on the road. One of the men could hardly get past me at all, overcome with amazement at his first sight of a blue-eyed creature in strange garments, the foreign barbarian woman. The road was rough, and he stumbled heavily almost at my feet. His companion laughed heartily. "That is what comes of staring at the elder sister!" he cried; but the astonished one picked himself up, passed on and out of sight with his head turned and his eyes still fixed on myself, as if expecting to see me turn into a fox on the spot, or send my head after him like the snake-woman of the Japanese ghost story.

We had a visit from a dear old woman pilgrim

one day, as we were sitting at afternoon tea out of doors. She was very old, and partially blind; but in spite of this was evidently the leader of two younger women who accompanied her. They were all peasants, burnt in face and limb from long standing in the rice-fields under the scorching sun. The old lady had her skirts kilted very high, and a blue towel tied coquettishly round her head. As she came up the path, she seemed to share the feelings of the lost charcoal-burner; for she kept exclaiming, "How beautiful, how grand! Whose is this honourable beautiful house?" The servant explained; and then she said that it was the first time she had seen a foreign house, or garden: might she humbly ask that she and her companions should be allowed to stay a little and look at it? Of course she might! So she went over the funny little domain, and looked with the greatest interest at the cooking arrangements, and inquired if that honourable animal (the Brown Ambassador) with the honourably long tail were really an honourable dog? Makotoni? Sōdeska? What great and wonderful people these honourable foreigners are, to be sure!

CHAPTER XXVII

THE AUTUMN TYPHOON. — THE LOSS OF THE "ERTOGROUL."
— LEGENDS OF FUJI. — THE GREAT UPHEAVAL. — CHINESE TRADITION AND THE SACRED MOUNTAIN. — THE STORY OF JOFUKU. — THE LOTUS PEAK

TOKYO, *October*, 1890.

OUR return to Tokyo was followed by the usual autumn typhoon, more destructive than ever this year. The catastrophe which has saddened us most was the loss of the *Ertogroul*, a Turkish battle-ship, which went down with the admiral and five hundred and fifty men. The poor admiral was always afraid that something would happen to his horrible old tub with her worn-out engines, and only a short time ago was heard to say that she could not possibly live through a bad typhoon. He had warned the authorities at home of the state of the vessel, and solemnly rejected any responsibility for what might occur. He was a charming man, and had made himself so much liked here that the tragedy has cast quite a gloom over our small circle. He had fifty cadets on board, and they were all lost. About sixty of the men were rescued, and have been treated with the greatest kindness by the Japanese. A Russian man-of-war offered to take the poor fellows home, and the offer was accepted by the Cabinet, and went up to the Emperor to be approved. To every one's surprise, the Emperor was most indignant; the men, he said, were his guests, and as such they should be taken home in one of his own battle-ships with all the honours. This is accordingly to be done. Our own fleet gathers in force just at this time, before going south into winter quarters, and we have been very busy. It is rather an imposing sight, when the European squadrons are all gathered in Yokohama Harbour.

I am always glad to return to Tokyo, and to greet Fuji San from my windows once more. With all the splendid scenery of the hills, I miss the great white mountain when we are in Karuizawa, and feel more at home in Japan when its perfect outline is the first thing I see in the morning, the last at night. There are a thousand beautiful stories told about the mountain; they hang round its name as the mists hang round its feet, and the love and reverence of a hundred centuries have wrapped it in a mystic robe of holiness, so that to look at it is to have the mind raised to higher things, whether one will or no.

There is a strange legend of the origin of Fuji, which connects it with Lake Biwa, the Lake of the Lute, a hundred and thirty miles distant, in the province of Omi. Many a pleasure-boat full of laughing girls glides over its surface in the harvest moonlight; and the girls slip back their long sleeves, and, leaning over the side, gather the water in the palms of their hands, and let it slide through their fingers, or throw it in silver showers on the dusky face of the night, each saying in her heart, "Now are my hands full of the sacred snows of Fuji San!" And perhaps at the same moment, far away in Hakone, a *gyōja*, or mountain-worshipper, standing on Fuji's crest after a long day's climbing, stoops and takes up a handful of snow, and bathes his face with its whiteness, crying out, "Now am I washing in the holy water of Lake Biwa!"

And to understand the legend we must go back to the dawn of time. Many gods had there been in reed-grown Japan; but they were not immortal, and faded away with the fading seasons, scattered on the air as the soft-blown down is scattered when rush-heads break their velvet coverings and a million winged seedlings wanton in the breeze. But at last came the god Izanami, and he said, "Where now all is water among the reeds, we will make dry land!" So, standing on the sevenfold radiance of the Bridge of Heaven, which we call the rainbow, Izanami plunged his coral-pointed spear down, down to the bottom of the sea; and when he drew it up again, little portions of sand and mud were hanging on it. These he threw on the reed-grown land, the land of twilight and water shadows and changing lights, where the moon danced among the reeds, and the sun stayed not, since there was nought for him to ripen in that bowl of tears. So Izanami shook the sea relics from his spear, and they spread out in the form of a dragon-fly, and made fair dry country, full of rich growths, and smiling in the sun. Then the god said: "It is well; and these green

PLEASURE BOATS ON THE LAKE.

lands shall be called Akitsusu, the Islands of the Dragon-Fly. Now let us fill them with men, like ourselves, but not immortal."

Then he called the great goddess Izanagi, his consort, and she came willingly at the sound of his voice out of her house among the stars; and he said to her, "Come, and behold the country I have made." And together they descended to the land, and separated, Izanami walking towards the sun, and Izanagi towards the moon; and they met, face to face, after walking for many days. And Izanagi, rejoiced to see her Lord after the days of loneliness, leaped forward towards him, crying out, "Oh, joy to behold the beautiful god!" But her husband was displeased, and said, "Dost thou speak first? That is unfitting in a woman. Walk round the islands once more, and repent thy immodesty!" So, weeping, Izanagi passed him, and walked many days, weeping at his rebuff; and because of her copious tears Akitsusu is a land of many streams and wet fields. And she said in her heart: "Is not my Lord right? Never shall he reproach me again!" And at last they met, face to face, in a green meadow, at the time of the sunrising. And Izanagi stood still, and the dawn mists were round her feet, and the sunrise on her brow; and she bowed her head in reverence. And her husband, seeing her submission and modesty, sprang towards her, crying out, "Now, indeed, do I behold a beauteous woman!" And Izanagi wept no more, but smiled on the wise god her husband; and he and she remained in the new country until she had borne him many sons

IN THE LAND OF REEDS AND SHADOWS

and daughters, and the land was peopled with their children, to whom they taught the true wisdom of the gods.

At that time the land was all one great plain, and there were no mountains and no lakes. Where the water lay, the people made rich rice-fields; and where the soil was dry, grew splendid forests; and all the foundations of the country were bound together in strength by wistaria roots, which stretch but break not. And at last Izanami and Izanagi said farewell to their children, and sailed away to found-

and people other lands. Centuries brought more and more power and splendour to the Islands of the Dragon-Fly, and then — the great earthquake came. One night the world was shaken to its foundations; all its bands of roots and armour of rocks could hold it together no longer. The sea seemed to be pouring down upon it from the sky; the sound of the storm was as the battling of dragons; darkness lay on the land, and black fear on the hearts of the people. That night seemed to them longer than a year of famine; and when morning dawned at last, many a head was white which had shone black the day before. But the morning was clear and peaceful, and Amaterasu, the sun-goddess, smiled on earth and sea, making all things white-faced in her shining. The people of Omi went out over the plain to till their rice-fields as usual, and as they went they shook their heads, fearing to find much damage done to the tender rice; but when they came to where yesterday had seen rice-fields spread in the sun, a great wonder met their eyes. No fields were there; in their stead a great lake, sixty miles long, and shaped like a lute, lay dimpling in the morning light. Had a piece of the blue field of heaven fallen there in the storm, or had the ocean crept in from the far coast and hollowed a bed for itself out of the heart of Omi? Who could say? There lay the blue jewel for all the world to see, and the people came from far and near to gaze on it; its depths were full of fish, and towns and hamlets soon grew up on its shores. Great wealth came into Omi; and because of its strange shape the lake was called Biwa, the Lake of the Lute.

But the great storm had not raged in Omi alone. Far away in Hakone the earthquake and the hurricane had been as terrible as in the more southern province.

FUJIYAMA FROM HAKONE LAKE

The people in Hakone had prayed and wept through the long dark hours, and many a home was shattered by the earthquake, many a farm devastated by the tempest. But peace came with the morning to Hakone as it had come to Omi; and when the sun rose, it shone on a glorious mountain, marble pure, perfect in majestic symmetry, Fujiyama. At first they too thought they beheld the vision of a dream, a cloud picture that the noon would melt. But the dazzling cone changed not, though all around it changed. The clouds that lay at its foot would rise and veil its splendour for an hour, then they passed away; but the new glory remained. By day it towered against the blue, by night the white crown seemed wreathed in stars from the Milky Way. The land which some god had scooped in the hollow of his hand from Omi he had built up in a lordly mountain in Suruya.

Its fame went forth even across the stormy sea to China and Corea. In the oldest Chinese books there is frequent mention of Horaisan, a sacred mountain of perfect beauty and shining whiteness, which was said to rise out of the Eastern Ocean. The word passed over to Japan with other Chinese lore in time; it came with the meaning which it then bore in China, Elysium, the Land of Happy Souls, Paradise, and has kept that meaning in Japan, where the name is in no way connected with Fujiyama. It occurs in congratulatory odes, and also in Japanese fairy tales, always in this sense. It is said that only of late years has the original allusion to Fujiyama been traced by Japanese men of letters.

In China wonderful stories were told about the half-mythical Horaisan. It was said to be inhabited by a number of holy hermits, and that whoever climbed to its summit would live for ever, immortal, untouched by death or decay. And a quaint story shows how profound this belief was. The Emperor Shin-no-shiko, who reigned in China some two thousand years ago, had everything that this world can give — empire, riches, beautiful children, perfect health. And all this was as poison to him, because he knew that he must die and leave it all behind. Night and day death was before him, as a patient enemy who could bear to wait because he must win at the last. And Shin-no-shiko vowed that he would overcome death; and he sent for all the wise men in the country, and spent enormous sums on trying to discover the elixir of life, and offered untold treasure to any one who could help him to find it.

And many came; but all their prescriptions seemed worthless, since those slaves on whom they were tried died unresistingly when Shin-no-shiko nodded to his green bannermen to slay them. He was almost in despair, and used to wander through the golden courts of his Palace and about his magnificent hunting-park always with the thought of death in his heart, and he became morose and cruel, and was a terror to all. But at last there came a very wise man called Jofuku, saying that in truth the other wise men were all fools, but that he, and he alone, could tell the Emperor where to obtain that for which he longed. He seemed so sure of success that the Emperor began to hope again, and sent for him at once. Then Jofuku told him that the hermits of the Holy White Mountain in the Eastern Sea possessed the water of life, and that to them the Emperor must send a mission begging them to give him a little, so that he might live for ever.

Then Shin-no-shiko rejoiced greatly, thinking that immortality was his at last. Jofuku offered to lead the mission, and the Emperor gladly promised him money and ships wherewith to reach the holy mountain. Jofuku asked for a thousand of the most beautiful youths and maidens of the Empire to accompany him, in order, as he said, to please the hermits; and he also took a quantity of treasure wherewith to reward them for the elixir of life, and he took, apparently without asking the Emperor's leave, a great number of learned and sacred books.

All this splendid plunder was put on board a fleet of ships which Shin-no-shiko fitted out for the crafty ambassador; and Jofuku sailed away, to the land of the rising sun and the holy mountain — for good and all. No thought of returning to China had ever been in his mind. His five hundred goodly couples, his treasure, and his books were what he needed for the founding of a colony in the country over the waters, and the Emperor waited in vain to see him sail into port with the elixir of life. Too late he found that he had been deceived, and in his rage made bonfires of all the learned books, and put to death all the sages of his empire. "The uneducated are more easily governed," ran his proclamation; and terrible was the destruction which followed it. But Jofuku was out of reach, and cared little for the Emperor's wrath. He founded a splendid colony in the Japanese province of Ki-shiu, and the valuable books which he stole (as if foreseeing Shin-no-shiko's wholesale destruction of learning) are to this day the envy and despair of Chinese scholars.

All this does not explain why the white and holy Horaisan of Chinese tradition is the Fujiyama of Japanese reality. As there are no less than twenty-eight characters which represent various meanings of the monosyllable Fu, it naturally follows that there is great variety in the characters used to transcribe the beloved mountain's name. The word *yama* which is generally added merely means mountain, and *san* may be translated either as a term of respect or as the Chinese *shan*, mountain or hill. The name has many forms; but Fuji San is the one I have most often heard used, and there is no authority for preferring one signification over the other. When it is written 不 二 it means "not two," unequalled, peerless; the characters 不 死 signify deathless, immortal, and are connected with Jofuku's story of the elixir of life. The scholar finds a likeness in Fuji's towering height to the superiority of the learned over the rest of mankind, and writes it "rich scholar." A young girl in her father's garden, so the story goes, once plucked a handful of the white and purple wistaria blossom, and called it Fuji, because of its likeness to the holy mountain when the twilight hangs a violet veil above the snows, and because its peak was shaped like the spotless flower. Then she remembered that the hair of a beautiful woman ought to grow in points, leaving her forehead the shape of the mountain. So she felt in her sash for her little mirror, and pulled it out of its embroidered case, and looked at herself as she stood in the sunshine under the wistaria trails; and as she looked in the mirror, she was so surprised at the gleaming whiteness of her forehead in the sun that she raised her eyebrows in surprise, and two white points rose towards her dark hair, and she was satisfied because her forehead was white and shapely

FUJIYAMA FROM IWABUCHI

as the holy mountain; and from that time the ideal feminine brow is called *Fuji Bitai*, the Fuji forehead. And so on, for indeed the legends about the beloved mountain are endless; every one loves it, and each calls it that which stands highest in his own imagination. The true origin of the name is probably to be found in an Ainu word meaning "to push forth," a combination alluding either to the eruptions of the volcano in past times or to the river which breaks impetuously from the mountain-side.

Fuji San is sacred to many gods, even as it goes by many names. Pilgrims of every sect crowd along its steep paths in the summer days, and, no matter how separated on other points, all agree that it is a very holy mountain; and I think each one, while smilingly tolerating the mistakes of his neighbours, feels that it is the home of one of his own deities or tutelary spirits. It is dedicated to a goddess — tradition calls her, "The Princess who makes the Blossoms of the Trees to flower;" but in spite of this fact the ascent was forbidden to women until quite lately. It is a rough and arduous undertaking, involving a night passed in the rude shelter-hut on the summit; and a young Japanese friend of mine, who went up with a party of Europeans, told me that nothing would induce her to go through such hardship again. I reminded her of the Japanese proverb, "There are two kinds of fools: those who have never ascended Fuji, and those who have ascended it twice."

The ordinary pilgrim must not be confounded with the *gyōja*, the true mountain-worshippers, who are supposed to practise great austerities, and to lead lives of great purity. They are rather despised by both Buddhists and Shintoists, on account of having fallen away from what is called the right teaching. This same right teaching must be either very easy — or very difficult — to find; for the opposing sects have all taken some of each other's dogmas and most of each other's gods, so that to an unpractised eye it is almost impossible to distinguish between them, except in the shrines of "purified Shinto," where no images exist. The *gyōja* is chiefly distinguished as an ascetic, who has so far overcome the flesh that he can perform amazing feats like those of the *yogi* of Thibet. It is rather amusing to find that one of his chief penances is reckoned that of bathing in cold water long and constantly; he must even stand under waterfalls in the mountain-paths (a thing which I have seen Englishmen do for coolness' sake, only the poor *gyōja* must do it in the chill hours before dawn); and the colder and cleaner he is, the more elevated does he become, until he can take command, as it were, of the forces of nature. He is not forbidden to marry, but may not look boldly at any woman whom he meets; the hardships which the genial club pilgrim undergoes in laughing company for a few weeks in the summer are the *gyōja's* life portion; the name means "the man of austerities," but his sect is called "Yama-bushi," the mountain-worshippers. The true *gyōja* can do things which would be terribly distressing to ordinary humanity: he can stand on the narrowest ledges at enormous heights without feeling dizzy; he can play with scalding water and walk over live coals unhurt; he can mount ladders made of fine-edged sword-blades without shedding a drop of blood; he can fast beyond the limits of human resistance; he has probably climbed every sacred peak in Japan, and becomes personally possessed of the gods on the holy mountain of Ontake. Fuji, steep and cold, has no terrors for him, and doubtless says much to him that the ordinary pilgrims cannot hear. The *gyōja* sees Lake

Biwa in Fuji's snow; the *gyōja* can hear when the alien grains of sand and dust that have come up in the sandals of the pilgrims go racing down the mountainsides at night, true to the mystic law which says that no unconsecrated soil may remain on the bosom of the holy mountain. The *gyōja* will tell you that, of all dreams, the dream of Fujiyama is the most splendidly auspicious.

There is one more name besides those which I have enumerated, and to my mind it is the most poetic of all the titles of Fuji San: the Buddhists call it the Peak of the White Lotus. To them the snow-crowned mountain, rising in unsullied purity from the low hills around it, was the symbol of the white lotus, whose foot grows green under its wide leaves in the stagnant water, while its cup of breathless white holds up its golden heart, its jewel, to the sky; and the wonderful symmetry of the mountain, with its eight-sided crater, reminded them of the eight-petalled lotus which forms the seat of the glorified Buddha. In the more learned odes, the mountain is called Fuyo Ho, the Lotus Peak; and the Buddhists say that the great teacher, Buddha himself, gave it this perfect shape, the symbol of Nirvana's perfect peace.

So the queen of mountains hangs between the stars of heaven and the mists of earth, dear to every heart that can be still and understand. As I said once before, Fuji dominates life here by its silent beauty; sorrow is hushed, longing quieted, strife forgotten in its presence, and broad rivers of peace seem to flow down from that changeless home of peace, the Peak of the White Lotus.

CHAPTER XXVIII

THE OPENING OF THE DIET. — THE ATTACK ON THE RUSSIAN
LEGATION. — *SOSHI* AT OUR OWN GATES. — PRINCE KO-
MATSU AND THE GRAND CROSS OF THE BATH. — THE
IMPERIAL CHRYSANTHEMUMS

TOKYO, *November*, 1890.

THE month of maples, chrysanthemums, Imperial garden parties, the beginning of our queer little gay season, has been marked by an important event, not unaccompanied by disaster. The event was the opening of the Diet in great state by the Emperor, and the disaster — the storming of the Russian Legation the same day. The inauguration of the Houses of Parliament has been the point towards which great preparations and precautions have been tending for many months past. The elections took place quietly and successfully in July, when we were in Karuizawa; the Japanese are a profoundly lawful people (if I may use the word in its old sense), and there were few or no disturbances. Of course here and there some irregularities crept into the proceedings, and one or two elections were invalidated on account of bribery; but as those things are not unknown in England, the very cradle of representative government, we must not be surprised at their occurring here on the first trial of the new methods, and doubtless many a strange scene will be witnessed before the huge unbroken team of deputies settle down into their working stride.

The present Houses of Parliament form a group of roomy wooden buildings, intended only to serve until the permanent and costly erections planned for the purpose can be completed. With admirable good sense the Government decided that, until the needs of the Diet had been shown during a working session, the permanent Houses for its accommodation should not be put in hand, and also that no national vanity should induce them to spend more than was absolutely necessary on these temporary buildings. A very small sum, 80,000 yen, was voted for the work; but as it went on, various portions had to be added to the original plan drawn out by Stegmüller, the German architect to whom the task had been entrusted, and the final cost has proved to be about 240,000 yen (£24,000), a small sum when one considers the necessities of the case. Although carried out in wood, the structure is dignified and harmonious. It covers a very large area; is surrounded, of course, by a garden, planted with full-grown trees; and contains Chambers of Session for the House of Representatives and the House of Peers, each containing three hundred and twenty-six seats, and accommodation in the balconies for four hundred visitors. Besides the great halls, there are over a hundred rooms fitted up as committee-rooms, libraries, and so forth; fire-proof warehouses for archives; and two official residences for the

Chief Secretaries of the Upper and Lower House. Huge stacks of chimneys show that the winter session need not be a cold one; and the electric light is used here as in the Palace. The decorations are in such beautiful colourings (pale rosy terra-cotta, dull green, and rather dusky gold) that the absence of elaborate ornament is not even noticed; and certainly the comfort of the mem-

H. I. H. PRINCE FUSHIMI NO MIYA

H. I. H. PRINCESS FUSHIMI NO MIYA

bers has been carefully consulted. The seats and desks look most inviting. In the Chamber of the Upper House, above and behind the President's table, a large alcove, almost like a chancel, has been built into the wall; and here stands the throne, where the Emperor will sit on the rare occasions when he attends a session. The President's seat and table would then be removed, and the sovereign would preside alone over his lieges. The decoration of the throne place is most beautiful, the baldachino and drapings of heavy Kyoto silks, and the front shut in by a richly carved railing. When the Emperor is absent, a curtain is drawn across the alcove, and the view of the throne shut out. The Empress, the Imperial Princes, and the Diplomatic Corps have boxes, made as comfortable and pretty as possible; and on the second floor a large reception-room for the Emperor is built over the entrance hall, and opens on a balcony, where he can step out and show himself to the people if necessary.

There had been some delay about the opening ceremony, arising from the fact that the whole organisation of the Diet had to be elaborated before it could take place. When the day came, the excitement was intense; although, apart from the invitations sent to the heads of missions, and other officials, only the most tardy announcement had appeared as to the hour when the Emperor would leave the Palace. From early morning the streets were crowded with people, and the great open spaces round the Houses of Parliament were packed with dense crowds, such as always gather eagerly when there is a chance of beholding the sovereign. The police had their hands full, as they were responsible for keeping the public back to a line drawn twenty yards from the main route on all the streets intersecting the road from the Palace,—this not to isolate the Imperial procession, but to keep space open for the hundreds of vehicles which must pass conveying visitors to the Houses of Parliament before the Emperor's arrival. The result was perfect; for there was not a single block of any kind, or the slightest difficulty in finding the carriages and jinrikshas when the ceremony was over. A very stringent regulation forbids that any one should look down on the sovereign from an elevated position. There were hardly any upper windows on the route, which passed by the great avenues along the Palace moats; but one or two youngsters who had audaciously climbed trees so as to get a better view were pulled down sternly by the police, and the attempt was not repeated. A very large body of troops lined the entire route four deep before the Emperor finally left the Palace; but this was done merely to add to the pomp of the procession, for his Majesty would have nothing to fear from any class of his subjects except too warm a demonstration of loyalty, and even that would always be tempered by the religious awe with which even the most violent Radicals here regard his sacred person.

The invitations named ten o'clock as the hour for arriving at the Houses of Parliament, and by half-past ten the rush of carriages and jinrikshas was over, and a broad empty way was left for the procession from the Palace. It was headed, of course, by Guards and outriders; and then came three carriages full of Imperial Princes (cousins and uncles of the Emperor) old enough to take their seats in the House of Peers; then the beautiful State coach, with its glass sides and golden phœnix crown, its six splendidly caparisoned horses and gorgeous attendants, passed slowly by, carrying the Emperor in his marshal's uniform and many

decorations, attended by Marquis Tokudaiji, the Lord
High Chamberlain, who sat on the opposite seat. A
body of Life Guards followed the Emperor's coach; and
then came a number of State carriages containing the
Cabinet Ministers and Court officials. When the Emperor arrived at the entrance to the Houses of Parliament, he was received by all the great functionaries,
headed by Count Ito (who has been elected President
of the Upper House), and then proceeded to wait in the
great reception-room while all those who had accompanied him were sorted into their places. A separate
reception-room was set aside for the Diplomatic Corps,
whose younger members were indignant at finding all
the windows impenetrably veiled to prevent their looking down from this upper floor on the Emperor's arrival. They had, however, the privilege of accompanying
him to the Chamber of Peers, and told me that it presented an imposing sight when he entered and took
his seat on the throne, surrounded by that great concourse of subjects and courtiers. The Commons were
all gathered in the hall, some of the lower seats having
been removed to give them standing room; the Empress
with the Princesses and her ladies (the only women present) took their places in the box prepared for them;
and the Strangers' Gallery, as well as every available
corner, was crowded with smart uniforms and brilliant
decorations. The members of the Lower House were
almost all in plain evening dress, and it was maliciously
remarked that they looked fluttered and delighted;
while the Peers, conspicuous in their gorgeous military

PORTRAIT AND AUTOGRAPH OF H. I. H. PRINCE ARISUGAWA TARUHITO

and official uniforms, preserved the impassive dignity and calm which mark the Japanese aristocrat.

When the marshals entered preceding the Emperor, the House rose and stood in breathless silence, and then bowed like one man almost to the ground as he took his seat. The first sound heard was the Emperor's voice, when, standing before the throne, he made his first speech to his first Parliament. It was one of those incidents which strike the hour, clear for all men to hear, in the course of a country's history; and no one then present will forget the solemn moment.

Here is the speech:

"We announce to the members of the House of Peers and to those of the House of Representatives: That all institutions relating to internal administration, established during the period of twenty years since Our accession to the Throne, have been brought to a state approaching completeness and regular arrangement. By the efficacy of the virtues of Our Ancestors, and in concert with yourselves, We hope to continue and extend those measures, to reap good fruit from the working of the Constitution, and thereby to manifest, both at home and abroad, the glory of Our country and the loyal and enterprising character of Our people.

"We have always cherished a resolve to maintain friendly relations with other countries, to develope commerce, and to extend the prestige of Our land. Happily Our relations with all the Treaty Powers are on a footing of constantly growing amity and intimacy.

"In order to preserve tranquillity at home and security from abroad, it is essential that the completion of Our naval and military defences should be made an object of gradual attainment.

"We shall direct our Ministers of State to submit to the Diet the Budget for the twenty-fourth year of Meiji, and certain projects of laws. We expect that you will deliberate and advise upon them with impartiality and discretion, and We trust that you will establish such precedents as may serve for future guidance."

So much for the event. Now I must tell you of the riot which broke out and threatened to wreck the Russian Legation while this majestic ceremony was going forward in the House of Peers.

As the Emperor was going thither, the procession had to pass the corner of the Russian Legation grounds, where two wide streets form an angle, and where a small pavilion perched on the garden wall gives a view down both streets. True to their orders, the police were keeping back the crowd which would have poured down from the side to the main street; and it may be that the people were indignant at seeing a number of foreign ladies and children standing on this point where they could see the Emperor from an elevated position quite forbidden to his own subjects. His Majesty at any rate entirely understood the situation, and glanced up, smiled, and nodded to Madame S—— and her daughter. I was not well enough to join them that morning, as I had intended doing; but they described to me what followed.

PORTRAIT AND AUTOGRAPH OF H. I. H. PRINCESS ARISUGAWA TADA

As soon as the Emperor had passed, the populace, composed largely of young students, tried to force the blockade of the main street. They were vigorously met by the police, who, seeing that they might soon be outnumbered, struck a few sharp blows with their sword-scabbards to reduce the mob to order. The ladies in the summer-house above were watching the contest with rather alarmed interest, when a cracker was exploded in the crowd with a snap and a puff of smoke, rather startling in the circumstances. Somebody in the pavilion gave a little scream, and there was a laugh among the rest, when they suddenly became aware that stones were being thrown at them from the crowd, first singly, then in showers, and increasing in size; a brick very nearly struck Mademoiselle S——, and, much to her mother's wrath (for Madame S—— is a gallant lady, who objects to retreating before a mob), the little group had to disappear from their position in the pavilion. By that time the stones were also flying over the front gates which open into the side-street, then crowded with a surging mob, and some terrified servants came rushing to say that the people were beginning to climb the gates. As all the gentlemen of the staff were absent with the Minister, there was no one to appeal to. Madame S—— sent the servants back to barricade the iron gates, which are fortunately strong and high, and then smuggled one man out of a little side-door in another part of the garden to call some of the policemen to enter by it and defend the place within. Her visitors and their children had taken refuge in a remote part of the house. Meanwhile, outside the gates, a pretty fierce fight was going on; the police were working bravely to get to the gate itself; and the men-servants had posted themselves in the pavilion, and were returning their assailants' fire by a shower of bricks, which had been piled for some new building in the garden, and which naturally did not tend to improve the temper of the mob. Madame S—— told me that her relief was intense, when she saw a little company of policemen file through the forgotten door and march to the gates and the pavilion. As soon as the crowd saw that the police were in force inside the enclosure, they lost something of their courage; but they were still surging against the gates in great numbers and much excitement, when the carriages containing the Minister and the Secretaries returning from the Diet drew up on the outskirts of the crowd, finding it impossible to penetrate through it. Knowing nothing of what had occurred, Monsieur S—— imagined that a fire must have broken out, and was much alarmed for the safety of his family. When at last a way was opened for him to drive up to his own gates, great was his amazement to see that they were held by a body of police, one of whose number sat astride the top bar with a revolver in hand, prepared to shoot any one who tried to follow him. The crowd quickly melted away after the Minister's return, but not before several arrests were made. The incident has naturally created a very unpleasant impression; but we are told that it really has no political significance. I have noticed that the actions of an excited crowd seldom have, especially if the apologist be a member of the Government.

Nevertheless there is a good deal of rampant *soshi-ism* abroad, and it manifests itself in quite unexpected ways. Hearing of the trouble at our friends' house, I ordered the carriage late in the afternoon to go and tell them how sorry I was for their fright. Just as I was ready to start, H—— came in and told me that he had sent the carriage back to the stables, as the streets were not safe for me to drive through. I was greatly surprised, as I have never been prevented from going out, even in last year's anti-foreign agitation. I learnt afterwards from Mr. G——, who was walk-

H. I. H. PRINCE KITA SHIRAKAWA

ing with him, that quite close to our own gates they had suddenly been surrounded by a band of *soshi*, armed with their favourite sword-sticks. An attempt had been made to distract the Chief's attention by hustling him behind, and at the moment when he was intended to turn his head a sword was drawn to strike him in front. But he refused to look behind him, and kept his eyes fixed on the face of the man in front, who lowered his sword at once. H—— laughed a little, and went on and finished his walk; but his companion told me that had he turned his head he would have been run through at once, for the *soshi* was closer to him than Mr. G—— when the thing happened. The Chief was in greater danger than any one had been in the riot of the morning. There was deep dismay in the Japanese Foreign Office when the matter was reported, and profuse apologies were of course made. H—— improved the occasion to insist upon the abolition of those horrid sword-sticks. Every turbulent *soshi* in Tokyo carries one, and they constitute a real danger in any excitement. We cannot imagine why the Government should be so shy of controlling the *soshi*, who are now wild misguided youths, and will be later very unmanageable and dangerous citizens.[1]

And now let us turn to gayer subjects. A pretty little compliment came out for Prince Komatsu the other day, the Grand Cross of the Bath, with which, I think, his Imperial Highness was very much pleased. We went with much solemnity to his Palace, and H—— gave the Queen's message and invested him with the collar, which is really a beautiful bit of gold and enamel work. All sorts of pretty speeches were made, and the Prince (who has the most good-natured face I ever saw, with a Disraeli curl on the forehead) kept us

[1] It is now an established fact that the *soshi* have often been employed by one party to frighten another into submission. A former member of the House of Representatives told me that he had found them extremely useful in this way. — 1898.

to lunch, and the Princess went through all the pretty speeches in her own royal-feminine language, quite a different dialect from the royal-masculine speech, which in its turn is quite apart from the speech of ordinary men, who must be careful when speaking to the Princes to use certain words consecrated only for the ears of royalty! Is this not a puzzling sum? Of course all the

H. I. H. PRINCESS KOMATSU

H. I. H. PRINCE KOMATSU

conversation is carried on with the help of interpreters; for though the Prince speaks some English, it is not enough to carry him through an official occasion, and the Princess will not admit that she knows any English words, though I suspect that she often understands what I am saying long before the interpreter has repeated it. She has the most lovely Paris frocks, and, though not pretty, is always extremely well put together. My wicked Dachs, the Brown Ambassador, fancies himself greatly in white satin, and generally picks out the smartest gown in the room to lie down on, with the air of paying its owner a great compliment. After the Prince had been invested with the Bath, he and the Princess came to dine with us. The Princess had a beautiful dress of white satin brocaded all over with gold feathers; and as we women were sitting in the drawing-room after dinner, Tip observed the gown from afar, and decided that it would suit his complexion. Giving one bound through the air, he landed on it with all his four fat paws outspread, and looked round to be complimented on the feat. The Princess screamed, taken off her guard by the sudden onslaught, the lady-in-waiting turned pale, and poor Tip was carried off in sad disorder. He is a source of the greatest amusement to the Japanese ladies who come to see me; they think his tricks quite miraculous; and he sits up before each one in turn to be fed with sugar and told that he is *rippai* (splendid). He is a born courtier; for he goes round on my reception days, speaking kindly to any strangers who come, holding out a solemn paw to be shaken by Europeans, but making a long Japanese bow with his head on the floor before the little ladies of the country, who go off into fits of laughter at the sight, and I am sure believe that I have taught him his absurd tricks.

I have at last seen the Palace chrysanthemums, which are extremely beautiful, and almost more interesting than beautiful, on account of the complete triumph of art over nature which they proclaim. The gardens devoted to them are those of the Aoyama Palace, on the eastern heights of the town. This was the Emperor's residence for several years, while the new Palace was being built, but it is now the home of the Empress-Dowager. The Emperor's birthday party is always given in the gardens of Aoyama, the chrysanthemum being his flower, even as the double cherry is that of the Empress, whose own birthday party is always given at the Hama Goten, the cherry-blossom Palace by the sea. As no party was given last year for the Emperor's birthday, this was my first view of these famous chrysanthemums, and I was quite dazzled by the extraordinary variety and size of the blooms. Those in the show gardens of Dango-Zaka do not approach them in splendour.

The Aoyama gardens are very large, and are laid out, according to Japanese rules, in lakes and islands, bridges and arbours, pavilions, rocks, little dells full of maple trees, and little hills crowned with strangely shaped stones of enormous value in the eyes of the Japanese. But at this season one hardly notices the other features of the grounds, because everywhere are armies of chrysanthemums, sheltered in large pavilions of pure white wood, open on one side of their length to the gaze of the admiring crowds who have been invited to behold them. These garden parties are wonderfully well arranged, and always seem to follow the same precedent. An hour is named on the card of invitation well ahead of the time when the Majesties intend to appear. The carriages put us down at the gate, and we have quite a long pleasant walk over the green lawns and through exquisitely kept grounds before we reach the place of gathering. All through the gardens the air is full of music, the bands being stationed in picturesque spots sufficiently far from each other not to distress the sensitive ear; the paths are full of all one's friends and acquaintances; the crowds of smart frocks and bright uniforms make the gayest of pictures under the trees. When the goal is reached, one finds a huge tent, all draped in the broad stripes of severe black and white, which are the mark of the Imperial Household; a tremendous feast (no better word quite expresses the fact) is laid out here for the world in general; and at one end is a smaller pavilion in which the sovereigns receive us, and where we have tea at little tables with the Court people. But the sovereigns are kind, and do not arrive until we have had time to walk about and look at all the show of flowers.

And what a show! There is one plant, standing alone under a carved roof, which has grown, as it was told, in the shape of a great junk, with a poop at either end, and double decks and all the rest of it. The central stem has become a tree, covered with solid bark; and it has thrown out this year nearly four hundred blossoms, all exactly alike, of the same size, and of a pale-pink colour, the whole thing occupying a space about fifteen feet long, and standing quite ten feet from the ground. When one can tear oneself away from this beauty, there are, as I have said, armies of flowers planted in terraces five or six rows deep, each entire row being so perfectly uniform that there is no single difference of petal or leaf all along the line; for the Japanese gardener would reject as failures the most beautiful blooms if the leaves grew unevenly up the stem. He succeeds in producing a hundred specimens, each flowering to the same point, with the leaves sprouting in perfect regularity at the same distances on the stalk. My simile of an army is really a correct one, for in looking down the lines there is no more dissimilarity to be discovered than in lines of well-drilled troops. And not only this, but between the lowest line and the topmost one our garden magician has managed to show us the growth from bud to bloom; the lowest line, standing hardly

CHRYSANTHEMUMS

a foot from the ground, is all in bud, the next slightly more advanced, the next still more so, and so on till the highest of all shows us the full-blown beauty of the flower. In the very long thin-petalled specimens now in fashion here, the disc is spread out like a white or crimson sun, over a delicate frame of copper wire, many inches across. In some specimens the petals are so long that they hang over the edge of the wire in a flowery fringe; in others they are spiked, and bristled with what look like fine hairs growing out of the surface; others are curled, thick, pompous; some like full moons in perfect roundness, some all rays like a midday sun. In every shade of rose and crimson, brown, scarlet, yellow, pale lilac, sunset purple, they almost fatigue the eye with colour; and I turned gladly to look at some lovely pale globes whose foamy petals curled inwards over a green as alive and transparent as the wave on the shore or the glow-worm's lamp in the grass.

Going from one to another with a Japanese friend, who was giving me the national appreciations on the subject of chrysanthemums, I was almost sorry when the Majesties' arrival was heralded by the Grand Master of Ceremonies, who waved us into two lines, through which the Emperor and Empress walked together, followed by the Princes and Princesses and the rest of the Court. The ladies' dresses were of lovely Kyoto brocades, as near the tints of the chrysanthemums as possible. The sovereigns merely bowed as they went by, and then a long procession formed after them in couples, according to the usual order of precedence.

I found myself in charge of the Minister for Foreign Affairs, and we played a decorous kind of "follow my leader" through the grounds, until the Majesties came to a halt in the pavilion marked out for them; their interpreters stood beside them, and we went in, in detachments according to precedence again, to have our little conversation and make our little bows, and slide off to leave room for the next batch. When all the greetings and bowings were over, the business of ices and champagne began, and was treated with proper solemnity. Then a tiny shower came down, and the Court rose as one man, the sovereigns took leave of us with some little precipitation, and they and their people made for the main building of the Palace, where they would at any rate be safe till the rain had passed. The last I saw of them was a string of little ladies carefully holding up their delicate satin gowns and racing along under black umbrellas.

We broke up at once — not at all according to precedence! We had no umbrellas, of course; but everything is foreseen in Japan. As we issued rather ruefully from the royal tent to traverse the long piece of wet garden which separated us from our carriages, a number of servants suddenly appeared from among the bushes, carrying sheaves of umbrellas, at least five hundred of them, all alike, ornamented with green silk tassels. One was put, ready opened, into each guest's hand, and, as we stepped into the carriages at the farther gate, another little army of servants was in waiting to relieve us of the precious umbrellas, which were all carried back in bundles to the Palace — to wait for next time.

CHAPTER XXIX

NIKKO AT LAST! — THE BRIDGE OF BEAUTY AND THE BRIDGE OF USE. — IN THE TEMPLE COURTS. — THE STORY OF IYEYASU. — HIS FRIEND, WILL ADAMS, THE ROCHESTER PILOT. — A PIECE OF IMPRISONED SUNSHINE. — MAPLES AND WATERFALLS. — CHUZENJI

NIKKO, *November*, 1890.

DO you wonder that I have waited so long to write the name of the most beautiful, the most solemn place in Japan? In truth, I have feared to write it sooner, have feared to visit it until now. It seemed to me that a certain initiation should be gone through, a certain standard of judgment on Japanese thought attained, before I went to stand face to face with the supreme expression of beauty and solemnity. So I visited other temples, stood in the shade of other groves, listened to other waterfalls and other nightingales, taught my strained Western senses to forget the golden-tinted ruins, the jewelled hills, the gorgeous colour feasts of our blazing South Italian home; and then, when the spirit's eyes were rested from the sunshine, when they had learned at last the value of cool shadow and grey distance and whispering pine branch under an autumn sky — then I was not afraid to come to Nikko, I could hope to understand.

I could not come all the way through the grand cryptomeria avenue, because the travelling now is mostly done by rail; but even from the carriage windows we could look up at the splendid trees through which the line cuts again and again, wantonly, as it seemed to me. The last two or three miles are done in jinriksha, and make up for the rest of the noisy smoky journey. One creeps slowly and with a certain reverence to the heart of Nikko, the village of Hachi-ishi, which is the centre of the district; for though we foreigners distinguish this one town by the name of Nikko, that properly belongs to the whole of this range of hills, which lie some eighty miles to the north of Tokyo.

To the north-east of Hachi-ishi rises the volcano of Nantai San, extinct since prehistoric times; and in its side is a huge cavern, from which in ancient times (so the story goes) there issued frightful storms which devastated the country every spring and autumn. Popular legends say that, on account of these twin storms, the country was called Ni-Ko San, or Two-Storm Mountain; and that the great saint and scholar Kobo Daishi in the year 820 exorcised the storm demons, and called the place Nikkō San, the Mountains of the Sun's Brightness, which name it bears to this day. But the demons were only temporarily appeased, and the exorcisms had to be repeated every year; so Kobo Daishi taught his formula to a Shinto priest, whose family continued to carry out the prescription for eight hundred and eighty years, when they seem to have given it up, persuaded perhaps at last that the equinoctial storms had their origin farther away than the big cave on Nantai San. Long before the days of Kobo Daishi, a Shinto temple had existed at the place we call Nikko; but for some reason it was removed, and sent downstairs, as it were, to be put up in Utsunomiya, the present railway junction, twenty-five miles from here. The next temple, built in 767, was a Buddhist one, built by the saint Shōdō Shonin, whose life, as told by Japanese chroniclers, is a tissue of beautiful marvels. Kobo Daishi succeeded him, and added much to the holy buildings, as did also another abbot, Jigaku Daishi, who came a little later into the same honours. From that time onward Nikko became always more holy and more beautiful; endless Buddhist saints have lived and prayed and been laid to rest among its groves; its temples are full of exquisite art treasures; and two of the country's greatest men, Iyeyasu and Iyemitsu, chose it for their tomb.

This atmosphere of a great past hangs over it everywhere, and even noisy tourists who respect few things are impressed and silenced by its calm majesty. Foreign residents from Tokyo and Yokohama come here in the summer and take houses, and have their futile picnics and tea parties, and make no more effect on the place than do the sand-flies on the face of the great bronze Buddha. One of my reasons for going in the autumn was that they would all have flown back by this time to thick carpets and coal fires; for though the maples are still in all their red beauty, it is cold in Nikko, and the river brings down icy breaths at night from the tempest-haunted caves of Nantai San.

Now the river is the first thing one sees, the central spot of all one's mind-excursions here. It divides the place in two, coming down very full and angry between the deep-green hills, and spanned, just where the sides of the glen are steepest, by a perfect bridge, thrown in one scarlet arch across the white water, from the black green of this side to the golden green of that, where the sun lingers longest ere he rolls down to the

THE BRIDGE OF BEAUTY, NIKKO

plains and the sea. Why are not all bridges scarlet, latticed, lying between green steeps? The inevitable wise man will say that they should be things of use, and not of beauty alone; but then, he has never been to Japan. This bridge is not for use; only grass-grown paths unopened to traffic lead anywhere near it. Should the Emperor come to visit the shrines, his sacred feet might tread its scarlet arch — his, but no others. He would have to walk alone, as of old the Shoguns walked; for the bridge is too holy for unanointed feet.

At one time pilgrims were allowed to cross, because of their consecrated mission; but this is no longer allowed, and the lovely bridge has not felt the tread of a mortal footstep for many a day.[1] Do the ghosts of holy men come to do the repairing in these autumn nights, I wonder? No human hand has mended it for two hundred and thirty years, and they say the wood is as fresh and strong across its eighty-four-feet span to-day as it was when it was put in place.

Lower down the river than the bridge of beauty comes the bridge of use; and when we have crossed it, to-day seems left behind, to-day with its hotels and railways and endless fuss and friction chafes us no more; we seem to have entered into the avenues that lead to changeless peace. The pines, the solemn, pontifical pines, are standing shoulder to shoulder in serried ranks, their enormous roots reaching up like brown buttresses against the central spire, their heads far away near the sky, whence their murmur comes down to us fitfully, like prayers that pass the lips long after they have been prayed in the heart. Between the trees long stairways of grey stone climb from terrace to terrace, ledge to ledge, of the dusky hillside, ending perhaps where stone lanterns are set as if to catch the early sun-rays, and whisper the good news of his coming to the deep shadowy courts from which the stairways rise. It must be highest noon ere the shadows

---

[1] When General Grant visited Japan, the Emperor had the bridge thrown open, and invited him to pass over it. The General was much touched by this mark of honour, but refused to accept it, saying that he considered himself unworthy to do so.

lift from those embowered courts, tracked with grey stones laid in leisurely sequence along the rich dark soil, showing the path to a favourite shrine, or to the well where pure water bubbles always for the pilgrim to wash in ere he enter the holy places. Beside the stepping-stones grey lanterns stand, stone too, each with a recess where a light may be placed, in memory of the giver or the giver's dear ones. In one a light is floating in its cup of oil; in another an incense-stick, just lighted, sends up its blue spiral of smoke, as it stands in the mouth of its rough bamboo holder.

The air is mild in these sheltered courts, and the ground dry and scattered with pine needles; so I sit down at the foot of a flight of steps, and my good Ogita, who has a bad cough, and cannot walk far in these days, tells me the story of Iyeyasu and Iyemitsu and of their coming to be buried here.

Iyeyasu was the son-in-law and the favourite general of Hideyoshi, the Taiko Sama of contemporary history; and when Hideyoshi died in 1598, Iyeyasu, following his leader's dying wish, recalled the great Japanese army from the invasion of Corea, and took the government of the country into his hands. He was one of the Minamoto family, and took the name of Tokugawa from the village where his immediate ancestors had lived. Hideyoshi had such confidence in him that when he was dying he left his son and successor, Hideyori, in Iyeyasu's guardianship, telling him to use his discretion as to placing him in the Shogun's seat, which Hideyoshi himself had filled in fact but not in name. Iyeyasu had no such scruples, and five years after Hideyoshi's death proclaimed himself Shogun. The son of Hideyoshi attempted to oppose him and win back his father's power; but Iyeyasu crushed all his pretensions, even as Hideyoshi had crushed those of Nobunaga, the rightful heir in his time. Hideyori committed suicide, and Iyeyasu founded the Tokugawa Shogunate, which lasted down to our own day, ending in 1868, when the present Emperor took the rule of his own dominions into his own hands.

But Iyeyasu's usurpation was not accomplished without much bloodshed, and constant resistance from enemies, who found it convenient to call themselves the defenders of the rightful successor of Hideyoshi. His last and decisive battle with these envious or loyal adversaries was fought at Sekigahara, a village on the Nakasendo, the chief route from Kyoto to Yedo. It seems to have been the first battle where firearms were used in Japan (October, 1600), and terrible slaughter ensued. Equally matched, equally valiant and determined, the two armies almost annihilated one another; but the victory at last remained with Iyeyasu, and two enormous mounds are still shown as the place where the heads of his opponents were buried after the battle. He himself does not seem to have been certain that this was the decisive victory for him; when the day was ended, he turned to his generals, saying, "After victory, tighten the strings of your helmet" — an axiom which is constantly used in Japan to-day. Iyeyasu knew how to tighten those strings effectually.

He crushed the rebellious, encouraged the more peaceful subjects, forgave his opponents wherever there was a chance of turning them into friends, and, as I have already said, established his family firmly in the powerful position which they maintained until our own day. He knit round him most of the great Daimyos, so that his rule centred in the strong feudal system of Japan. The powerful nobles were all drawn to him by his subtle good sense and power of influencing others, and before he died had recognised that they must stand or fall with the House of Tokugawa.

Before Iyeyasu died, the conquered neighbour Corea was again upon a friendly footing with Japan, and peace was cemented with China. The greatest blot upon his memory is the destruction of Hideyori and his mother; but doubtless he considered this an absolute necessity to assure his own safety. His persecution of the Christians, then numbering a notable percentage of the population, was one of the most frightful ever instituted, and went so far as to break up those sacred ties of parental and filial duty which stand at the head of all moral obligations here. It is said that Iyeyasu was instigated to this course by the suggestions of English and Dutch traders, who, jealous of the power and influence of the Jesuit Fathers, told the Shogun that they would usurp his rule. But it now seems proved that his desire, like that of Hideyoshi before him, had always been to suppress the foreign religion, which had been warmly accepted by many of the powerful Daimyos; and that the moment he felt strong enough to do so he set about the task, or rather set his agents to it. These gaily took it in hand, and invented barbarities impossible to even describe. With the exception of one uprising, in which the Christians, tortured beyond endurance, made common cause with a number of peasant insurgents driven to rebellion by the cruelties of their feudal lord, no opposition, except that of constancy and endurance, was offered to the persecution, and Christianity was practically stamped out in Japan through the wholesale martyrdom inflicted by Iyeyasu and by his successors. To the everlasting shame of the Dutch traders, it is recorded that they assisted the Government with guns, powder, and their best ships in the final conquest of the Christians, who, when their last fort was taken, were massacred to the number of forty thousand.

The period in Iyeyasu's life which followed on all this active work was devoted first to the elaboration and consolidation of the feudal system (by which great privileges were granted to the *samurai* as compared to the civil or non-fighting part of the community), and then in the development of literature and of useful arts. In these last he was greatly assisted by Will Adams, the pilot of a small fleet which went out round Cape Horn to trade for the "Indish Company." After fearful hardships and privations, Adams and a few companions reached the coast of Japan, and were kindly received by the authorities. Iyeyasu, interested in the strangers, kept Adams near himself for many years, learnt all that the ex-pilot could teach him, loaded him with riches and honours, and finally kept his bones in the country; for poor Will never saw his beloved Rochester again, and lies buried near Yokohama beside the Japanese wife whom he had taken to himself.

Iyeyasu retired from the Shogunate in order to establish his son firmly on his own seat during his life-

A TEMPLE GATE AT NIKKO

time, and his last years were spent in the encouragement of literature and in writing his remarkable work *The Legacy of Iyeyasu*, in which he treats of every subject connected with good government, whether of the family or the country. He chose to pass his last years in Suruya, probably in sight of Fuji San; and a year after his death (in 1616) his body was brought to Nikko, and lies, according to his wish, in this most splendid of the temples of his country. His portrait shows a humorous face, with smiling eyes, and shrewd mouth somewhat cynically curved at the corners, the face of a man who made his world believe in him, while he believed — in success.

When his body was brought here, with magnificent pomp, in a car which is still shown in the Temple, the reigning Emperor (an unknown being called Genna) awarded him posthumous honours and the high-sounding title of "Supreme Highness, Orient Radiance, Great Saint"; and it is by this latter title that he is still known among the people. As Gongen Sama he is worshipped here at his tomb, and is supposed to return from all the shadowy peace of Nirvana to ride for one night in the year in the gold-lacquered carriage which bore his body hither. Are there any Christians in his Nirvana, I wonder? If so, I wonder what they say about his saintliness?

As usual, I have been carried away by the human associations of this great home of great shadows, and have told you nothing as yet of the visible treasures which it contains. Behold, are they not all written down in the indispensable pages of Murray? And yet I wish I could show you some of them; for it seems as if specimens of every art had been stored here to honour Iyeyasu's memory. From highest to lowest, his country-people have contributed their gifts. Ogita tells me (but I find no corroboration of this in any of the handbooks) that the famous avenue of cryptomerias was planted by a great Daimyo, the Prince of Chikuzen, before Iyeyasu's body was brought to Nikko, that the road might be worthy of the traveller. The first gate is a splendid granite *torii*, sent by this same Prince from his own quarries two years after Iyeyasu's death; then comes an exquisite pagoda, over a hundred feet high, and richly decorated, presented a little later by one of the great vassals of the family. The Gate of

ONE OF THE NIKKO TEMPLES

the Two Kings is a marvel of carving and painting and symbolism, which it would take days to describe; whichever way one turns, the most amazing elaboration of ornament meets one's eyes, and yet all is harmonious and subdued, dominated by the great stone stairways and the dark pine trees, and lit in the luminous even whiteness of Japan's noonday. The light here, as elsewhere in the Islands of the Dragon-Fly, is soft, yet entire; the magic mountains seem to cast no shade; in the depth of the woods, as in the golden Temple storehouses, everything is calmly clear to the eye.

There is one tree which stands alone, surrounded by a stone railing — the square stone railing of temple architecture which gives such character to all these scenes. The tree has a right to special protection; for it is, says local tradition, the one which Iyeyasu (who must have loved pines as I do) carried about with him for years in his palanquin, when it was a tiny sapling in its pot. Near it stands a stable, where a white horse is kept, in case Iyeyasu should return and want a charger in a hurry. He must have sent for it this morning, for the stable is empty. Then we are taken to see various relics of Iyeyasu, his helmet and shield, bronze objects so overlaid with green patina that their very shape is obscured; then a wonderful library of Buddhist books, in a revolving bookcase, scarlet and gold. But that which pleases me most are the finely carved panels of the splendid halls intended to accommodate the Shogun and his train when they came here to worship. Every bird and beast seems to have been pressed into the service of decoration, every device which unlimited treasure and redundant imagination could produce has been lavished on these temple rooms, each more beautiful than the last. The very architects seem to have feared the envy of heaven for their perfect work; and one pillar has its carvings done upside down, that the voluntary defect might appease the jealous gods. It is named the "Pillar of the Aversion of Evil."

The tomb of Iyeyasu is beyond all these splendours, a small pagoda cast in a single piece of bronze, of a golden colour, standing alone on the hillside. And this reminds me of the splendid tomb of Yung Chung, in the northern hills beyond Peking, with its vast hall, its hundred scarlet pillars, its lonely state; and beyond it, on the hillside, a nameless green mound, as large as the Temple itself, in whose depths the great Emperor's bones were laid secretly and unmarked, so that no enemy might disinter them, no envious god shatter their resting-place in his jealousy of its beauty.

Only one thing will I tell you of the tomb of Iyemitsu, great Iyeyasu's grandson. In a small iron storeroom, entered by a low and heavy door, I saw the finest piece of illumination which the world contains, eight feet long, four feet wide, the whole surface covered with a series of paintings so delicate, so patient, so perfect, that I have never seen anything in European collections to approach it. The artist seems to have actually dipped his brush in sunshine and stardust when he painted it. It represents the Buddhist heaven, with glorified spirits crowding round a central figure, which makes the impression of giving out light. In that small dark treasure-house, the old priest spread it out for me to see, and murmured explanations of the picture; to me it was like a piece of sunshine imprisoned since the morning of the world, when the sun must have been more gladly golden than now. How strange to think that grey pine-shrouded Nikko should keep this jewel buried in its bosom!

At last we left the temples, and wandered back to the bridge, near which a flight of stone steps leads up to other holy spots, temples and shrines crowding one another on the hillsides. One stone marks the grave of Iyeyasu's favourite horse, the one he rode at the great battle of Sekigahara, which was the turning-point of his life. The old horse was turned loose in these sacred hills after its master's death, and lived many years in freedom among the pines. At the end of the walk from the bridge, by the bank of the river, stand a long, long row of strange little Buddhas, all exactly alike, their gentle faces quite obliterated by moss and spray, only their outline telling what they are. The torrent keeps them always wet, and sings here such a loud rushing song that one's senses get dazed, and no one ever counts the moss-shrouded images right. The Japanese call them the five hundred Buddhas; but there is nothing like such a number as that. I think they object to being counted. Tradition says that no two people have ever counted them alike; and, indeed, when the river is running high, it is not easy to get to them all. They look intensely weird and lonely, and a profound melancholy seems to hang around the long grey line. Some time ago, in a violent storm, one of them leapt from his place, and went bounding down the stream as far as Imaichi, the village at the foot of the hill; then he turned and stopped, with his blind face towards his old home, and there he stands to this day; but none of his companions have found courage to follow him.

THE LONG, LONG ROW OF BUDDHAS

Wisely had we chosen the moment of our visit to the Nikko hills; for, beyond the sombre mantle of the pines, the mountain-sides were clothed in a curtain of scarlet and gold, a curtain woven of the star-shaped leaves of innumerable maple trees, hanging to the cliffs as children hang to the skirts of their mother. The path up to Chuzenji was all aglow with them; and where it wound directly under their branches, fired from above with the noonday sun, the effect of colour was so strong that it caused sudden dizziness, and I had to close my eyes for a moment before I could support it. All the waterfalls on the way (and Nikko is the home of waterfalls) were studded with a spray of jewel-tinted leaves, mingling with the iridescent showers; every pool was the harbour where thousand-sailed fleets of golden leaves rose and fell on the delicately ruffled surface of the flood; the path was all paved with crimson stars, laid on a soft mosaic of bronze and orange; and everywhere was that delicious fleeting smell of autumn woods where the summer has breathed its parting sigh. I was happily surprised by finding the maples up here so late in coming to their glory; for ours in the Tokyo gardens, exposed to sharp winds, are already curled and brown. But the woods were always gracious to me, their worshipper; and the leaves have hung on in the sheltered dells to give me the greeting that Cæsar heard of old, "Morituri te salutant."

At last the wooded steeps are left behind, and we reach a level road that leads, with a bend and a sudden turn, right out on the edge of a lake; an upland lake, of crystal water and sun-searched deeps, with all the sky to dream over it, all the daylight, the transparent living daylight of Dai Nihon, to smooth its frets of blue and gold to one wide white calm. The hills fall back a little from its sides; the woods stand shyly off from its silver strand; all the world just now seems to

CHUZENJI LAKE

culminate in this perfect jewel, held up in the palm of the hills for heaven to gaze upon. I too will gaze, for I shall not see the like of this untouched peace again. The rest may wander and climb, and even try the steep ascent of great Nantai San; but not I. I will sit and drink the light here, and learn the silences of peace, and hear the wordless music of the ripple at my feet, as soft and even as the breath of infancy.

Space to breathe with one's face to the sky, solitude, and the ceasing of this world's voices, speechless beauty all around, and the blue dome of the heart's home above, — why go farther? Here is the City of Rest.

CHAPTER XXX

ANOTHER CHRISTMAS TREE. — BABIES, EUROPEAN AND JAPANESE. — IDEALS OF HOME AND SCHOOL. — A DAY AT MEGURO. — A LITTLE *SAMURAI* GIRL. — A VISITATION OF INFLUENZA. — MIYANOSHITA AS A SANATORIUM. — BURNING OF THE HOUSES OF PARLIAMENT

January, 1891.

THE New Year has come round again; but it has brought such a frightful visitation of influenza that our little society has hardly had strength to exchange the usual greetings and good wishes. I am told that the scourge was let loose in Tokyo at an innocent Christmas party in our house, where we had ventured to gather together all our European and Japanese friends round a huge Christmas tree, to the great delight of the little Japanese children, to whom the sight was as surprising as it was to the compound children last year. We had placed our tree in the inner part of the hall, where the great staircase makes its three turns round a square space, usually filled with plants and easy-chairs. That day everything was turned out, and the tree spread its branches right up to the level of the second floor, where, by the way, a kind of fire brigade was stationed in case of accidents. All this was impenetrably curtained off from the entrance hall, until all our guests had arrived and the whole of our Tokyo world gathered together; then, at a given signal, one of the old Christmas carols burst from a choir hidden in a recess, the curtains were drawn aside, and the pyramid of light shone out in all its completeness. The sight was fairylike, and the cry of pleasure that rang from one end of the hall to the other quite repaid me and the many kind friends who had been my helpers for any trouble and fatigue that the thing had cost.

Then came the distribution of our little gifts (a serious business, for there were at least two hundred children, besides all their grown-up relations); and this was followed by a sight which to me was as pretty as the tree itself. The house is not very large for a gathering of this kind, and all the available rooms on the ground floor had been turned into supper-rooms for the grown-up guests; so we were obliged to lay the children's feast in the long gallery on the second floor, running the whole length of the hall below. This had been decorated with green wreaths and quantities of lanterns, and here little people of every nationality sat side by side and made friends over the bonbons and crackers. Count Saigo's three splendid boys, in the gold-laced uniform of their military school, insisted on helping to wait on the others; and it was pretty to see the dark aristocratic heads bending over the fair-haired English babies, who smiled up confidingly at the kind big boys. Everybody sat down where they could find a place; a small Princess Sanjo, dressed in dazzling garments of crape and gold, her hair held up with gold and amber chrysanthemums, made friends with a dear little person of three who is one of my great cronies, a Yorkshire Margaret, with the reddest hair and the bluest eyes I have ever seen. Her little fat fingers, already sticky with sweets, were eager to explore the wonders of the little Japanese lady's embroidered pocket-book, with its gold and coral chains hanging out in a fringe over her splendid sash. The tiny Saigo girl, another small friend of mine, had been to foreign parties before, and ran about as if the place belonged to her; while her mother followed her everywhere with an amused smile, and making many excuses for her daughter's forwardness.

ONE OF OUR GUESTS

The grown-up people crowded in such numbers round our beautiful battalion of children that there was hardly room for the attendants to wait on them at all; but the European little ones looked after themselves pretty effectually, and Japanese children of the upper classes will not eat in public; they take a bonbon out of politeness, but it does not enter into their code of manners to be eager about food or to partake of it before strangers. They would, until quite lately, have expected to have their portion of the feast packed up in pretty boxes and put into their carriages, or sent to their houses after they had gone home. A reminiscence of this custom has brought me a charming collection of Imperial wine-cups; for whenever H—— lunches or dines with the Emperor, one of these is put into the carriage wrapped up in Palace paper. They vary a little in design, but are always of transparently thin white porcelain decorated with gold chrysanthemums. At the dinners given by the Imperial Princes, the parting gift is generally a silver or enamel box, sometimes of beautiful workmanship, filled with bonbons; and wherever one dines, we women at any rate carry away baskets or bouquets of most lovely flowers.

But to return to the Japanese children. I told you, I think, last year, how charmingly the servants' little ones behaved (the tree was repeated for them this year too); and I was glad to compare their manners with those of the small nobles whom we had gathered together this time. Well, except that the nobles showed rather more gravity of demeanour, and were far more beautiful to look at, there was really nothing to choose between the classes. The same suave calm manner, the same quiet thanks for gifts bestowed, the same self-effacement and consideration of others, were shown at both my parties; and I feel that there must be a great deal to say for a system of education which, without robbing childhood of a moment's bright happiness, can clothe little children of every condition with this garment of perfect courtesy. I have rarely seen its match, except once or twice among little Austrian and Italian royalties; but there inheritance and environment, as well as the high standard of behaviour insisted on in all noble Catholic families, royal or otherwise, had had full scope, had moulded the little personality from the very outset of life.

Here, explain it who can, it is in the blood, and can be counted on with absolute certainty. It is, to me, most comforting to see that all that is desirable in the little people's deportment can be attained without snubbings or punishments or weary scoldings. The love showered upon children simply wraps them in warmth and peace, and seems to encourage every sweet good trait of character without ever fostering a bad one. Japanese children are never frightened into telling lies or hiding their faults. Open as the day, they bring every joy or sorrow to father or mother to be shared or healed, and their small likes or dislikes are quite as much taken into account as those of their elders. True, from the time they can begin to understand anything, axioms of honour, kindness, filial duty, and above all patriotism, are repeated and explained to them with a good faith and solemnity which would send our English schoolboys off into fits of scoffing laughter. The nursery catechism takes somewhat this form in Japan.

"What do you love best in the world?"

"The Emperor, of course."

"Better than father and mother?"

"He is the Lord of Heaven, the father of my father and mother."

"What will you give the Emperor?"

"All my best toys, and my life when he wants it."

And so on—and it is all true, and has been and will be proved again and again. But there are no scoffers in Japan. There are bitter haters, and perhaps as many criminals as can be reasonably expected after only thirty years of intercourse with civilised nations, the delays in extending the railways, and the tiresome perfection of the police system; but the most hardened criminals have not yet learnt to scoff at virtue and patriotism, to heap contempt on honour and courage and humility. This grave belief in abstract things (which in England to-day could only be mentioned with an apologetic smile for one's own weakness) is still the foundation of education in Japan, and gives the parent or the teacher a strength and authority in dealing with the young spirit which our poor schoolmasters can never exercise. I have known many of these unhappy men, and have not yet found one who was believed in by his pupils. Indulgent tolerance from big boys, who can afford to say, "Old So-and-so is an awful humbug, but not half bad when you're big enough not to be afraid of him"; hatred and fear from the little fellows, to whom all morality is made horrible because their chief torturer is probably their preacher as well, — this is what our dominie gets at home, this is what I have seen and shuddered at for so many years in dear Protestant England, that it is an unspeakable relief to be among people where the teacher is still venerated, where the position of master in a school is considered honourable enough for the eldest son of a great noble to accept it gladly, where education leads youth unblushingly back to the feet of those great schoolmistresses the cardinal virtues, and still has for its object to make gentlemen, scholars, and patriots out of Japanese subjects. In this reverence for truly great men and things lies the real strength of the people — a strength which may or may not be assisted by modern armaments and modern legislation. I am certain that it will never be called upon in vain, and will never be finally vanquished by evil.

No one can deny that there are turbulent students in some of the Japanese colleges; and occasionally where a teacher has given real dissatisfaction (generally from wishing to introduce some unpopular innovation) the whole class or the whole college will strike, and refuse to attend any of the lectures until the obnoxious professor has been changed. But there is no want of respect for his office involved in the rebellion, in which as a rule the strikers are warmly supported by their relatives. It is the man, the individual teacher, who, as they consider, fills the office unworthily; and since there has never been any necessity for promulgating laws forcing attendance at school in this country, the scholars are not breaking the law by staying away. They troop back to their classroom the moment that the grievance is removed, and, as far as I can judge by reading accounts of such *pronunciamientos*, do not abuse their power. On the whole, they do not much care about foreign teachers; and though some have become greatly beloved, others have been violently unpopular, on account of their rough methods, more approaching the familiar brutalities of the English clergyman-schoolmaster when dealing with very small and weak boys. Terrible trouble has been caused here in girls' schools, chiefly in those recruited from the upper middle classes, when a foreign mistress has so far lost her temper as to strike a pupil. Then the whole body of girls would leave at once, and only consent to attend again when a proper apology for the insult had been offered and accepted.

A terrible scene took place in one of the college playgrounds some time ago, when two foreign teachers, instead of entering by the proper gate, jumped over a fence to join the boys (youths of seventeen and eighteen) in a game of football. The lads flew at them, and maltreated them very severely, one gentleman having the impression that he had barely escaped with his life. The onset was cruel and unprovoked, as far as the victims of it knew; but some slight excuse may be found in the fact that it took place during a time of intense anti-foreign excitement, that *soshi* principles and false views of patriotism were everywhere in the air, and that every boy in Tokyo was boiling with rage at an absurd story which had got about that a well-known missionary teacher in Tsukiji had refused to take off his hat when the Emperor drove by. The unfortunate teacher in question had to claim British protection, and was so pestered by threatening letters and excitable young patriots that he wisely decided to leave the country for a few months and take a short holiday. All this sounds very absurd and unreasonable; but is it not the *défaut d'une qualité*, the one weak point in a tower of strength, the hard shadow cast by a blazing sun of patriotism where none would have been visible in the dull grey light of indifference?

I have wandered from the congenial subject of Japanese children to the more puzzling one of their elders; and yet it was about the children that I meant to write to you to-day. I have several small friends amongst them, and I think, when they are not made to play tunes on the piano or repeat French fables for me, that they are really glad to see me. They do not readily join in the noisy games of our young English friends, who invade the compound on Saturday afternoons, and make the place ring with those delightful squeals of joy such as only English lungs can produce.

But in their quieter way they enjoy things quite as much. One of the prettiest sights of last year was a fancy-dress ball, where the little Japanese nobles came in costumes of war or the chase, the most elaborate and splendid that I have ever seen. Every detail was carried out in antique stuffs; the weapons and ornaments were the original ones used by children of the family hundreds of years ago, and kept as precious relics through all wars and revolutions. The solemnity with which these were worn was pretty to see. Evidently the little boys attached something of religious veneration to the things which they were permitted to handle on that one day. The girls were quite as splendid; but their every-day dress is so brilliant and rich that one noticed the change less in them than in their brothers. One or two had on robes given them by the Empress, who is fond of children, and often sends for the little ones to come and see her. When they were all assembled, the master of the house (an artistic, appreciative Englishman, who is legal adviser to the Japanese Foreign Office) marshalled the small people in a long procession, where fierce-looking young gods of war led fair-haired Red Riding Hoods by the hand, where a little carter in his smock-frock and long whip was accompanied by a small damsel out of a fairy tale, wearing trailing robes of purple and gold, looking as gay and delicate as a Brazilian humming-bird. One of the loveliest there, little Madgie M——, an English child, so beautiful that we all took a sort of national pride in her, has passed away to the country where she will be young and fair to all eternity. One misses the little angel face at this year's gatherings.

A little while ago we went out to spend the day at Meguro, Countess Saigo's beautiful place in the country. I say Countess Saigo's because her husband laughingly disclaims having anything to do with such a feminine domain. "Look at all these flowers, and the silkworms, and the children!" he says; does it look like a rough sailor's house?" And it certainly does not, though the way everything revolves round the First Lord of the Admiralty tells how he is loved and honoured there. After an elaborate lunch, we women rose from table, and my hostess beckoned to me to follow her. I knew whither she was leading me — to look at the portrait of her eldest son, a brave and brilliant boy, who died while at school in Europe, and whom she never forgets, even when surrounded by all her other children. There is always a little sadness in her smile, a grave note in her gentle voice as of pain accepted and forgiven. I followed her in silence; and her three-

ONE OF THE CHILDREN

year-old daughter caught her dress and toddled along at her side. A little off the hall we entered a small quiet room, where, near a window, so that all the daylight illuminated it, was the portrait, a life-size head, of the dead boy. There were fresh flowers on either side, incense-sticks burning fragrantly, and in front, on a small table like those used in the temples for presenting offerings, a collection of tiny plates containing atoms of food from all the complicated French dishes of the lunch from which we had just risen.

It is some years since the boy died; but from every meal partaken of in the great house his share has been set aside — he is not forgotten. The little sister, who never knew him, stands up on tiptoe in her flowery robes, and gravely examines the small dishes to see if all is in place. She would no more think of touching the dainties than of striking her mother's beautiful face. "My brother," she lisps proudly, as she pulls at my dress and points to the picture. But the mother has turned her face away, and, with one deep salutation to her son's picture, leads us out. We join the rest, and spend a long gay afternoon in wandering about the grounds, picking flowers, and examining the great house full of silkworms, who provide all the clothing for our hostess and her daughter.

"I send it to Saikyo to be dyed and woven," says the Countess. "See what a pretty pattern I have chosen for my daughter's new *obi!*" and she holds out a piece of French ribbon, with Louis XV. bouquets and love-knots in pink on a pale-green ground.

"But it is a European design!" I cried. "Don't you think your own are much prettier?"

Then the Count spoke, laughing as usual. "Yes, please tell my wife that she should not venture on European costume. She looks as large as — a saké-tub in those tight-fitting things." Which was a deliberate untruth, for he and we and the Countess herself know that she is one of the few Japanese ladies who have what our dressmakers call a figure — the only one who looks as well in our costume as in her own.

"Don't listen to him, Mrs. Fraser!" she retorted, laughing gaily. "He only lives to tease; and if it hurt, I should long have ceased to live."

Then the Count has a portrait to show me, and I am taken indoors again to see a most villainous full-length painting of the little daughter in her *kimono* which was given by the Empress; and I try to conceal my feelings about the crude production, which is barely recognisable as a likeness. Both father and mother seem to worship the small girl, who is the most benignant of family tyrants now, and whose character is forming visibly in the maturing sunshine of her home. I was much impressed last autumn by seeing her, tiny as she was, insist on taking part in some egg-and-spoon races which were going on at a children's garden party composed chiefly of Europeans. The little Saigo girl was the youngest there; but when asked if she would run with the others over the grassy little racecourse, she nodded gravely, took the egg and spoon in both hands, and started off, her long robe with its delicate colours sweeping the turf, her little feet scurrying along under it in their miniature sandals, and her whole soul concentrated on getting the egg to the goal in the spoon, although she had not the slightest idea why the feat had to be performed. It was evidently a highly honourable thing for a *samurai's* daughter to do, so — come on! She was so small that the roses and lilies of the garden over-topped her little head, and in a minute or two all the other children had left her far behind; but she would not give in, and pressed bravely round the whole course, her lips quivering, large tears rolling down her cheeks, which had lost all their colour except the two spots of rouge, her little chest heaving pitifully while her mother, who walked by her side, tried to persuade her that the game was for bigger and stronger children. No; she had begun, and the *samurai* spirit would brook no defeat. A hundred eyes were on her when she neared the goal, and something uncommonly like a cheer went up from the society crowd when she reached it. She did not break down even then, but gravely returned the dreadful egg and

CARRYING DOLLY

spoon to her hostess, bowed her due thanks when a prize dolly was presented to her, and then walked back to her seat beside her mother, as if egg-and-spoon races were her usual exercise!

Yet she is not very strong. When the cold days came she pined, and lost her appetite (she and her brothers are brought up on European food); and her mother took her down to Numadzu, where the sun shines warm among the pine woods even in winter, because the Kuro Shiwo, the warm stream in the sea, bathes all that coast. I went to see them when they returned, and found them installed in the official residence, a big European building in the town. "How is O'Ione San?" I asked. "Much better," her mother replied. "Dr. Hashimoto has ordered her to learn dancing as a gymnastic exercise, and it has done her so much good!" Just then a servant held open the door, and O'Ione San entered, and came to greet me. "Will you dance for me, O'Ione San?" I asked; and the sweet round face lighted up with pleasure. "Then," said her mother, "O'Ione San must go and put on her dancing clothes." "I like dancing clothes," she replied. And at a nod from her mother the maid carried her off to be dressed.

This was evidently rather an elaborate business; but at last the doors were thrown open with some pomp, three women musicians in dark silk gowns entered, bowed profoundly, and ranged themselves on the floor against the wall; they were followed by a maid, who spread a square of fine matting over the carpet; and then came the little lady herself, dressed in a strange black-and-white costume, much more severe than anything she usually wears, and opening robe over robe in front to give her small feet play. Her hair had all been done again, and was full of ornaments; and her expression was as grave as her gown. She came and stood on the mat, then knelt down and touched her head to the ground, and then the music began, strange strident notes, with a strong humming accompaniment, and quick beats through it like pursuing feet and sobs as of labouring breath, that weird Japanese music which is to me the saddest in the world.

But this time I hardly noticed the music in my wonder at the precision and freedom, the grace and the strength, of the child's dancing. Every movement had been learnt to perfection; her little body swayed over to this side or that, recovered itself at the right angle, seemed to be rising from the ground on those long winglike sleeves, or striking it in anger with a little white heel that stamped with the sharpness of a hammer on the ground. She turned and twisted, whirled her skirts like a wheel, or slid round her square with them clinging closely to her childish limbs; and when the dance was over knelt again and knocked her head on the floor, and stood up to begin another, giving her orders to the musicians in one authoritative word. They were women with refined faces and delicate hands, women of the *samurai* servant type; and they smiled proudly at their little mistress as she showed off her new accomplishment, mastered in a wonderfully short

YORKSHIRE MARGARET AND HER BROTHERS

time, for she had then only been learning for about three months. The finest dance she kept for the last; it consisted of some wonderful evolutions with a fan, which flew hither and thither, opened and shut, and wheeled about with such rapidity and verve that it seemed like a live thing, and the sharp click of its slats opening and closing kept time to the hurrying music. When she stopped at last, it was without a sign of fatigue; and I found, on rising to go, that she had been dancing just an hour!

All our pleasant engagements have been broken up by the influenza, which seems to have taken the gathering of our small world round my Christmas tree as a convenient occasion for spreading itself over Tokyo. The next day whole households were in bed, and within a week the town was one large hospital. In the Palace there was hardly any one left to attend on the Empress, who was very ill. One lady-in-waiting only was spared, and she was nursing all the others and the Empress as well. In many houses there was not even a servant who could light the kitchen fire; and one of my friends, too ill herself to go downstairs to do it, kept her family alive on Liebig's extract cooked over a spirit-lamp beside her bed. As for us, we fared better than some of our neighbours, because our loyal little servants endured everything rather than let the kitchen fires quite go out; but — we had thirteen people in the house down with it at once, including ourselves. My own first notice of its arrival was an attack of such sick mental despair that I thought I must be going out of my mind; then I felt myself falling on top of my little *amah*, O'Matsu, and just called out to her not to get killed — and the rest was black darkness, from which it took me a long time to recover. Every engagement was cancelled; people were too ill to ask if even their best friends were still alive; and as soon as we could crawl down to the carriage, we went off to Miyanoshita to try and recover strength. Miyanoshita was soon full of other victims, who came on the same errand; but as we were all suffering from the inevitable after-depression which the scourge leaves behind it, we avoided each other sedulously, and when we had to meet were all as grumpy and reserved as if we had just left England for the first time and were afraid of making " undesirable acquaintances."

Miyanoshita worked wonders, and the weather was glorious, though bitterly cold. Enormous icicles hung over all the bridges; the fairy waterfall on the road to Kiga was just a film of frozen spray. But the sun shone in the daytime; we made roaring fires of pine logs and cones in the sweet-smelling wooden rooms; Kelly and Walsh, the beneficent booksellers in Yokohama, sent us piles of new books and papers; and in a fortnight we found that we could answer a plain question civilly, look at food without nausea, and trust our feet to take short walks. Then uprose the great question of neglected work, unread despatches, unregulated affairs. "Let the things lie," I pleaded; "who wants to hear from such a hotbed of sickness as our unlucky compound?" But my arguments were ruled away as beside the mark, and, feeling still rather shaky, we returned to our stricken home.

"I wonder if there is a session going on," I said, as, driving up from Shimbashi to the Legation, I noticed a crowd gathered at the end of the wide road which leads to the new Houses of Parliament. Then the coachman turned, and drove down the road itself. There were no Houses of Parliament there. Forty brick chimneys rose straight from the ground, which was layered with ashes. Smoke was still rising from them in a dull spent way here and there. The Chamber of Representatives, the Chamber of Peers, the committee-rooms and reception-rooms and fire-proof archive-rooms, had all been burnt to the ground. The electric wires had ignited, and the fire had taken exactly five hours to consume the whole building, in the early morning of the day on which we travelled down from Miyanoshita.

A formal reception at the Palace has had to be given up. All the electric wires there were at once disconnected after this catastrophe. No other means of lighting the huge place was ever contemplated, and the ladies of honour say that really it is better to go to bed by daylight than to sit up with one candle — after one has had the influenza!

CHAPTER XXXI

A READING SOCIETY. — STORIES FOR THE JAPANESE LADIES. — THE EMPRESS'S VERSES. — THE EXAGGERATION OF A VIRTUE. — MARRIAGE, EASTERN AND WESTERN. — MOTHERHOOD AND FATHERHOOD. — PARENTAL TIES. — NEW LAWS OF INHERITANCE

TOKYO, *February*, 1891.

WHO was the Irishman who declared that the population had been "decimated by one-third"? The description might apply to Tokyo since the visitation of influenza. It spared nobody, falling first upon the foreign community, and then on the Japanese; from the Emperor and Empress down to the last coolie, every one seems to have had it. Society has put up the shutters, and Tokyo is so dull that I find myself regretting the mountain walks round Miyanoshita, where, as I told you, we went up to recruit. The last of my walks I took late in the day before we left, and the memory came home with me here. The sun had set, but had left a crystal clearness in the sky, which was just beginning to turn lilac behind the enclosing hills. A new-born moon, like a silver feather, hung over the flush of amethyst, and the pine trees were beginning to make black fringes on the mountain-edges against the sky. The air was intensely cold, but full of the sound of unconquered brooks, some boiling hot and sending up wreaths of smoke as they rushed down in a neck-and-neck race with a cold rival fringed with icicles, as if to see who could reach the gorge first in the sight of the watching woods. I went up into the valleys behind the house, right towards the sunset. I relapse into savagery in the country, and commit many *bassesses* to get my walks alone. There is only one thing in life which for dear comfort equals a solitary ramble among the hills on a grey winter afternoon — and that is the Ninth Symphony!

The universal epidemic has broken up some little readings in which I had been much interested from two points of view — a selfish and an unselfish one. As most actions are none the worse for being shown off in the best light, I will tell you of the unselfish one first. In some of our long conversations with Japanese ladies, I noticed how eagerly they listened to any story of valour, heroism, or filial piety. Very often, not knowing quite how to amuse our visitors, we have shown them pictures and engravings, all of which had to be explained and illustrated clearly to their minds. They think it impolite to pay a short visit, so as a rule there has been plenty of time to develope our themes. I have found the strongest interest excited by anything connected with our Queen; and a splendid old copy of Pyne's *Royal Residences*, out of my American grandfather's library, was almost the most popular of the picture-books. Then, seeing how shut off from intellectual amusements is the life of the

Japanese lady, a friend and I put our heads together to see if we could not provide some little entertainment for these dear women, who have shown us such endless kindnesses since we came. My friend

A JAPANESE PROFESSOR AND HIS FAMILY

should have by far the greater credit for any success that we achieved. She is spending all her time, money, and strength on helping the Japanese ladies in those directions where from tradition and circumstance they are narrow and stunted. She is frankly a missionary, in her own quiet independent way, and can talk to them of Christianity as it would be quite unfitting for me to do. But she is so *grande dame*, so Japanese in her intense consideration for others, that she has won their complete confidence; they send their boys and girls to her to be taught English and English modes of thought, even where they are not inclined to become Christians themselves. I constantly meet the Saigo children there, and little Princess Kujo, Princess Sanjo and her daughter, and many another; and no one ever speaks of the mistress of the house except as "Dear Mrs. K——." She looks upon me as a bigoted Catholic, and I tell her that she will be saved by her invincible ignorance, *i.e.* good faith; and then we leave controversy on one side, and work our little schemes out together with perfect harmony and success.

Now for the other motive, the selfish one. I want to be brought nearer to the lives of these Japanese women, both from the interest and sympathy I feel for them, and because, although on some points my knowledge is wider and more accurate than theirs, yet there are many others where I am glad to learn from them.

I think it was in October that I had what the papers called an official tea party, at which we collected all the women of importance in our little world, and asked them if they would care to come to me once a fortnight to hear "pretty stories" read and talked over. I could give them as an example my English reading society, where twenty or thirty women meet and read and discuss English literature with very keen interest. The idea was new, and pleased them greatly; though

I think one or two feared that, as my coadjutor worked so frankly for Christian interests, this might be a scheme to forward them. However, they all accepted, and have been most faithful about coming. Of course there were many things to be thought of and prepared. The first story had to be one which would appeal to their sense of all that was fit and proper. After much deliberation, we fixed on a tale of filial piety, the immemorial "Exiles of Siberia," with its wonderful story of a daughter's devotion to her parents. Then the translation had to be put into flowery language full of pretty conceits, or else the sensitive ears of these dainty Court ladies would not listen to it for a moment; and the business of finding a proper translator brought me into contact with my first friend of the professor class in Japan — a woman so cultivated and modest and charming that I shall always feel the richer for having known her. Her husband is a professor in one of the colleges; and she has had a very modern education, and writes for Japanese reviews and magazines (how funny it sounds!), of which more are published here than foreigners imagine. She had long desired to be of use in cheering the rather monotonous lives of her countrywomen, and, while deploring, as in (Japanese) duty bound, her own unworthiness, yet set about the task of translation with great enthusiasm. The long story had to be abridged, and much left out which would have been incomprehensible to our audience; but at last it was ready, and our little ladies gathered in force to listen to it.

It was with a new sensation, called, I believe, shyness, that I found myself explaining to them what we were going to do. Our translator-reader had arrived, dressed in softly tinted blue crape with her little monogram on back and shoulders. Every detail of her costume was fine and harmonious, her hair piled in a shining crown on her small head, and her splendid *obi* — the most expensive article in a Japanese lady's dress — kept in place by a thick silk band buckled with pure gold. At first she stayed near the door, explaining to me in her pretty deliberate English that she was too small and humble a person to go up to the top of the

TYING ON THE OBI

room among all those great ladies. As it was impossible for them to hear her from the door, she was at last prevailed upon to take a more prominent seat. The others quite understood the hesitation, but received her very graciously, and expressed their thanks beforehand for the trouble she had taken. Then I was asked to read the English before each paragraph of the Japanese, as some of my guests, especially the Empress's ladies who understand it, wished to compare the two. And at last we began. Well, it really was a success. The translation delighted them by its elevated style; and the story was after their own hearts: an unhappy parent, a devoted child, an all-powerful Emperor who grants her prayer, — why, the whole thing might have happened in Japan! Who would have thought that foreigners had such a high morality? (This of course was not said to me.) Evidently there were devoted children all the world over, — and so on!

Every two weeks we have a meeting, alternately with my English one, which is one of my great interests now. We finished Elizabeth, and then gave them a tale of wifely heroism, Lady Nithsdale's rescue of her husband from the Tower, which appealed to these daughters of the *samurai*, and drew tears of admiration from their eyes. They laid aside their studied calm for once, and became absolutely enthusiastic over the heroine's courage and wit. When I went out in the world, the husbands of some of them came and thanked me for the "splendid story," which had been repeated all through the family circles word for word. At the end of every reading the Empress's ladies make the same polite little request to be allowed to take home the manuscript, "so as to read it again." And that is what happens to it, being read aloud to the "august ears," only too glad of some new thing, I fancy, in the dulness and pomp of a childless life. The Empress is fond of writing verses — a very touching one appeared the other day: "The world is great, and full of men and women, who can tell each other of the grief or joy in their hearts. My heart is also full; but that which it containeth I tell to God alone." She composes music too, and is, it is said, the author of the national anthem, a very solemn and stirring chant. I sometimes have fancied that the extreme faithfulness and earnest attention of her ladies to our little readings was not given entirely on their own account. The next story on our list was a life of gracious Queen Margaret, the saint of Scotland, whose shipwreck on its shores was a very sunrise of love and faith and gentle rule for the rough country and its rougher Court. Where, in these stories, the action turns on faith, we give the religious element its full value; and the audience never takes offence. "Hearts are alike in Europe and Japan," one of them said to me; "English ladies are very brave and true to their duties — that is what we admire." "You could teach us more than we could teach you on that point," I sighed, thinking what Japanese women would make of our just laws, our honourable equal marriage rights (equal in all except evil, where our prosaic old legislators must still argue on the ground that woman is a naturally pure and elevated creature, and shall never enjoy the indulgence necessarily extended to her fallen companion!) — of what my little friends here would be, surrounded by the chivalrous institutions of the West; and I was also thinking of what we Western women could make of our world, had we the heroic humility, the faithfulness to duty, the divine unselfishness of our Eastern sisters.

You will say that the exaggeration of a virtue is revenged in Nature's exacting balances by the formation — somewhere — of a fault. I must grant that, and unnatural heroic unselfishness does often encourage a distorted selfishness in base natures quick to seize their own advantage from another's generosity; and Japanese husbands, especially those of the upper classes, have fallen into this sin, and do fall into it every day. A man who for his father and mother will support every privation, make every sacrifice, is cold and indifferent, perhaps, to the blameless woman at his side. She is too much a part of himself for him not to be ashamed to lavish outward testimonies of regard upon her. She is the other self of the inner life, which, for all their apparent disregard of privacy, is so truly the inner life that a Japanese never even speaks of his wife unless absolutely obliged to do so. As far as European life has touched them, the Japanese are willing to conform to our usages as regards the treatment of women in

A JAPANESE LADY

public. The wife of an official accompanies him to pay me a visit. Since the husband is in office, the wife may only appear in European costume, and she passes before him according to European traditions. Perhaps the next time they call he has resigned his portfolio; then Madame is in her own pretty dress, and Monsieur enters first in his own pretty way!

The truth is that marriage is not, and never can be here, the supreme relation of life, as it is in Europe. Love, in our sense of the word, has nothing to do with the matter; and the experience of this great passion, which holds such a paramount place in Western lives, is here an exceptional thing, a destiny, generally condemned to be a sorrowful one, and eliciting pity, and something of the praise we accord to martyrdom, when, as constantly happens, the poor lovers, seeing their union impossible in this world, commit a double suicide, and travel to the Meido together, sure of reunion in the shadowy realms, where, for us, marriage ties are said to be dissolved. As marriages are always arranged by parents or friends, the young people's consent only being asked at the moment when they have had their first interview, a very small amount of personal feeling enters into the contract — at any rate in its early stages. An English bride would blush angrily were it hinted that she was not, as the phrase runs, in love with her new husband; that rarest of passions, pure love, is supposed to preside even at the most fashionable weddings. Not so in Japan. The young girl here would reply that such passion is for the women whom she need never meet; the very name of it is unknown to her, unless she has seen it illustrated in a play at the theatre; who would think of mentioning such a low feeling, where the solemn duty of wife to husband, and husband's father and mother, is concerned? Her marriage is the passing from childhood's happy careless life to the responsibilities of reason. Body and soul, mind and spirit, must all tend to one thing — the giving entire satisfaction to the new master and his family.

This seems very dreary and cold to us; and the best European woman, educated in the full consciousness of her own value, would feel that she lost her integrity by entering such bondage. That it is done by hundreds of girls every year without any thought of love or duty either, but simply for the sake of having a luxurious home and plenty of fun, does not touch the case at all. Our typical high-minded English maiden despises these weaker sisters, is ashamed for them as for some blot on womanhood itself. The best of her gods is still naughty Cupid; and if he is to be shut out of her life, she would rather give up the struggle at once.

And yet all English history can show no record of higher, stronger love than the Japanese wife has again and again laid at her lord's feet. It would seem as if that rare passion of which I spoke just now may, in fact, be born in what we call bondage; may grow great in its nameless glory in these quiet lives; and when the time comes, may claim life, and everything which is dearer than life, with the certainty that all will be given entire. You exclaim, as you hear of some amazing piece of heroism, "How the woman must have loved the man!" And your friend, your little Japanese friend, looks up into your face with her childlike smile and some surprise in her dark eyes: "Oh no, it was her duty; he was her husband."

A little while ago, in the coldest time of the winter, the constable on duty after dark in one of the great cemeteries heard the sound of bitter weeping for two or three nights, and in the darkness could not discover where it came from. At last he found a newly made grave—the grave of a young man. Incense-sticks were burning beside it, and on the earth, her face turned downwards to the buried face beneath, a young woman lay weeping. The policeman roused her, and asked who she was. "He was my husband; we had been married but a few months; they buried him here. Do not send me away," she prayed between her sobs. "Weep in peace, O'Kami San," said the constable; "was he not thy husband? It is thy right to be here."

It seems to me that the common amusement called "falling in love" has absolutely nothing to do with the affectionate and careful fulfilment of the duties of married life, and that the crown of an all-absorbing worship of one human being for another may be, and often is, granted without that passing preliminary ailment having been contracted at all.

Nor does what is mistakenly called "the plurality of wives" seem to interfere materially with the true wife's happiness, or her regard for her husband. Steeped as we are in the laws and prejudices of the

West, it is not easy for us to judge of these questions; but since my sympathies naturally go with the woman, the wife-woman, who alone can carry the noble name, alone takes the responsibility of all the children's education, no matter who their mothers may be, we shall at any rate apprehend one aspect of the truth if we can grasp her point of view — a point of view which in ordinary circumstances would not have the defect of over-leniency at any rate.

In the first place, there is but one wife properly speaking, and it has rarely, if ever, been heard of that any attempt was made to intrude any other woman into her place. Her dignities as responsible head of the household, as wife and mother, as ruler of the home-world and dispenser of its hospitalities — these could never be taken from her; nor would they ever be given to a concubine, if the lady of the house were to die. Into her hands is given her husband's income, great or small; she apportions it as the best interests of the family require; and the great ladies show a profound power of organisation, making property yield its highest value, controlling all expenditure with a good sense and economy seldom shown by European women, unless they have had very special training in the management of great affairs.[1]

Where the property is very large, the lady employs a steward to collect the rents and see to the more out-

---

[1] This part of her duties has only been laid upon the Japanese lady in recent times. Formerly she was supposed to know very little of the value of money.

side matters; but she never drops the reins, and it is to her, and not to the master, that all claims or complaints are made. The steward is always called *her* steward, and may never come into contact with the master at all. This all entails very hard and constant work, and quite precludes the possibility of spending a very idle life, as rich men's wives are popularly supposed to do. Her other task, twin to this, is the entire management of the children's education while they are still young, and her responsibility for their health and morals.

Motherhood is what may truly be called the supreme relation of life for the Japanese woman. It crowns her with honour and glory; and although her children, if they be boys, are considered superior beings to the mother who bore them, yet she shines with every glory or distinction they achieve; every success of theirs is a jewel in her crown. As in the Bible, so here, the names of great men's mothers are handed down with those of their sons; and the nation says, for instance, of the Empress Jingo Kogo in her brilliant conquest of Corea, "No wonder that she did valiantly! Was she not carrying her great son Ojin[1] in her bosom at that time, to inspire her with wisdom and courage? Like son, like mother!"

It seems like a compensation to Japanese women for their judicial inferiority to men that the ruling passion of a woman's heart, love for children, is recognised as a national virtue; that the reverence for child-

[1] Ojin was after his death deified as Hachiman, the god of war.

hood has developed a system of kindness and care and protection of childhood such as would be the dream, the unrealisable dream, of many a broken-hearted mother in England, powerless to protect her children from the drunken cruelty of the brute who is their father, or, in a superior class, from the more refined torture inflicted by schoolmasters and other bullies. There is no baby torture here, no beating, no starvation, none of the indescribable horrors exposed and punished in some degree by our only too necessary Society for the Prevention of Cruelty to Children. From one end of Japan to the other, a child is treated as a sacred thing, be it one's own or a stranger's. Each little one carries its name and address on a ticket round its neck; but should it, indeed, stray from home, food and shelter and kindness would meet it everywhere. Do not shudder — a man will kill his child outright, scientifically, painlessly, if he sees that there is nothing but want and misery before it; but while he lives the child will not suffer.

A terrible case came under my own notice last year, when something very like famine desolated the land. The rice-crop failed, and the want was terrible. Relief camps were opened, soup and bread distributed from various centres in the city, one of the most efficient managed by Archdeacon S——, the (Protestant) Legation Chaplain (he and his wife people of such merciful goodness that everybody in trouble flies to their house, and is sure to find refuge and comfort there. Their hearts are of pure gold, and their house must be built of india-rubber — I wish one could say the same of their income!). But it was impossible to reach everybody, and starvation ploughed the poorer quarters of the city. At the worst moment a coolie came to the gate of our Convent in Tsukiji, leading two little girls. All three were frightfully emaciated. The poor father entreated the nuns to take the children, and bring them up among their orphans. He said he could no longer earn a livelihood for them; their mother was dead; he had nothing left in the world. Alas! he was not the first who had come on the same errand. During the few weeks before, one child after another had been brought to the good nuns, or left helpless at their gates, the parents certain that it would be cared for by them. Every corner was filled with sick and hungry people; the nuns had given up their one sitting-room, and were living in terror of the supplies giving out, for many a time the Superior has gone to bed not knowing where the money for the next day's marketing was to come from — and this with over three hundred mouths to feed! "It is God's family," she has often said to me; "so it is God's affair, and the money will surely come, or the food. He does not intend that we shall make debts!" But on this day the Sister was frightened. It did not seem right to crowd the children's dormitories any further, and people were sleeping on the floor in the passages already. She gave the poor man food, and a tiny sum, all she could possibly spare, in money. "Leave me your address," she said; "and the moment I have room I will send for the poor little girls. Have courage; I will not keep them long waiting." So the man went, taking his children with him; and the nun, seeing the despair in his eyes, was troubled all night about it, and sent down the first thing in the morning to tell him that she would risk it, he might bring the little girls back. Both children were dead. My dear blameless Sister Superior weeps whenever she remembers them, and that is very often. In that famine-time she saved many a child from being sold to a much worse fate than death. The parents were mad with trouble; the Yoshiwara man offered money, would never be unkind to the girls; prostitution was a misfortune certainly, but no disgrace, no crime; why not let them go?[1] Then the poor little girls, in their terror of the unknown, would cry out, "My cousin or my friend is with the Tsukiji Virjen Sama; take me to them, Ottottsan!" And that was one reason why the Convent was so terribly full just at that time.

I must say a few words more about the woman's life here before leaving these grave subjects for gayer ones. Perhaps it is really a hardship that a young and charming woman should have to call herself the

[1] Such traffic is forbidden by law, but is unfortunately still carried on in secret. It is quite distinct from the apprenticing of girls to masters who train them as *geisha* (or dancing-girls). These are highly educated according to Japanese ideas, and are not necessarily disreputable. Their training is extremely severe, and every gift of mind and body is developed to the highest point. Many have married men in prominent positions, and those whom I have known, although not warmly welcomed by Japanese ladies, have shown great sense and dignity in the conduct of social and domestic affairs.

mother of several big girls and boys who could not by any chance be her own children. I am always inclined to smile when such a woman gravely speaks of "my daughter," nodding to a girl nearly as old as herself, and perhaps without a trace of her own delicate features and innate high breeding; but my impression is that my friend herself sees nothing derogatory in it, although she may be very well educated and a Christian as well. The *mekake*, or concubine, is in her own

COMING FROM THE BATH

way a perfectly respectable woman, probably taken from the class of small shopkeepers, who do not consider her accepting such a position as any disgrace. The woman herself very likely acts as a servant in the house; always kindly treated and provided for to the end of her life, she yet has no part in her children, and must only tend and love them as an upper nurse might do. This is the real hardship of her lot; but in the simplicity of the Japanese points of view there are many things which soften it for her. Although never for a moment usurping the mistress's place, she is treated with a good deal of consideration by the whole family, on the principle of her being a favourite with the great lord and master, round whom they all revolve in different circles indeed, but all with equal dependence on the domestic sun. If he be a very rich man, he will probably give the *mekake* a home to herself in another part of the grounds; but there will be no enmity between her and the great lady, the true wife, who mothers all the children. A young married woman came to see a friend of mine, arriving rather late for an appointment. "You look tired," my friend remarked to the visitor. "I am very tired," she replied; "we have had a dear new baby born in the house. I was up all night with the mother. We thought she would die, poor thing; but I am glad to say she is all right now!" This lady was a Christian too; but — the King can do no wrong in Japan.

One very good result comes from the frank way in which these matters are treated. There are no illegitimate children, as we understand the term, because every child takes its father's name, and he is forced to provide for its maintenance. Even in former times the son of the true wife was looked upon as a man's natural heir; but failing him, the inheritance passed to his brother, whoever the latter's mother might have been. Failing a half-brother, it passed to a daughter of the true wife, and failing such, to any other daughter whom the man might have had. Such was the rule; but where each man was absolute master in his own house, distinctions of favouritism were often arbitrarily exercised. A man could, in fact, choose which son should inherit his honours and estates, or he could put all his own children aside, and install a stranger as head of the family. Nothing mattered except that my lord's whims should be carried out. But now things are different. A man is responsible for all his children, whoever their mother may have been; but his title can only be inherited by the eldest living son of his true wife, and, failing such, must go to the nearest collateral legitimate heir. The next heir to the throne after Prince Haru must be the son of his Empress, or, failing him, the son of the true wife of the Prince nearest to the throne. This new regulation is a death-blow to the old system of adoption; and, while rendering far higher honour to the true wife than she had heretofore enjoyed, inflicts disabilities on the children of concubines, which will gradually bring discredit on the whole system. At least, so it strikes me. It seems to be the thin end of the wedge of external respectability according to Western ideas, applied to the spot where its touch will be most keenly felt — the honour of the family. I doubt if the new regulation will add to the happiness of the Japanese home, which for decorum and harmony so far compares more than favourably with the ordinary European one; and I see in it a danger to the permanency and strength of the tie between father and child.

I hope that my plain speaking will not give the false impression that I undervalue the splendid privileges which the Church bestowed on Christian men and women when she instituted Christian marriage. There is but one state higher, the angelic life led in religion; and certainly we Western women owe all our freedom and honour to the Catholic Church, which told the slaves that the King of Heaven had died for them, which took the slave-woman and called her wife, which to-day in the marriage service says to the man, "Remember, I give thee a companion, and not a slave."

But where the man is no more a Christian than the ordinary society man in London; where he has taken no vows, however flippantly, binding him to one woman; where every day humanity does not take the sacred name of love in vain, — there I think that decency, order, and the family ties are less outraged by the existence of the quiet faithful concubine and her children than by the revolting arrangements resorted to in Europe, where men, who as the saying goes "are not straight to their wives," are brought without shame or regret into the society of women from whom the poor Japanese *mekake* would shrink with horror.

The counterpart of that class exists here. Compared to the poor creatures who compose it in Europe, the Japanese women are models of refinement and disinterestedness. But society shows stern disapproval of the men who frequent their company; a wife may protest against such lapses without any infringement of the respect she owes her lord, and it would be considered her duty to do so.

As a last word, I should say that there are many Japanese families of the upper class where it has been for generations the custom to make the wife supreme in every way, and to admit no *mekake* into the family. Concubinage is an expensive luxury confined to the upper classes, and is greatly on the wane even among them; among the poor it is unknown; and divorce, though still fatally easy, is not often resorted to.

CHAPTER XXXII

THE DEATH OF PRINCE SANJO.—A STATE FUNERAL.—A BRAVE DAUGHTER.—OGITA'S FAREWELL.—THE SHIBA TEMPLES.—A FEAST OF BEAUTY

March, 1891.

A PROFOUND gloom has been cast over the capital by the death of Prince Sanjo; he was such a familiar figure at all the Court functions, he and I had sat through so many dinners, walked in so many processions side by side, that I had come to look upon him as an old friend; he was always kind and cheery, and the wife and daughter had been among those whom I saw most constantly. They are in terrible grief; and I shall not see them for many months, as a long period of seclusion will separate them from the world. They were all with us on Christmas Day, and the poor Prince took influenza almost immediately afterwards. His lungs were never very strong, and he could not weather the attack of inflammation which set in. If companionship is any comfort in grief, his family ought to be comforted; for the whole country mourned for the Emperor's friend and councillor, the quiet, duty-loving statesman, who has done so much for progress, justice, and peace.

If there were a Libro d'Oro in Japan, the name of Prince Sanetome Sanjo would be among the very first in its pages. A Kugé (or descendant of an Imperial Prince), his pedigree goes back to Kamatari (A.D. 626), the founder of fourteen out of the sixteen Kugé families existing to-day.[1] Prince Sanjo was always devoted to the Imperial cause, and in very early youth flung himself, his influence, and his fortune into the struggle to put down the usurpations of the Shogun and restore the sovereign to the reality of power. I have described this struggle in an earlier letter. Prince Sanjo was but a boy when it began; at its close, after fourteen years of constant warfare, he was only thirty years old, and had proved his devotion and ability so completely that he was at once raised to high rank in the Government, and was ever after looked upon by the Emperor as the most trustworthy of his councillors. In 1871 (he was then thirty-four) he was given the post of Chancellor of the Empire, the highest in the Administration. He held it for fourteen years, by far the most difficult years in Japan's stormy history — years during which all the changes that we admire to-day were introduced and consolidated without the slightest shock to the national strength or integrity. The country came through the ordeal, accompanied as it was by civil war, rebellion, intrigues without

[1] If pedigrees may be trusted, there is no body of peers in Europe who can out-class the present peerage of Japan. It numbers four hundred and seventy-three members of the old nobility, and, of these, four hundred are the direct descendants of Emperors, and possess written records going back for thirteen or fourteen centuries.

and within, with perfect safety; with the Emperor firmly seated on his throne, never to be touched again by the ambitions and intrigues of the Shoguns; with enemies transformed into loyal servants, friends rewarded for faithful service, the empire ready to work like one man at the task of setting its army and navy, its legislation, its organisation on the footing which befits a great power. It is, I fancy, rare to hear of a Prime Minister holding uninterrupted office for fourteen years; and it is in our experience unparalleled that any nation should so have transformed itself in that period of time. Prince Sanjo had no personal ambition, and several times begged for permission to retire from public affairs, which were then advancing safely and smoothly. This permission was at last unwillingly granted, in 1885; he was made Keeper of the Privy Seal, and did not again enter public life till the end of 1889, when he reluctantly took the leadership of the Cabinet at the Emperor's command after the attempted assassination of Count Okuma. Every one recognised in him a man of intense conscientiousness, wisdom, and intrepid courage, whose every good quality acquired a double value through his complete integrity and disinterestedness.

There are distinctions in Japan which are only granted to dying greatness. When we heard that the Emperor was about to visit his faithful servant, we knew that but one visitor would succeed him in the quiet house; the sovereign was the herald of death, and he conferred the honours which Sanetome Sanjo must take with him to the Meido, the shadow realm, for he could not enjoy them here. As soon as his desperate condition became known, the Emperor hastened to his house; and while the Prince was still conscious, told him that he had come to thank him for his life-long devotion,

PRINCE SANJO

and to bestow on him the highest rank that it is possible for a subject to hold. The people who accompanied the Emperor tell us that all his assumed calm fell away from him when he looked on his friend's face, and that it was with the greatest difficulty that he controlled his emotion as he spoke words which must have been very sweet even to dying ears. This is what the sovereign said:

"In the early years of my reign, while I was still but a youth, you were my greatest help. You, not shrinking from the gravest responsibility, lent me assistance so constant, so ready, and so true, that you were to me as a teacher and a father. Never did you fail in the discharge of your great duties. All my subjects should look up to you as a model. In recognition of your great services and faithfulness I confer upon you the First Class of the First Rank."

This last, Sho-ichi-i, is a distinction which has not been granted to any subject for over eleven hundred years, when it was borne by one of Prince Sanjo's ancestors, who died in 738. They say that the poor Prince made violent attempts to rise and salute the Emperor properly. A few hours after the visit he passed away, and the world is much the poorer by the loss of a good man.

The Imperial family practice the "pure Shinto" form of religion, and Prince Sanjo's State funeral was arranged altogether by Shinto rules. These forbid pomp, but enjoin the use of white robes, white woods, quantities of flowers, everything simple and cheering and pure. I have heard the reproach of heartlessness again and again made to the Japanese, on account of the calm and cheerful countenances with which they accompany their dead to the grave. But their long and tender remembrance of the dead surely exonerates them from the accusation. Their belief is that those who die beloved, and for whom remembrance is constantly made, do not suffer in the shadowy peace of Meido, the home of departed spirits, which is not a prison, and from which they constantly come to visit the living, to protect and comfort the bereaved. Is it possible that this humble impersonal faith can sustain the survivors in the dreadful emptiness of the stricken home? I think it helps them so greatly, because it is a part of eternal truth — just that portion of it which they are fitted to apprehend now. The great Teacher does not insist upon making all His children learn the same lesson the same day.

Our friend's funeral was very beautiful and very simple, its greatest pomp being that which we should all love to share in — the true sorrow of grateful hearts. The white-robed priests and mourners, the white lotus flowers with their silver leaves, the exquisite white-wood coffin with its snowy panoply — all seemed to fit the passing of his pure spirit to its rest. But the whole country mourned his loss, and there never has been seen such a concourse of people in Tokyo as that which lined the route of the procession. The procession itself was two miles long, and passed over some six miles of distance, from the solemn house among the fir trees where he died, to the Gokakuji Temple, where the funeral rites were to take place. It is a beautiful place, with great gardens full of flowers, in which wander young bonzes from a college kept here for them. The Temple is the mortuary chapel, as it were, of the Imperial Cemetery, a part of the grounds

THE SACRED LOTUS

having been set aside for that purpose, now that Emperors live and die in Tokyo. The place is never opened to the public except when some silent Prince or Princess comes knocking at the gate.

All along the line of march really sorrowing crowds watched the train go by, amid a hush of intense respect. The troops who accompanied it remained outside the gates, and the rest passed in, up long flights of steps which led to the sanctuary where the service was to take place. All those invited to the funeral had already assembled here. The heralds of the train were a number of white-robed men, carrying quantities of green branches of the *sakaki* (*Cleyera Japonica*), sacred to the dead. Then came the offerings, which would later be placed before the coffin; these were enclosed in a case, white and plain like all the rest. A great troop of Shinto priests followed, all white-robed except the high-priest, who wore purple. Then, to the sounds of the weirdly sad Shinto music, came a great white banner, on which were inscribed all the Prince's titles and honours; and after that quantities of people carrying the *sakaki* sprigs, the placing of which forms a part of the funeral ceremony, and others carrying silver halberds and enormous trophies of flowers such as people here send to a funeral instead of our wreaths and crosses. Eight separate decorations, the most honourable in the Emperor's gift, had been bestowed on the Prince at different times; and these were carried on cushions by eight bearers, all dressed in white; and then came a goodly company in the same costume, the chief servants of the family. It was their privilege immediately to precede the bier, which was of a lovely shape, like a small temple, all carved out of spotless white wood, the spruce which the Japanese call *hi-no-ki*. It did not look like a coffin, but like a closed litter, with beautifully chased golden mountings, and fresh green bamboo blinds closing its little windows. The roof rose at the four corners in delicate ornaments; and tassels of pure white silk hung against the blinds. Raised on a system of poles crossed and recrossed, the bier was carried by fifty men, all dressed in white. We were told that it covered a double coffin, made also of white wood. A thrill of real sorrow seemed to run through the great crowd as it passed, and then all hearts went out to the boy and girl who followed as chief mourners, for their mother was too prostrated by grief to appear. The girl was my little friend, Princess Chiye, her beautiful face absolutely rigid, and white as the robe which showed under her black cloak and brown *hakama*, the kind of divided skirt worn on all occasions of ceremony. Her little feet were roughly sandalled, and she walked the whole way from her father's house to her father's resting-place, bareheaded, without betraying a sign of fatigue. Her brother, dressed in black and white, and wearing the same common sandals, walked at her side; and behind them came four little girls, the younger sisters, who wore no black, but white crape robes without a single ornament, and having their long hair tied back with white ribbon and hanging far below their waists. They were followed by a crowd of relations, and in this order the procession passed at last in at the Temple gate, and up the many steps, till they stopped under a tent or porch which had been erected before the door of the Temple. Here were two pavilions, in which the family took their seats, together with the Imperial Princes, the Ministers, the Foreign Representatives, and the other guests.

The tent was all draped in the sombre black and white stripes that I have so often seen used for Court functions. In the centre, just before the steps, the bier was placed on a stand prepared for it; the banners and flower trophies were disposed on either side of the space leading up to it; and the Prince's Orders were laid on little white-wood stands around. Then came Shinto chants; and the two chief priests with their acolytes prayed before the bier, and bent in homage to the dead. Then the chief priest took the offerings of food, and placed them on other stands prepared for them; and he read aloud, in a high-chanting voice, two orations of farewell to the dead. In these all the good and great acts of the Prince's life were recounted; and at the end came the phrase, "May thy soul have eternal rest and peace in heaven," so like our "Requiem eternam dona eis, Domine, et lux perpetua luceat eis," that a very deep chord of sympathy was touched in those who could understand the words.

But the ceremonial was terribly long for the poor children, who went through it, as *samurai* and nobles should, without a single change of expression on their young pale faces. How the eldest Princess bore it I know not; for she worshipped her father, and the tie between them was that of the most complete confidence and intimacy. When the orations were over, the priests distributed sprigs of the *sakaki* to every one, beginning with the young Prince, the Imperial Princes, and the envoys of the Emperor and Empress. When these had reverently laid the branches before the bier, the poor little Princess and her four sisters slowly advanced, holding the sacred boughs in their hands, bowed to the very ground in the last act of homage to their beloved father, and laid the green boughs on those already lying before his coffin. This was a terrible moment, and seemed likely to be too much for the eldest daughter's fortitude; but she conquered it, laid her offering on the rest with a hand that trembled pitifully, and led her sisters back to their place, unconquered by grief.

Something like two thousand people followed to render this green tribute to the Prince's memory; and when that had been done, most of the guests returned home, only a very few having been invited to attend the actual burial in the cemetery. The road to the grave was all a double wall of flowers, standing high on either side of a long carpeting of fine matting. Every lovely bloom that could rob death of its terrors had been collected there; under the bright Eastern sunshine a beautiful canopy of white wood hung high over the open stone vault. In the gardens around, all life was rising to its spring, and stately trees, the guardians of the place, seemed to have been waiting long for this honoured and welcome guest. When the white coffin had at last been placed in its quiet home, amidst a silence woven of love and reverence; when the green boughs and the flowers and the insignia of earthly glory had been laid at the door, through which the honoured dead must pass alone,—then those who had been bidden to his farewell crept away, leaving the poor children to say their last good-byes alone. And in that morning smile of nature, in that perfect peace which seems to have robbed death of its fear and bereavement of its sting, I trust that the good-byes were not despairing ones.

These things happened in the end of February, and this is the beginning of March. Alas! the spring has robbed me of another friend, and one whose like I shall not find again. Ogita, our *samurai*, guide, interpreter, my right hand in a thousand matters of life, has passed away, unable to recover from the effects of that awful influenza. He had been ailing for long, coughing, and looking very thin. We think he hurt himself by giving lessons in the exhausting Japanese fencing, which Dr. Baelz, one of the strongest men I know, and trained, as all Germans are, to such exercises, told me was so terribly fatiguing that the learning of it nearly broke him down. Poor Ogita was a great swordsman, his family was large, the Government pay none too generous; so nothing was said when it was found that he was giving lessons in his spare time. After Christmas we sent him down to Atami to keep him out of the way of the epidemic; but he took it there, and came home at last, with death written on his face. Do you wonder that I tell you so much about a mere servant, a Chancery writer? He has been so helpful and faithful, has carried out all my whims with such gentle patience, has piloted me through so many journeys, taught me so many quaint stories, that a part of my Japanese life has died with him.

He had a little house in the grounds, where I went constantly in the last days. The old mother, the wife, the five girls and boys, always received me with an air of gay satisfaction, and never let me see them break down at all till quite the end. In the bare little house on the worn mats lay my poor friend, too weak to speak, but with a light of welcome always shining for me in his eyes. He was a tall man, of soldierly bearing, and there was something very pitiful in seeing him lying, so long and weak, on the floor of the tiny room, which seemed so much too small for him. Behind him, to keep off any draught, was a six-leaved screen out of my sitting-room, with gay summer landscapes and dancing waterfalls painted on the panels. What comforts could help him he had; and though the rooms were small, at any rate the house was his home, and he was surrounded by all the love of mother and wife and children. The children were greatly on his mind; but when their future was provided for to his satisfaction, he was quite content to die, and said to me once or twice, "Okusama is very kind; I would get well if I could; but I can never travel with her any more, and I am too tired to live." To the very last his two hands always went up to his brow when I entered, even after he could not speak; and I used only to stay a minute or two at a time, for fear of exhausting him. We had had many a conversation about the future life; but, alas! he had lived too long among careless Christians to have any special regard for Christianity. He had seen in his twenty years of Government service bad men and good, among the Christians as among the sects of his countrymen — less good, perhaps, among the former than among the latter. There was no ground for a conversion here, and he went out among the shadows a valiant, humble, upright soul, a *samurai* and a gentleman to the last; and I do not believe that any true gentleman was ever shut out of heaven yet. They left me alone with him for a while the day after he was dead; he lay very straight and stiff, with a smile of peace on his thin face. His hands were crossed on his breast, and his long blue robes were drawn in straight folds, all held in place with little packets of tea, which filled the room with a dry fragrance; the coffin was lined with these, and his head rested on a pillow of the same. Beside him on a stand lay his most precious possession, his sword; and before the weeping wife left me kneeling there, she touched my shoulder, and pointed to the sword, bowing her head in reverence, and whispering, "Samurai, Okusama!" Incense-sticks were burning in bronze vases at either end of the sword, and freshly gathered flowers stood on the floor near the coffin head. Behind was still my screen, not turned upside down, as it should have been in the presence of the dead (perhaps because it was mine); and in the little room, bared of all except that which was left to honour my poor friend, the summer landscapes and dancing waterfalls spoke of hope and new life and a world where a tired spirit might rest earth's weariness away.

So they took our *samurai* home; and after the first bursts of grief, far less restrained among the poorer women than among the nobles, I think the old mother and the wife and the little girls have found comfort in visiting the quiet grave in Shiba, where Ogita lies. All little gifts are stored up to carry there; O'Ione San, the baby girl of three, whom her father worshipped devoutly, saves up all the pretty cakes that find their way from my tea-table to her little brown hands. "Ottottsan's!" she says when they are given to her; and a piece of paper has to be found to wrap them in, and they are put in the alcove in the place of honour till she and her mother pay their next visit to Shiba; and then they are laid with many a tender word on *Ottottsan's* grave, to comfort him if he is lonely or hungry in the Meido. Good-bye, kind friend and

THE SHIBA CEMETERY

faithful servant. "May thy soul have eternal rest and peace in heaven!"

And now, as I have spoken of Shiba, I must tell you something of those Shiba Temples which are the pride of Tokyo — temples built mostly as tombs or temporary mortuary chapels for the Shoguns of the Tokugawa Dynasty. Its founder, Iyeyasu, lies at Nikko (as does his grandson, Iyemitsu); but during his lifetime he suddenly realised that he had no especial temple of his own; "and that," said he, "is a thing unheard of for a great general! I must immediately select a temple, where I can pray during my life, and where others will pray for me when I am dead!" The result of these pangs of conscience was the choice of the great Temple of Zōjōji, in what is now called the Shiba Park, as the one where his *ihai* (mortuary tablet bearing his posthumous name and titles) should be set up. The Temple was administered by priests of the Jōdō sect of Buddhists; it was extremely rich and splendid, but was burnt, in revenge it is said, when in 1873 the Buddhists were banished, and the Temple given over to "pure Shinto." A smaller and poorer one was built, which seems out of place behind the magnificent triple gate (Sammon) which remains from the days of its predecessor. But the mortuary temples (not intended for public worship) were fortunately not burnt, and contain wonders of lacquer and painting and carving. The great red gates, with their scarlet columns and big lanterns and wheeling flights of pigeons (tame as those of San Marco), are quite beautiful to look at; and I often drive past them just to see the pigeons gathering round the feet of some girl who stands in the great opening feeding them with grain bought at the little booths which line the terrace, while behind her the sun touches hundreds of huge stone lanterns in the grey inner court. And when the spring has come, when the tall camellia trees are flinging the petals and the perfume of their single rose-coloured blossoms all abroad (petals so delicate that it seems wrong to walk on them, perfume so fragrant that one longs to store and carry it away), then the courts of the Shiba Temples are happy places to wander through; its flights of grey stone steps make seats where one can rest and dream a sunny hour away with much profit. For the sun is the master of the house; and unless you find him at home, you may as well leave your card and come another day. The dusky splendours of the sacred buildings will be invisible to you unless he illuminates them; the paintings and carvings withdraw into space, and none of the fairy-work will show itself rightly, except at the touch of the great magician.

The friend who took me there the first time had spent days and weeks in making drawings of some of the wonders of decoration on panel and roof; and he would not let me go near the temples, until one glorious morning when it seemed as if a hundred suns were shining at once. Then the wide courts, with their armies of lanterns, their limpid fountains for the washing of the worshippers' hands, their stately stairs and fern-set walls, all seemed so attractive that I had no great desire to enter the dark buildings. But my want of enterprise was taken no notice of, and I was glad, for the contents of the casket were equal to the outer covering. Through a splendidly carved dragon-gate, we passed to an inner court, where are two hundred and twelve bronze lanterns, very stately to behold. Beautiful, also, is the cistern for holy water, perpetually brimming with a crystal flood which never overflows. Then we pass to an inner court still, whose galleries are adorned with elaborate paintings; over our heads a beautiful winged woman hovers, painted in the purest and most brilliant colours; and everywhere are endless interweavings of those wave and wind patterns which symbolise the original principles in nature, the Fûng Shui (wind and water spirits) of

GATE OF THE SHIBA TEMPLE

China. It would take many days to note all the changes, the beautiful elaborations worked from these through hundreds of developments, in each of which the artist gives a new shape and meaning to the rush of the hurricane, the curl and spray of the wave. But we pass on from the gallery intended for the Daimyos, who accompanied each Shogun when he came here, to his own temple, to pray. They might not go with him to the inner sanctuary, the Honden; there he entered, and offered up his devotions alone, while they sat, the greater divided from the less, in perfect silence without. All this painting and gilding and carving must have proved a great interest and solace, if the Shogun was long at his prayers. We passed on to the inner sanctuary, having slipped off our shoes so as not to scratch the polished and lacquered steps with our hard heels.

I believe there is in the human being a profound hunger and thirst for beauty for its own sake; there are chords in our hearts which thrill at the sight of piled gold and rippling jewels, at the miracles of perfect, priceless decoration, as they thrill at great music or a splendid sunset. Now and then in life this hunger is satisfied by a feast, and more than a feast, of beauty; the soul is intoxicated with the new wine of gold and colour and magnificence, and understands in that triumphant flush some secret of the permanent and divine essence of beauty which it never can apprehend, or affects to forget, in the sober daylight of its working existence. When I found myself face to face with the marvel called the Octagonal Shrine, I felt that I was in presence of the supreme effort of art in one particular direction — that this vision of the eight-sided shrine of pure gold lacquer, from whose depths trees and hills, birds and beasts, have been as it were resolved for us to see, whose sides and pinnacles shine with gems and fairy-work of rainbow enamel, this indeed could rank with my visit to the green-draped shrine in the Dresden

Gallery where the Sistine Madonna reigns in the silence, with golden hours passed under Michelangelo's cypresses in the gardens of our home, with our sailings in the summer moonlight past the islands of the syrens to the violets of Pæstum: here was one more piece of perfect

THE HALL OF THE BOOKS

beauty, mine for ever in the inalienable kingdom of remembrance. I have but to close my eyes, and there rises before me this golden flower of beauty blooming on its petalled base in hazy glory; the sun falls on it down the softened air, and seems to kiss it into warmth and life. The columns all around reach up, as if they had grown of themselves in bars of pure gold, to fence the treasure in from floor to ceiling; and the roof itself, with all its sombre splendour, seems a shadowy reflection of the jewelled casket below. It contains —— But who cares what it contains? The perfume of the rainbow and the elixir of life, most like! No, only a little image of the Shogun Hidetada and his mortuary tablet; and the Shogun himself lies deep in the ground below our feet, rolled in vermilion and charcoal to preserve his bones. Gladly must his spirit hover over the place where his memory is enshrined in all that beauty!

There are other chapels and other shrines in Shiba's magic courts — shrines of surpassing richness and loveliness; and if we ever go there together, you shall visit them first: we will linger in the great hall of the books, where the sacred scrolls lie swathed in silk, each in its lacquered box on its lacquered stand; we will see paintings and carvings, angels and demons, peonies and lotus flowers in a hundred lovely tints; and then, when you are inured to hardihood through this orgy of colour and decoration, we will visit the tomb of the Second Shogun. We will see it undazzled, sober still, if possible, but shall want no more sights afterwards. *Sufficit!*

CHAPTER XXXIII

IN THE EMPRESS'S OWN GARDEN. — A WHITE SAIL SET SQUARE TO THE WIND. — THE BOYS' FESTIVAL, ITS ORIGIN AND MEANING. — HIDEYOSHI AND HIS BATTLE STANDARD. — THE MONGOLIAN INVASION

TOKYO, *May*, 1891.

THE Empress's own cherry blossoms were in all their glory in April, when she invited us to come to her Palace garden by the sea to look at them. Something interfered with the festival last year, so this was my first visit to the Hama Rikyu, or Enryō Kwan. Everywhere the cherry blossoms have been perfect this year; our own garden is a dream of loveliness. There has been just enough rain to bring on the flowers without drowning them, and at one moment the whole place was like the rose-coloured wedding that we once had in the family. Do you remember the transformation of that December day? Winter seemed a thousand years away, when we went down to see the Empress's cherry blossoms. The Hama Rikyu consists more of gardens than palace; for the house, though pretty, is small, and is chiefly used for the accommodation of illustrious visitors. It was there that our two young Princes were received when they visited Tokyo. The Empress stays there for a few weeks in the late spring to enjoy the freshness of the sea breezes, which blow in at the wide windows. The sea rolls up to the foot of the walls on one side; and the garden is built out into the water, like Miramar, near Trieste. The flowery alleys wind about amongst lakes and canals, where real waves come beating boldly against the toy bridges. There are islands with quaint pavilions perched on their green summits, and arbours, and boats, and all the furniture of a fairy tale; and everywhere, above the floating strains of the gay bands, above the murmur of talk and singing of the wind in the trees, comes the august chant of the sea — the chant that began when all this rich country was a reed-grown marsh, when the wild foxes were the only courtiers, and Emperors and Empresses of Japan were called Prince Fire-Shine and Princess Fire-Subside, and the Flood-Tide Jewel and the Ebb-Tide Jewel, in the play-grounds of mythology. The sea is with us still, and has never turned courtier. As we walked through the gardens in the usual official procession behind the sovereigns, we looked, with all the uniforms and finery, like some huge dazzling snake, gliding in and out of all the narrow paths, hanging on red bridges, losing its lengths in green dells; and the breeze rioting in from the bay rained down cherry blossoms on our heads.

Suddenly we came out on a wide terrace close to the sea; the salt water was lapping against the stones at our feet; the sea-gulls flew inland with wild cries, the afternoon sun turning their wings to dull gold; the gardens stretched back towards the town, their mountains of rosy bloom seeming to break like spray against the black-green pines on the steeps of Count Ito's garden. And just then, in the tearing breeze, a native boat, with its great white sail set square to the wind, seemed to be rushing down on us for a moment — came so near that for one breathless space we heard the water cutting cold against the prow; the brine

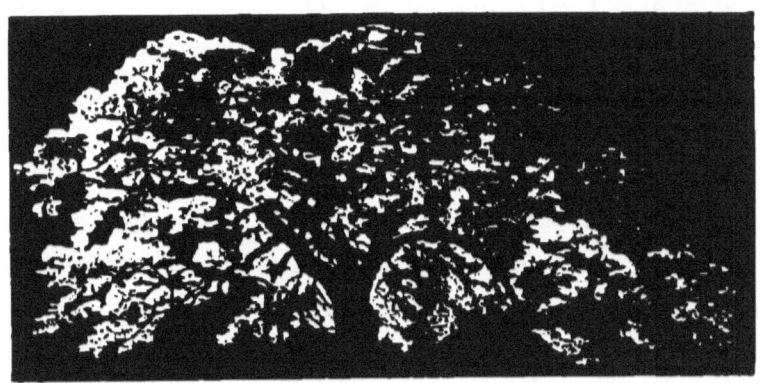

A VERY OLD CHERRY TREE IN BLOOM

from the new-made wavelets came salt on the air, and a rim of spray hung between us and the sun; then the boat turned and tacked, and fled up the bay, carrying some stray pink petals lodged in the hollow of the sail. It was just a piece of bare delicious nature, let down before our eyes as a contrast to all the artificialities of the Court. Perhaps even that is less artificial here than it would be over the water. Our dainty Empress, who has the soul of a poet, had ordered from her own looms a robe of pale apple-green brocade, with bunches of rosy cherry blossoms scattered over it. The effect was quite lovely. A soft green velvet mantle, and a bonnet of white lace and jewels, made one forget that the gown had to be made in European fashion; and the Empress herself seemed very happy that day, as if she were frankly enjoying the flowers and the sunshine, and even the bonbons, cherry blossoms and brown twigs and fairy grasses, all done in sugar by that famous Court confectioner! She kept me with her longer than usual, asking many kind questions about some theatricals which we had had for a charitable object, an infirmary which was much wanted, and for which she had kindly sent me a generous cheque.

It was the first time that I came away with regret from one of these stiff parties; the whole thing was so wonderfully pretty and fresh. But I suppose we shall soon see the gardens of the Enryō Kwan again, since the Cesarévitch, who is expected for a visit to Japan, will be lodged there.

Very great preparations are being made for this royal visit. The apartments in the Palace by the sea have all been furnished and decorated anew; there are to be triumphal arches and illuminations and Court balls; and the Emperor intends to lavish honours — and fun — on his guest. The S——s at the Russian Legation have transformed their somewhat dingy house into a bower of flowery beauty; I have just been going over it, and rather envied the Grand Duke the two thousand pots of lilies in bloom which are to line the great staircase. They must have spent an enormous amount of money, for they have had to build an immense ballroom out into the garden; and as there was no time for painting and papering, the whole place has been lined with Japanese crapes in brilliant colours, palms, and ferns, and creeping plants. I could not help condoling a little with Madame S—— on the endless bother of the whole thing. " How can you say such a word!" she cried, with flashing eyes, "*Bother!* It is a joy to do anything for our sovereign's son. I wish we could have done fifty times more!"

And now, since it is May, and since the Cesarévitch cannot be here for a few days yet, let me tell you of the strange symbolic rejoicing called the Boys' Festival, which is peopling the town with flying-fish, rising and falling from their gilt poles on every breeze—fish of every size and colour, but all of one shape, the shape of the *koi*, the undaunted, unconquerable carp.

When the fifth day of the fifth month has come, the streets of Tokyo and of every city in the empire are alive with these quaint banners fluttering in the wind. A stranger might congratulate himself on having arrived at a moment of public rejoicing; and I shall never forget the amazement with which I regarded the flying-fish and their golden rice-balls, when I first arrived here, in May, two years ago. Now they are a part of the spring; and it seems as if its best days were past when they no longer hover over the low brown roofs.

For all its festal aspect, no crowds or knots of holiday-makers are to be seen in the streets of the city; no drums are beating the time of a religious festival: everything is quiet. The shops are open; customers are coming and going; brown little children with bare legs play with bean-bags in the roads; the young girl walks slowly along in her clattering *gheta* (clogs) and silken *kimono*, followed by her attendant maid, who carries her books from school; the business man in native costume and "bowler" hat wheels by in his jinriksha to his day's work. Busy life seems going on everywhere, undisturbed, beneath the rustling wave of bright colour which floats over the town. Bright, indeed! The banners which fly from almost every house are all in the shape of gigantic fishes, painted blue or red or grey, with silver scales, made of paper or cotton cloth, and hollow so that they swell and rise, shrink and fall, as the wind takes or leaves them. Very realistic, indeed, are their gaping mouths, huge eyes, and fins, and the sheen of their scales glinting in the sunlight. They are of various sizes, though always large, and all made after one pattern — that of the *koi*, or carp.

The *koi* is the emblem of a male child and of luck; and this is the Boys' Festival, *O Sekku* or *Tango*, as the Japanese call it.

Fish in Japan takes the place of beef in England, and next to rice is the staple product of the country. On the birth of a son, the support of the house, the relations and friends send or bring with their con-

THE FISH FESTIVAL.

gratulations live *koi* swimming about in tubs of water; and at this feast parents are entitled to display a paper fish for each son, the younger the child the larger the fish, and *vice versa*. This toy fish is attached to a long bamboo pole, which is hoisted in front of the house, often with other ornamental flags and signs, such as a wind-wheel or a gilded wicker basket, which may stand for the puffy ball of rice paste with which the real fish are fed. Several fish may often be seen flapping around one pole; and proud is that house, for it means that the master is blest with many sons.

But the carp does not stand (or swim) only for luck and good cheer. That wonderful feat, only accomplished after persevering efforts, of swimming up the rapids (*taki nobori*), is, as I think I said before, the symbol of the brave youth who overcomes the difficulties and obstacles of life. I do not think European carp ever attempt the enterprise, and it was only when I came to Japan that I learnt that it is possible. Here it has passed into a proverb, and is a favourite subject with the native artists, the valiant carp being now synonymous with the abstract virtues of perseverance and fortitude. The legend says that when he has scaled the waterfall a white cloud from heaven sweeps down and catches up the triumphant fish, who then becomes a dragon. The brave *koi*, undaunted by the most fearful difficulties, is pointed out to the boy to impress upon him that the prizes of life are not for the sluggard or the coward, and its presence in lifelike similitude at his birthday feast is meant to act as an incentive to manly action and unflagging courage.

His birthday feast it is, at whatever time of the year he may have been born. Except for the purpose of casting a horoscope, the real day of his birth will be seldom remembered; and just as every girl's festival is March 3rd, so every boy's festival proper is May 5th, although the whole month is more or less his, and the fish float triumphantly from their ,enormous flagstaffs until the heats of June. It is on May 5th that the little feast is kept inside the house — every house, rich or poor, that Heaven has honoured with a son. And in all we should see the same symbols, the same flowers; for sons belong to the poor as well as to the rich, and are counted as the props of the home.

First of all, in the matted dwelling, one notices that in the floral arrangements, which are a distinct part of every ceremonial, a marked preference is shown for the long graceful leaves and spirited flowers of the iris. On the raised daïs, the place of honour, in the chief room, one will see a fine lacquer table supporting a vase, or more often a flat dish, of these lovely flowers, every leaf and blossom shooting up at exactly the right angle of strength and grace — the result of an hour's work or more, but looking so exquisitely natural that it seems incredible they should not have grown so by themselves, up from the limpid water where a tiny wedge of bamboo is really holding them all irrevocably in place. In another room is a wicker basket, or bamboo hanging vase, pierced in two or three places; and from this the swordlike leaves emerge with a will of their own, and the delicate flower-de-luce hangs its petals over them like white and purple flags, well-wishing them through the fight.

At this time of year the table at a Japanese dinner party is a study of what can be done with these most characteristic flowers. I was at one a little while ago, where all the decoration consisted of green bamboo, of the most perfect and polished surface, cut into sections

A PLEASURE-BOAT ON THE CANAL

of different lengths, and set upright in perfect gradation in three groups, spaced down the long table. In these natural organ pipes were arranged thin screens of iris flowers, ranging from deep purple to pale mauve, with their pointed leaves shooting up like swords among them. Every grace of stem, every vigorous breaking of flower from sheath, or leaf from leaf, was displayed with unerring knowledge and decision; and the result — forgive repetition — was the most perfect picture of strength and grace that it is possible to see.

But to return to our little Japanese boy and his festival. To-day Yasu, or Saburo, or Takenori would in old times have expected to find the entrance of his house all decked with iris leaves in the morning; and he and his friends would have plaited little toy swords, and have done some sharp mock fighting, just to mark the day. For fighting was what the young *samurai* had to learn; and a friend tells me that, in order to harden young boys and make them absolutely indifferent to suffering, he and his young townsmen were obliged to rise from their warm beds between three and four on a winter's morning, and go in a single robe, bare of head, and bare of foot, to the fencing-ground, where many a hard blow was dealt, and the young blood, warmed by the fight, threw off the rigour of the icy cold, and knew that it had won one victory more over sloth and weakness. He was quite accustomed to this terrific *régime* when he was eight years old!

So while our Japanese boys are playing, like others, at war, they know more of its hardships than one would think who only saw them with green swords in the mild May morning. The bath has preceded the play, and in the bath the irises too have their service. It is still credited with strength-giving powers, probably on account of its remarkable vitality and the varied character of its growth through the changing seasons. Great bunches of the leaves are thrown into the ocean of hot water called a bath in Japan. Thus used, the plant was supposed to inspire the spirit of patriotism and valour. Tradition held that the dew was an indispensable agent in developing this property in the herb, which was therefore employed the day before the festival in decorating the house-roof, being exposed there all night, to be taken down in the morning for the bath, in which the eldest son was the first to bathe.

But in the best room of the house, the honoured "guest apartment" as it is called, there are many things besides flowers set out — warlike figures, and toy weapons, such as would appeal to any boy's heart, in East or West. But here the figures are not toys — they are portraits; and each one tells its tale of glory in the ears of the Japanese child. These models of men, clad in armour, standing in attitudes of action or menace; the horses, richly and minutely caparisoned, pawing the ground as if impatient for battle, — they are the images of the warriors and heroes of this strange land, accompanied by their chargers, whose names have also been handed down for veneration. That warrior to the left of the bronze bowl is Iyeyasu, the maker of Yedo, the general whose tomb we have seen among the solemn pines of Nikko, the man whom the Japanese consider the greatest ruler the country has ever obeyed. Beside him is that famous charger, who outlived him for thirty years, wandering free among the sacred groves. His tomb also we have seen. Yonder is the figure of the mythical Raiko, the Japanese giant-killer, who delivered Kyoto from a fearful cannibal demon; and shoulder to shoulder with him is the effigy of another hero, Momotaro, the peach-born boy, who accomplished prodigies of strength, and freed his country from a stronghold of devils.

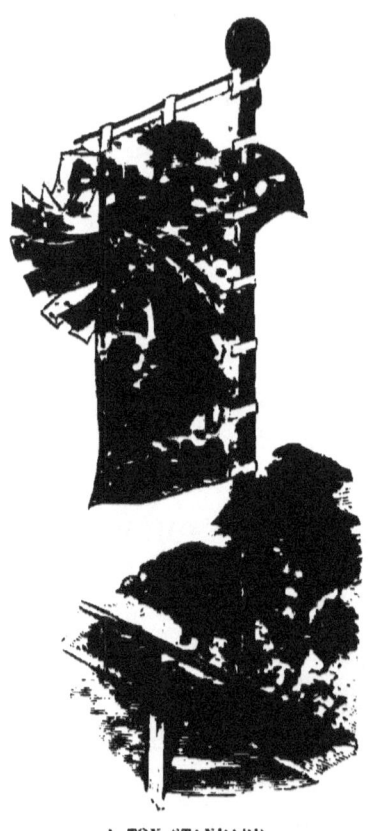

A TOY STANDARD

Standing up among the bows and arrows, the swords and spears, may be seen the model of a very strange-looking battle standard, or *umajirushi*. The head of this banner is composed of a number of small gourds, golden in colour, clustered round a larger one, and all placed on a rod. Underneath the gourds, a little way down, strips of bright scarlet cloth are suspended round the stick. No one looking at the pretty toy could imagine its romantic origin or the wonderful part it has played in the history of Japan. The gourds and scarlet cloth represent the *umajirushi* of Toyotomi Hideyoshi, the greatest adventurer, and perhaps the greatest general, in Japanese history. He was born of poor parents in 1536; and it is said that before his birth, which was marked by the appearance of a new star, his mother dreamed that the sun was within her. As a child, he was so unmanageable that his parents placed him with bonzes in a temple to be trained for the priesthood; but he soon proved too wild for them to manage, and was dismissed. The same thing happened at thirty-eight places in succession, Hideyoshi finding no master who would suit him, although he seems to have tried all the trades in turn, from a crockery-maker, to whom he was apprenticed, to a robber chief, in whose gang he served for a time. He was already distinguished amongst his companions by his courage and dexterity in fencing, by his constant readiness for a fight, and by his ugliness, which gained him the name of Saru-no-suke, or monkey.

Undaunted by misfortunes that would have crushed others, he at last determined to enter the service of Oda Nobunaga, a minor baron, who had gained possession of the provinces of Suruga, Mino, Omi, Mikawa, Ichizen, and Ise. Without waiting for his friends to petition for an audience for him, or for the ceremonious introductions necessary at that age before a commoner could approach a noble, Hideyoshi forced his way into the presence of Nobunaga when the latter was resting in his tent after a day's hunting, and fearlessly said that he had come to enlist himself in the Baron's retinue, and that he had chosen Nobunaga as a master worthy of his services.

Nobunaga, impressed by the young man's spirit and bearing, appointed him to take the place of one of his foot soldiers of the lowest rank who had fallen ill. Soon after this event he was called upon to show his strength and courage in single combat with one of the other retainers. In those days every warrior of any renown whatever possessed his own battle sign, and by this he was known. Hideyoshi, a young and poor adventurer, low in rank withal, could not obtain one; but he would not do battle without a banner of some kind to distinguish him. A gourd was growing by the wayside; he tore it up by the roots, and rushed to the contest, flourishing it aloft. His opponent, though an experienced warrior, was overcome; Hideyoshi won the day, and with it great renown, rising high in the estimation of his lord, who loudly praised his valour. Ever after, Hideyoshi had his battle standard made of gourds, and vowed that for every victory he won he would plant one of these vines. Whether he was able to fulfil the ambition he then formed, that of numbering a thousand such trophies, we are not told; but his banner is still known as *Sen-nari-hisago,* or the one thousand gourds.

By dint of hard work, indomitable will, and brave fighting Hideyoshi soon became the most capable and trusted retainer in Nobunaga's Court, and on the assassination of the latter subdued the whole country, and forced the other Daimyos to own him as their lord. The Mikado installed him in the office of *Kwambaku,* or Regent; and by his wonderful power of organisation, and the instinct which led him to choose such men as Iyeyasu for his generals and administrators, comparative peace and harmony was brought to reign in the country in place of the strife and bloodshed and revolt of the last two hundred years. So Hideyoshi rose by his own efforts from the lowest rank of the people to be the ruler of his country; and the effect of his work lasted for more than two centuries after him.

Such are the stories of brave deeds and wonderful lives told to the boys of Japan, when on May 5th their gentle little mother gathers her sons together, and takes them to the *ozashiki* (honourable drawing-room), where they all sit round her on the matted floor, and gaze reverently at the array of emblematical toys, standards, and weapons. They see the bright gourds, and know the meaning of the strange toy; and with deep-drawn breath they answer the questions put to test their knowledge in the leading events of their history.

Then the sliding-door opens, and the old nurse, with blackened teeth and shaved eyebrows, carrying the infant son on her back, crawls in. The *okkasan* (honourable mother) stops in her talk, and turns to welcome the newcomer, whose head is bent and patted into a bow by the nurse, as she makes a profound reverence before taking her place behind the mistress. Some more stories are told, and then the mother dismisses her children, telling them that if they wish to please their "honourable father" they must follow the example of such men as the heroes before them, and to do this they must be brave in battle and persevering in difficulties. Thus only can they hope to repay the many blessings they owe to their own father and to the "Father of the Land," their Emperor, in "this reign of enlightenment." The children bring their little dark heads to the floor in low obeisance before their mother. Then they run along the smooth verandah till they come to the block of stone which serves for a step into the garden. Sliding off the verandah, they slip into the wooden clogs which lie waiting there, and go perhaps to watch the sign of their existence floating from its pole in the garden; or to the pond, where, in answer to the clapping of their hands, the favourite carp come to be fed, jumping up from amongst the yet closely furled lotus leaves, and opening and shutting their mouths in appreciation of the food thrown to them by their little masters. At midday a maid comes to the edge of the *yengawa* (verandah), waves her hand from the wrist downwards out of the large falling sleeve, calling, "Waka sama, waka sama" (Young master, young master), "come, the food is served!" And they run in merrily, and more quickly than usual, in anticipation of the red rice which they know will be provided to-day in honour of the feast, instead of the usual plain white *gohan*. As they pass their mother's room, they see her busily lifting cakes wrapped in leaves, from a huge plate in which they are piled, into square lacquer boxes. These, daintily tied up in a *furoshiki* (the cotton, silk, or crape wrapper in which presents are always sent — the crest of the family is stamped on the *furoshiki* used on ceremonious occasions), are to be sent to different friends with congratulatory greetings. In a few minutes, having given directions about the different boxes, she comes into the children's room with a plate of the same cakes, *okashiwa*, made especially for this festival, and, sitting down on the floor, serves out with *o'hashi* (chopsticks) an equal number on each child's tray.

A small lacquer table, called an *osambo*, is set before the suits of armour and the models of warriors; on it is placed a little offering of the ceremonial food of the day; namely, a dish of the *okashiwa*, sweetmeats, and the usual blue-and-white porcelain bottle filled with saké, in which petals of the iris have been scattered.

The *Tango*, or Boys' Festival, has always been the occasion for giving boys some part of their martial accoutrements; and so when the *ottottsama* (lit. honourable father Mr.) comes home, there may be a crowning pleasure to this day of happiness in store for them in the shape of a gift of arms. Although the ancient picturesque armour is now laid aside for the modern soldier's uniform, the sword and bow still hold their own in the fencing and archery schools, which preserve the remembrance of some of the old methods of warfare threatened with oblivion and disuse by the march of civilisation. It may often only be a toy rapier or gun which the little *musuko* receives; but it sends him, happy as a king, to marshal out his playmates in mock battle, or to strut in their ranks with the seriousness of reality.

The story of the origin of this gala day is often repeated to the children; and I will give it to you as it is generally told here.

The festival is said to have been instituted in commemoration of the repulse of the Mongolian invasion of

Japan, A.D. 1281, an event which seems still fresh in the minds of the people, and a favourite subject for paintings and carvings. From 1274 to 1281 Japan was greatly troubled by expeditions sent against her by Kublai Khan, the friend and patron of Marco Polo. Fired by the description of the riches and beauty of

KUBLAI KHAN
From a very ancient Chinese painting

the Eastern islands, which in Chinese legends had always figured as a kind of earthly Paradise, the great Mongol ruler fancied that Japan was politically weak, and would at once submit to his own overwhelming power. During this period, though the Minamoto Shoguns were the nominal rulers of the country (the Mikado was, as we have seen before, kept in helpless seclusion), the Hojos, their retainers, held the military Regency under them; all real power was in their hands, after the murder of Sanetomo Minamoto in Kamakura. In pursuance of his idea of annexation, Kublai Khan sent one embassy after another to demand submission from Japan. The first embassy was dismissed with indignity; an expedition followed, which took possession of an island belonging to Japan; then new envoys were sent, but they were promptly beheaded on the beach of Kamakura by Hojo Tokumine in 1275. Determining to give Japan a signal punishment for her defiance, the Mongol chief collected a hundred thousand Chinese, Mongolians, and Coreans, and despatched this mighty army to Japan in 1281. The Japanese, invoking the aid of the gods, met the swarm of invaders off the coast of Kiushiu. Several engagements were fought, and at last, as if in answer to their prayers, a mighty storm arose, the enemy's fleet was scattered, and the Japanese, taking advantage of the opportunity, made a desperate and vigorous onslaught on the intruders and completely annihilated them. It is recorded that only three escaped to tell the tale.

Since this memorable repulse of the Mongolian invaders, no foreign enemy has ever attacked Japan; she regards herself as invincible; and the Japanese, looking upon the delivering storm as a miraculous intervention on the part of the gods to save their country, instituted the *Tango* to be a lasting memorial of thanksgiving and of the wonderful victory gained by the "land of the gods" over the barbarians.

By telling these stories to their children, the Japanese believe that they sow the seeds of reverence and admiration for the best and noblest examples of their ancestors, the seeds of self-reliance and belief in the invincible power of their country; and though to us, perhaps, the courage seems exaggerated and the ideals unattainable, yet I think it bears no mean fruit in the Japan of to-day. Loyalty and courage are the undoubted inheritance of the nation.

And so for the little boys of Japan the brightly coloured banner and the gay toy warriors have a real and moral significance. The children's hearts are stimulated, unconsciously at the time, no doubt, and their ambition roused to become worthy compatriots of the brave men gone before them. I think the hour will come again, as it has in time past, when these things will be of use to them, whether in the war with evil for good in their own hearts, or on the battlefield face to face with the foe.

CHAPTER XXXIV

THE ATTACK ON THE CESARÉVITCH. — LOYAL WOMEN. — TSUDA SANZO AND HIS LIFE HISTORY. — A NATION IN MOURNING. — COURAGEOUS JUDGES. — A *SAMURAI* MAIDEN

TOKYO, *June*, 1891.

THE most terrible blow fell on this unfortunate country on May 11th; and now, weeks afterwards, it is still impossible to think or speak of anything else. The Cesarévitch, whose coming was so eagerly anticipated, for whose entertainment every resource of the empire was to be called upon, whom the Emperor intended to honour as no foreign Prince has ever been honoured before — the Cesarévitch was attacked, deeply wounded, all but killed, by one of the policemen set to guard his way.

No words of mine can describe the consternation and dismay which took possession of this place, when on the afternoon of the 11th those horrible telegrams came pouring in, to the Russian Legation, to the Ministries, to the Palace. It was a lovely afternoon, and I was returning from a drive, when I met, not far from home, my friend Mrs. K——. She stopped her carriage, and got into mine, telling the coachman to drive to the Russian Legation, and on the way she told me what she had just learnt from one of the officials. The Cesarévitch had been attacked; no one knew yet whether the wound was mortal. We were met at the entrance to the Russian Legation by scared-looking servants, who led us up the big staircase where all the beautiful floral decorations had just been completed in expectation of the Prince's visit to-morrow. The fear of death seemed to be on every one, and the very gloom of it to hang over the great flower-filled house. What made it more terrible for Madame S—— and her daughter was that they were alone there, the Minister himself being in attendance on the Cesarévitch. As yet no one knew whether a riot had taken place, whether Monsieur S—— were also hurt or not; but to tell the truth, I do not believe the two poor loyal women could have then suffered more anguish of soul if he had even been killed. I learnt for the first time what loyalty meant; with what a passion of devotion the blood of some races leaps to the call, mad to be spilt for the sovereign and his family. My poor friends were utterly prostrated by the blow, which had fallen some two hours before, while I was far out in the country. They had wept till they could weep no more, and Vera S——, a most charming and brilliant girl, was raging up and down the room, wild to slay the doer of the deed, who, I think, would indeed have had a short shrift if her little fingers had once met on his throat. "Our Prince, our Prince!" she sobbed; and there were no other words but those. "Our Prince, our Prince! God have mercy on our Prince!" I am certain that at that moment both mother and daughter would have gone to death joyfully and unhesitatingly, if by so doing they could have assured the Cesarévitch's life. The Russian Bishop was there, doing what he could to comfort them; and telegram after telegram was brought and read to us by the Secretary, who himself looked as if he had heard his death-warrant. "Two deep wounds on the head; recovery impossible," the first message had run; then, "Prince better; most courageous," "Returning to Kyoto at once," "Great loss of blood — I am safe" (this had been added at last by Monsieur S—— to reassure his family a little); I do not think he himself cared two pins whether he was safe or not, and he very nearly killed himself by running for three-quarters of an hour to the Otsu Station, holding one side of the Prince's jinriksha, while General Bariatinsky, his Governor, ran on the other to defend him from any further possible attack.

How it all happened is a strange tale. The Cesarévitch came over from China on April 27th, attended by a squadron of Russian war-ships, to begin a tour through Japan which was to occupy a month, and during which he was to be shown everything which could possibly interest or amuse him. The visit had been under discussion for many months, and was intended to cement the bonds of friendship already existing between the two countries. We had heard of the many negotiations on the subject, and the coming of the Cesarévitch was to be the event of the year in Tokyo. When all the arrangements were completed, Monsieur S—— still felt uneasy about the safety of the heir-apparent. The Czar was allowing him to come on the Minister's representation that no danger whatever could possibly assail him on Japanese soil; but the Minister himself (I remember his telling me of it) was not absolutely satisfied with the arrangements made, and finally told the Emperor of Japan that he did not consider the guarantees sufficient. Then the Emperor made an answer at which some of his own people were almost indignant. "I take," said his Majesty, "the personal responsibility of the Cesarévitch's visit. His person shall be sacred as my own; I answer for his safety with my own honour."

After that there could be no more hesitation, and the Cesarévitch came, accompanied by his cousin Prince George of Greece, and by a numerous train, including a number of Russian officers. Prince Arisugawa was deputed to meet him, and the people were honestly and truly glad to see him. The Emperor's guest was received with the most hearty enthusiasm, when he landed in Nagasaki from the *Pamiat Azova*, the war-ship devoted to his especial service. The road from the quay to the Governor's house where the Cesarévitch lunched was lined with crowds for the mile and a half of its length — crowds who received their Emperor's guest with every mark of welcome. From Nagasaki he went to Kagoshima, where he and Prince George and the whole party were the guests of Prince Shimadzu for several days. There some splendid shows were organised, all the sports of the old feudal Court were revived in a kind of tournament,

KYOTO
From a water-colour drawing by John Varley, R.A.

and the Russian Minister told me afterwards that the display of antique armour and weapons had been quite wonderful. Presents of great value were offered to the Prince and his companions, and he is said to have much enjoyed all the novelty of the entertainments provided. From Kagoshima he came up to Kobe, where he landed and took train for Kyoto. He was attended by several great Japanese officials, among others dear Mr. Sannomiya, whom we always call the guardian angel of the foreigners here. While the Cesarévitch was visiting Kyoto, Mr. Sannomiya came up to Tokyo to see that everything was in readiness for his reception here by the Emperor; and it was during his absence that the blow fell. I shall never forget his face, when he came down to the

Russian Legation that evening, just before the special train started carrying most of the Princes and all the Ministers down to the scene of the disaster.

Of course, we sat there speculating wildly on the motive of the horrid crime, and longing to hear more of the details, for it was as yet impossible to gather from the excited telegrams anything but the merest outline of the facts. But more accurate news came on later in the evening, and by midnight we knew pretty well all that there was to be known, and could also estimate the gravity of the misfortune. The poor young Prince suffered a great shock, with after-pain, fever, and weakness. But Japan seemed to have been suddenly arrested in her march to the vanguard of nations, to have been thrown back fifty years in her history of civilisation, to have fallen into a great abyss of bitter and humiliating trouble.

And yet it was such a simple story! Had it happened in Europe, it would have been looked upon as a great misfortune, but no more. No deductions would have been drawn from it; no enemies could have brandished its record in the stricken face of the nation to show that no civilized peoples should have friendship with her, that treaties were an absurdity, equality a dream. All that happened to poor Japan, smarting under the wound, to her the most bitter of all — a wound to her honour. The Emperor's welcome guest had been betrayed.

He had gone from Kyoto to see Lake Biwa, the Lake of the Lute, whose waters are called the melted snows of Fuji. The party had lunched with the Prefect of the District at a little place named Otsu, the usual centre for some lovely excursions in the neighbourhood of the lake. As the roads do not allow of using carriages in that part of the world, the Prince and his following were in jinrikshas, each drawn by two coolies. The Cesarévitch was in the fifth of these little vehicles, those in front being occupied by the Governor of the Province, the Chief of Police, and two inspectors. Behind the Cesarévitch came another Japanese official, then Prince George, then one or two other members of the party, and finally Monsieur S——, the Russian Minister. The streets were lined with police on both sides, the men being set at short intervals from each other, all picked men who could be relied on to do their duty. But no one dreamed that their services would be really needed. It is the boast of new Japan that the foreigner can travel from end to end of the empire without ever receiving the slightest molestation; and this foreigner was the beloved Emperor's guest!

Among the policemen stood one called Tsuda Sanzo, an old sergeant-major in the army, where he had earned a decoration for services rendered in the Satsuma rebellion. A self-centred and somewhat bigoted man, he was yet one of the quiet, steady, tried servants who would be chosen for such a post as this. As the Cesarévitch passed him, he drew his great Japanese blade, and aimed a deadly blow at the Prince's head. The jinriksha was going at a fair pace, and the sword slid, caught the hat, and inflicted a second blow.

Then it fell as Tsuda himself fell; for one of the coolies, dropping the shafts, hurled himself unarmed on the policeman, and the second coolie snatched the sword and dealt the assassin two serious blows with it while he was still wrestling with the first man. The Prince himself, blinded with the flow of blood, leapt from the jinriksha as the shafts dropped, and ran forward towards the ones occupied by the Governor and the other Japanese officials. In an instant the Governor was supporting him, and led him aside into an open shop, while the whole train was thrown into the wildest confusion. Guards threw themselves on Tsuda and secured him, and Prince George, in intense anger and excitement, came and struck him violently with his stick. Monsieur S—— jumped from his jinriksha, and flew past the rest to where the Prince was standing in the little shop. He was bathed in blood, but refused to sit down; and when Monsieur S—— in his wild anxiety threw himself at his feet with a cry, the Prince raised him quietly and said, "Do not be anxious. *Ce n'est que du sang.* I am not really hurt!"

He was very much hurt, poor young fellow; but not dangerously so, as in the terror of the moment somebody wired that he was. They bound up the long cuts on his head, thanking Heaven that the hard hat and the thick hair had helped to turn the blow; and then they got him back to Otsu, Monsieur S—— running by the jinriksha, and holding it on one side, while General Bariatinsky did the same on the other. A special train brought him back to Kyoto, where, in spite of his calm cheerful manner, he was only too glad to lie down at last and have his wounds properly dressed.

And Tsuda? Of course after the event there were plenty of people who were sure that the man was insane, that he should never have been chosen for the service which brought him into such close contact with the heir of the Czar. It transpired that there had been insanity in his family, that one or two of his intimates had heard him speak with fear of the aggressions of Russia, just as a certain small class here write and speak. Their minority makes them insignificant; and nobody has done more than laugh when these wiseacres pretended to see the visit of a spy in the coming of the Cesarévitch; when, in obscure newspapers, they reminded the people of the Russian principles of aggression; as shown by Russia's taking Saghalien, which was, after all, deliberately exchanged for the Kurile Islands. Japan is rich in fanatics. One of the men who held these doctrines committed suicide before the landing of the Prince, in order, as he said, to be spared the sight of his country's humiliation. A legend exists to the effect that the late General Saigo, the chief leader of the Satsuma rebellion, was not really killed, but had succeeded in escaping to Russia, where he is supposed to have remained all these years, awaiting a favourable moment in order to return to Japan and once more raise the standard of revolt. A story got abroad that the Cesarévitch was bringing him back in his suite, and the absurd rumour caused a good deal of excitement in some districts. Such ideas had probably preyed on Tsuda's mind, apt to be unhinged because of that strain of madness in his family which was quite unknown to the authorities; and when he was named as one of the guardians of the road for the Russian Prince, the insane resolve to make away with him probably formed itself in his brain. The instant onslaught of the two jinriksha coolies prevented him from taking his own life, which would undoubtedly have been his next act.

But he has brought profound sorrow on the whole empire. So much was expected and hoped from this visit, in the way of friendship with the great European Powers. It was to have been in a way Japan's first step in the Social Polity of the world; and one cannot but feel the most profound sympathy with her in her distress.

Two hours after the first news of the attempt reached Tokyo, a Cabinet Council had been held, and a special train was starting for Kyoto, carrying Prince Kitashirakawa, with the Emperor's own surgeon, Dr. Hashimoto, and various officials to the spot. An hour or two afterwards another train went down with some of the Ministers, more of the Court people, and all the distinguished medical men of the capital; and early the next morning, amid an outburst of public grief and indignation, the Emperor himself, with all his staff, started for Kyoto. But before he left, an Imperial Rescript appeared, which told the nation of what had occurred, and of the intense pain caused in the Emperor's breast by the horrible deed. Here is the Rescript:

"It is with the most profound grief and regret that, while We, with Our Government and Our subjects, have been preparing to welcome his Imperial Highness, Our beloved and respected Crown Prince of Russia, with all the honours and hospitalities due to Our national guest, We receive the most unexpected and surprising announcement that his Imperial Highness met with a deplorable accident at Otsu whilst on his journey. It is Our will that justice shall take its speedy course on the miscreant offender, to the end that Our mind may be relieved, and that Our friendly and intimate relations with Our good neighbour may be secured against disturbance."

The Ministers paid a visit to the Russian Legation before they left for Kyoto — a visit in which it was intended at any rate to convey the expression of the profound regret of the Government to the wife of the Russian Representative. It was a most distressing ordeal for everybody, the officials finding absolutely no words sufficient to convey their dismay and sorrow; while Madame S——, who is always a delightfully impetuous and impulsive person, and who was just then in a frenzy of loyal indignation, seems to have found no difficulty at all in expressing her feelings.

Meanwhile there was one person who could do nothing to help the poor young Prince or to punish his assailant; the valiant gentle Empress forgot all the repressions of her up-bringing, all the superb calm which as a part of her rank she has shown in every circumstance of her life, and for the whole of that wretched night walked up and down, up and down, weeping her heart out in a flood-tide of grief. Those who told me of it said that all night long and for days after the Empress had but one cry; not a cry of despair for her country, humiliated in the eyes of the whole world, condemned perhaps to find bitter enemies where she had looked for friends — all that seems not to have touched her at all at first; her only thought was for the boy — and his mother. "The poor mother, the poor mother!" she wailed. "She cannot see her boy! She will not believe he is safe! Poor mother! How can I comfort you?"

That was all. And she who is supposed never to change expression or show the smallest weakness before others walked up and down her lovely rooms like a caged creature, with the tears raining down her face. Her ladies were terrified and overcome; they thought she could not live through such a storm of grief. Message after message was sent to the Czarina, assuring her of the profound heart-broken sympathy with which the Empress regarded her trouble, and promising that the Cesarévitch should be nursed and tended as if his mother were with him. As soon as she recovered from the shock sufficiently to travel, she went to see the wounded boy, who was deeply touched by her sorrow and her kindness.

He behaved all through like a Prince and a gentleman. Not the slightest sign of rancour ever appeared in his voice or manner; and when, at his parents' command (it is said, at his mother's entreaty), he gave up the rest of his Japanese tour, and was carried back on board his own ship to be nursed, he softened the act by every kind word that could possibly have been used, thanking the Emperor warmly for all his kindness and saying how great a deprivation it was to him not to visit the Emperor in Tokyo; because " for reasons of health, as he was still somewhat weak, it was considered wiser that he should return to Russia at once."

Mr. Sannomiya told me that the meeting between the Emperor and his guest was affecting in the extreme. As for poor Princess Komatsu, who went to visit him, she utterly broke down when she saw the poor boy, deathly pale from loss of blood, his head enveloped in bandages, and yet smiling at her kindly as she entered the room. The lady-in-waiting thought the Princess would faint; but she pulled herself together, and only cried quietly. Indeed, though perhaps it sounds heartless to say so, I should think the Cesarévitch (who has had a good deal of fever) would have got over his accident more quickly with fewer visits and less excitement. However, sympathy is a great thing; and this atrocious attempt has called forth such overwhelming expressions of national sorrow and sympathy that the Prince can never forget it as long as he lives. And as for the Emperor, I doubt if even he knew what his people felt for him until it was announced that the Emperor mourned — was in sorrow for his subject's sin — and the whole of the population in all its millions left its work and its pleasures, deserted the farm, closed the shop, turned from all its recreations and amusements — to sorrow with him.

I have never seen anything like it, — and you see I am learning lessons in loyalty! The theatres were closed, the shops and markets abandoned; everywhere people spoke in groups and with profound sadness in their tones. The little daughter of Viscount Aoki, the Minister for Foreign Affairs (she is ten years old), heard the announcement of the outrage with a stony face, and went away in silence to her room. There, for hours, she lay on the floor in an agony of grief and shame, moaning, "*I* am a Japanese! *I* must live with this shame! I cannot — I cannot! I cannot bear it!" At the Nobles' Club there was one opinion only — how could those at the head of affairs, those who were responsible for the Prince's safety in his journey, support life any longer? Why had they not already wiped out their dishonour with death? There was only one thing for a gentleman to do in such circumstances — commit *hara-kiri* or some other decorous kind of suicide!

THE DAUGHTER OF VISCOUNT AOKI

Among the people the sorrow took two forms: one, the intense desire to make reparation to the illustrious guest and his family for the insult and outrage which he had suffered; the other going deeper still, the yearning — no other word quite expresses it — to lift some of the load of sorrow from the Emperor's heart, to do something by which the "august" would cease to mourn. "Tenshi Sama Go Shimpai" was the word in every mouth — "Great Augustness, worshipped Sorrow;" and rich and poor, old and young, strong men and little children, all did what they could, gave more than they could, to undo the wrong.

People who were on board the Cesarévitch's ship told me that it seemed like to sink with gifts; the decks, the saloons, the passages, were encumbered, and still they came and came and came! The universality and spontaneousness of the manifestation gave it an overwhelming value, which the Prince here and his parents at home were quick to appreciate. Rich people gave out of their riches, and objects of unexampled beauty and rarity were brought out from the treasure-houses and sent with messages of love and respect to the boy who lay healing of his wound in Kobe Harbour. The poor sent the most touching gifts — the rice and *shoyu*, the fish and barley-flour, which would have fed the little family for a year; poor old peasants walked for days so as to bring a tiny offering of eggs. The merchants sent silks and porcelain, lacquer and bronze, crapes and ivory, according to their merchandise; telegrams poured in, expressing intense sympathy, and more intense indignation at the outrage. In the first twenty-four hours after the occurrence, so many thousands of these were sent that it was almost impossible to deliver them; twenty thousand persons called during the first two days at the hotel in Kyoto where the Prince lay before he was removed to his vessel; every corporation and community, town and village and guild sent either a deputation to carry its condolences or a letter to express them; and many who could ill afford the outlay telegraphed messages of sympathy to the Czar and Czarina in St. Petersburg, and always added a protest of horror at the wicked deed.

A BRONZE INCENSE-BURNER

The perpetrator of it is not yet judged, and some care has been necessary to keep him from being torn to pieces by his indignant countrymen, who "are ready to eat him," as the saying is here. The newspapers vie with one another in condemning the criminal, who, after all, seems to have been a common madman, all the more dangerous from having earned the confidence of his superiors.

Rather an amusing story is told here.

The Emperor, it seems, sent word to the judges

that the wretched Tsuda must be executed at once; the judges replied, "Your Imperial Majesty may remember that you have graciously granted a Constitution, in which it is promised that criminals shall only be judged and condemned according to the laws which have now been promulgated; in those laws such a case as this was not foreseen, and therefore we can only award to this man the punishment incurred by one who assaults and wounds any other person of any class whatever. We regret that we cannot carry out your Imperial Majesty's wishes. Tsuda Sanzo will undergo a term of imprisonment."

"Tsuda Sanzo will be executed," the indignant Emperor replied. "Let it be seen to at once."

"Then," said the courageous judges, "your Imperial Majesty will dispense with our poor services, and find some one to carry out your august commands who has not taken the oath to administer the laws according to the Constitution."

But the Emperor was too upright not to

INCENSE-BURNER IN THE SHAPE OF A JUNK

see that they were in the right, and it is said that he was pleased with their justice and courage. Tsuda is undergoing a term of imprisonment — I think ten years is the time mentioned; but I am sure that if he ever comes out alive, he will have to change his name.

The two coolies who undoubtedly saved the life of the Cesarévitch have been magnificently rewarded by the Russian Government. They are young, good-looking fellows, who, from being members of the poorest class of Japanese subjects, have suddenly become rich men, with decorations and reputations of which the Japanese think even more than of money. Their own Government awarded them each a medal, and a little pension of thirty-six dollars a year for the rest of their lives — a sum quite enough to keep them from want, living as they would with the ingenious frugality of their race. But the Russian Government has done things very magnificently. Each man has been awarded a thousand dollars a year for life; the Cesarévitch himself has presented each of them with a sum of two thousand five hundred dollars, and a Russian decoration has been added to the Japanese one. The two heroes, it is said, were completely stunned with this munificence. The sailors of the Prince's vessel made a tremendous feast for them on the day when they came on board to receive their reward; and I hear that they have gone back to their homes in a distant province to buy rich farms and live at ease, doubtless to marry the girls of their hearts, and to tell the tale of their courage and good luck to the third and fourth generation.

But the last note is a sad one. It is impossible not to be sorry for the Governor of the Province and the Chief of Police, who were held responsible for the outrage, and who really and truly had done all that it was possible to do to ensure the Prince's safety. They have both been dismissed, one degraded as well. In spite of all messages of forgiveness (and the Russians have been very generous), a most painful feeling remains, and painful memories must be carried for many years. The sovereigns and their people mourn together for the wicked madness of one man.

A little *samurai* girl, a mere child of sixteen, I think, was in service near Yokohama. She travelled to Kyoto, dressed herself in her holiday robes, composed her poor little body for death by tying her sash tightly round her knees after the custom of *samurai* women, and cut her throat in the doorway of the great Government offices. They found on her two letters: one a farewell to her family; the other containing a message, which she begged those who found her to convey to the Emperor, saying that she gave her life gladly, hoping that though so lowly it might wipe out the insult, and she entreated him to be comforted by her death. Her name, they say, was Yuko, which means full of valour.

CHAPTER XXXV

THE COTTAGE AT HORIUCHI. — THE DEAR DEAD. — GIFTS FOR THE SPIRITS. — THE BOTTOM OF THE SEA. — FISHING IN THE EMPRESS'S SEA GARDEN

July, 1891.

MY third summer in Japan is well on its way. I shall not see a fourth — in succession, at any rate; for we go home on leave next year. Europe draws one back with a thousand cords; but even there I shall regret the little Palace of Peace among the Karuizawa pines. Before transporting the family to those heights, I have been taking a long holiday by the sea at Horiuchi, a place about an hour's drive from Kamakura; Dr. Baelz has a Japanese cottage there, and kindly lent it to me for the time. Our station was Dzushi, and there I alighted one warm afternoon with one friend, one interpreter, and Rinzo, Matsu, and our "Big Cook San," the gentleman who tumbled through the bridge last summer. The poor fellow has been suffering from bad lungs ever since the influenza epidemic, and I thought a change would do him good. I only mention him because when they all turned out of the train I was so amused by the mass of baggage he had brought. Evidently the rumour had gone abroad that

Horiuchi was a place quite in the wilds, and that all our comfort there would depend on what we brought with us. Big Cook San descended to the platform, jingling like a gypsy tinker with all the sauce-pans that he had hung round himself at the last moment. An omelet-pan and a bain-marie, miraculously tied together, hung over his shoulder; a potato-steamer from his waist; in one hand he carried a large blue teapot, and in the other a sheaf of gorgeous irises, carefully tied up in matting, for fear that there should be no flowers at Horiuchi! A whole vanload of goods had preceded us, so these were after-thoughts, trifles gathered up at the last moment. We let the servants and baggage start before us from the station, and followed in a leisurely fashion, stopping our jinrikshas every now and then to admire the lovely glimpses down green gorges, through which the road winds and turns again and again before it comes out on the beach near Horiuchi. This is a tiny village, built in the round of a bay within Odawara Bay. The hamlet is as poor as possible; but the air is so pure that people have been tempted to build a few villas there for *villeggiatura*. The Italian Minister has a gorgeous one on the ground that rises from the beach; but it does not compare with the doctor's cottage for beauty of situation. This is planted so that when one enters the front door one looks right through the house, and the most beautiful picture of Fuji across the bay is seen framed in by the pillars of the verandah; and when one comes, as in duty bound, to stand beside the pillars and salute the queen of mountains, the sea is almost rolling to one's feet, just stopped by a low stone wall and a green dune, planted with pines that sing night and day as the salt breeze rustles in from the sea.

There are but six rooms in the house, all floored with sweet-smelling mats the colour of wheat; the bath-room is of clean polished woods, and the great tank in the floor is always bubbling with oceans of hot water,

BY THE SUMMER SEA

where one washes all fatigue away in these warm days. As the house was meant merely for a bachelor's bunga-low, it contains one jug and basin, which are kept on a shelf in the bathroom, where we went in and used them by turns. At our first lunch we discovered that, although the table was gorgeous with Cook San's irises, nobody had thought of knives and forks; two sets were found in a luncheon basket; and then a runner was despatched over the hills to borrow some from the hotel at Kamakura. But I did not mind at all. The irises were far better than knives and forks; and with the sight of the sea rolling in so close in crisp wavelets, the music that sea and pines made together, and above all, that vision of Fuji San and the Hakone Mountains across the blue spread of the bay, one felt ashamed of needing food at all. All the first day the beloved Fuji seemed to be gazing at us, making us feel small, but very happy. This morning a little good-natured gale has been tossing the trees about, and the sacred mountain has wrapped herself in clouds. I suppose I have said it again and again; but I feel impelled to say it once more, — in Japan one cannot think of Fuji as a thing, a mere object in the landscape; she becomes something personal, dominating, a factor in life. No day seems quite sad or aimless in which one has had a glimpse of her.

Last night her black shadow looked intensely solemn, with the stars above, and hundreds of torches in the fishing-boats floating on the sea beneath. I asked today why the sea was so full of stars last night — I had never noticed it at other times, but only in these July days. And then I was told the story of the Festival of the Dead, which I had heard spoken of in Tokyo in a scornful, superficial way, but which I hear is kept religiously in the provinces still.

The dear dead! Little children and old people, and all the souls that pass out of earth's family day by day, disrobed of their fair garment of the flesh, they love not the short winter days or the long dark winter nights;

but when summer broods over the land, when the night is welcome because it brings a breath of coolness to those whose work is not yet over, then they, who have laid by the wholesome tasks of earth, come back, in shadowy myriads, to visit their old homes; to hover round those who still love and remember them; to smile, if ghosts can smile, at the food and money, clothing and sandals, and little ships for travelling, all made ready by the loving souls to whom only such earthly needs are comprehensible, but who, in preparing their humble gifts, are investing them with the only present the spirits may take home again — the gift of love, which never forgets, or disbelieves, or despairs.

Just for these three days of July — the 13th, 14th, and 15th — heart-broken mothers feel the little lost son or daughter close at hand, brought back perhaps by Jizo Sama, the god who watches over the spirits of little children. The lights are lit before the small *ihai*, the death tablet, set up in the place of honour, and inscribed with a name that the little one would not have turned from his play for here, that never passed his mother's lips till he was carried away from her — his dead name, the one by which his shadowy companions call him in the yonder world. Full of comfort must these three days be for the faithful souls who are always yearning to offer some service or some token of love to the dead. Now they come back; and though no one sees them, they take their old places in their old homes. They find the house decked and garnished for their coming; the holy lotus flower, never

A GREETING

used save for their honour, is gathered and set by their shrine; and many another lovely plant and sprig, all with symbolical meanings, are brought in. Rice and vegetables, fruit and cakes, are placed for them; no animal food is offered, as pure spirits would consider that a sinful nourishment, but tea is poured out with punctilious ceremony in tiny cups at stated hours. In some towns there is a market or fair held expressly that people may buy all they need for the entertainment of the ghosts. As these always come from the sea, torches are stuck in the sands to show them where to land; and when the three days are ended, and the travellers must go back, reluctantly, to their shadow homes, then tiny ships are launched — straw ships of lovely and elaborate designs, freighted with dainty foods, and lighted by small lanterns. Incense, too, is burning before they set forth; and then they go, by river or stream if the sea is distant, with their little cargo of love-gifts visible, and their spirit-travellers invisible, back to their joy or their sorrow in the underworld.[1]

The Japanese remind one of sweet, wise children, whose play will always be an imitation, a childish rendering, of some great truth — overlooked, as often as not, by their elders in the rush and bustle of life.

I have been boating in the little Horiuchi Bay, and have gazed down for hours into the depths below through a glass-bottomed box let down over the side of the boat. It is a perfectly simple contrivance: the glass rests on

[1] See Lafcadio Hearn's beautiful and complete description of the Festival of the Dead in *Glimpses of Unfamiliar Japan* (1894).

or just under the water, and the wooden sides shut out all reflection; a series of small holes allow any water that splashes over the glass to run off, — one looks through it, — and suddenly one seems to be at the bottom of the sea. Great fish and little fish go darting in and out among the wet, sun-touched forests of the ocean bed; the rocks are shining palaces, guarded by fierce red starfish, who crawl slowly backwards and forwards on their beat. The shells open and close, and

GREAT FISH AND LITTLE FISH

swim about full of the strange soul-bodies which are their only life; there is colour, movement, expression; continents of clean silver sand, bordered by little reaches of golden woodland waving lazily on the water as our tree boughs wave in the wind; the fish have physiognomies, and meet, and fight, and bend, and dart away, all with their own little life to see to, their own extremely important affairs to conduct. And the sun laughs down through the moving liquid sheen, and makes many a pool of radiance in the quiet spots, and flings on the sand whole networks of living light that recall the flashing mail of the goldfish, or the pattern that wind and sunshine will ripple into the corn, or the gleam that the warmth of æons has flushed into alabaster, where milk and honey made marble still let the light shine through. Ah! these are all the vintages of the wine and the warmth of life; whatever the shape they take, the source of their beauty is one, — and would I could know its name!

And all through a pane of glass and a bit of wood? Ah! well, a less thing than that may open a world to our eyes. The glass makes the surface calm, the wood shuts out the misleading reflections of other things. It would be good to apply it to life sometimes, I think.

All my peace took wings at the sight of a telegram calling me back to Tokyo long before I was ready to go. Very cross, indeed, I was to leave the cottage in the bay; and my temper was not improved when I found that the summons meant an unqualified series of official *corvées*. Some people who had a right to ask it, wanted to be presented to the Emperor and Empress, who, alas! are in anything but a gay mood just now; but they were kind and good-natured, and so were the Princes; and my philosophy, which had suffered greatly at being recalled to Tokyo and audiences, was made quite serviceable again by finding one of the dearest of old friends waiting for me in town, whose coming I would not have missed for worlds. We talked of nothing but Rome and Villa Doria anemones and old friends for days, and took a deep draught of the wine of pleasant memories laid by in the Roman summers of our youth.

There was one bit of that week in Tokyo which will be added to the store of my memory picture gallery. A lunch was given for our distinguished visitors in that Palace by the sea where three months ago the Empress's cherry-blossom *fête* took place. It is called a Palace; but it consists mostly of a series of pavilions, lovely little Japanese buildings open to the view, and having hardly any decorations except the exquisite quality and colour of the woods used, and the perfect taste which makes them seem as much a part of the scenery as the fairy islands on which they stand or the blue water lapping round their steps. For in this dream garden (forgive me, if I told you of this before!) the real salt sea is everywhere, running its tides in and out of tiny lakes and winding canals, spanned by red bridges, delicate as if built with the slats of carved fans. The great sea fish come swimming in, and a number of fishermen had been brought with their boats that we might see the fishing with the circular net, which is an old Japanese amusement.

The boat is low and slender, and one man sits in the stern with a long single oar rather like the one used by the gondoliers in Venice. He pushes hither and thither till the spot seems promising for a throw. The fisherman his companion stands on the prow, which rises a good deal at the point. I do not know whether these were picked men, but I never saw straighter or goodlier lads than these fisher-boys. Their firm brown limbs looked as hard as bronze; their bright eyes and set resolute faces showed the resource and courage that come of long training in a difficult art. The pose of the one who was waiting to throw the net was the most perfect expression of strength in rest, but ready for the hunter's spring. As they floated across the lake, whose water was ruffled by a coming storm, I longed for an artist to be at hand, and make the picture one that would

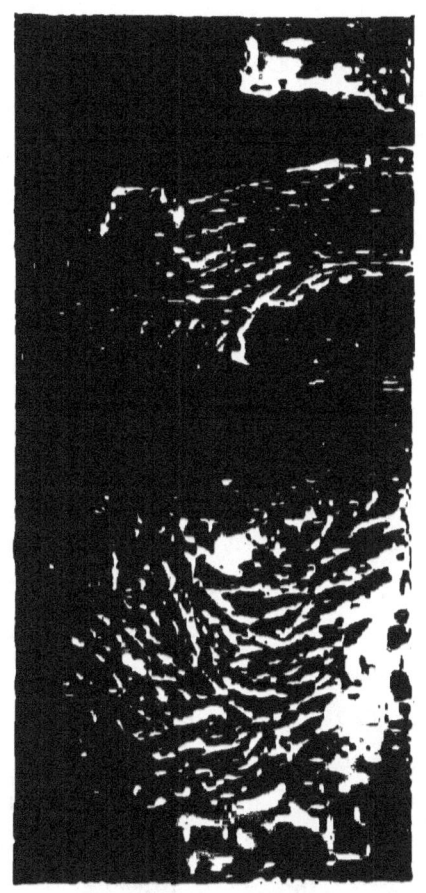

A SHOAL OF FISH

keep for ever. Do you know that lurid light which comes before a storm, when all the sky goes black as ink, but from some sharp rift an angry shaft pours down and seems to be absorbed by the greens of the trees and grass, until they positively glow as if with some indwelling radiance of their own? So it was that day in the Hama Rikkyu sea garden. The black of the sky, the gold greens of the foliage, the red of the bridges, and the storm light on the water made a harmony almost too vivid to be borne; and on that background floated the slim boat, twisting and turning like a water snake, while the boy standing high on her prow gathered the black coils of his net under one bare arm, poised his body in a bold curve far over the point, and with a sudden movement flung the net with a rushing noise out on the water, where it lay, a perfect round, for a few minutes, before it began to sink in search of its prey. Then slowly and very gently it was drawn back by a length of rope to the hand that had thrown it; the thrower sprang down from his point of vantage, and sat in the boat, drawing in fold after fold of the fine black mesh, and taking from its snares great fighting fish whose scales gleamed unbearably bright as they turned and leapt in their furious struggle for life under the dun glare of the coming storm.

Then I looked up, and outside our green embankments a great square sail, blown out with the strong south wind, went hurrying up the bay before the storm, as sublimely indifferent to Empress's gardens as its white companions the sea-gulls, who flew backwards and forwards from the free sea outside to the captive lagoons within, shrieking news to each other about the storm.

CHAPTER XXXVI

KARUIZAWA AGAIN. — FURIHATA IS RESTORED TO US. — OUR OWN VOLCANO. — THE MOUNTAIN'S OUTER COURT. — THE IRIYAMA TOGE AND THE CATHEDRAL ROCKS. — SUNSET LILIES. — A FORGOTTEN MONASTERY AND A DYING MAN

KARUIZAWA, *August*, 1891.

OUR Palace of Peace seems even cooler and greener than last year, and has already some of the atmosphere of home about it. It is a very wet home to-day; this is supposed to be the last day of the rainy season, and our world of woods and hills is drinking in the gracious flood, and promising, to the ears that can hear, a rich harvest of wild flowers and woodsy shadiness and emerald turf to make up for these grey wet hours, which, by the way, we are all enjoying after our own fashion. The Chief is writing, as usual; it is now past five o'clock, and ever since nine or thereabouts this morning the sounds of dictionary work have reached me from the other side of the wooden house, where Mr. G—— and his writer Okamoto San discuss and disagree over the possible and impossible meaning of all the Chinese words in the language. The third volume of the precious dictionary must have grown as much as the grass and the trees during this long day of rain. The very dogs are subdued and quiet, lying recklessly where people are sure to walk over them, gazing out with the calmness of despair, knowing that no human being in his senses would take down hat and stick to give them a run across country to-day. One beautiful Gordon setter, eldest son of Floppy Flo (a British subject, who came to us off a kind of pirate sealer, where several murders had been committed, and whose captain, when sent to prison, made the most careful arrangements for his dog's welfare), began to weep pitifully the first time he woke up, in the cold dawn of the hills, far from his mother and his sister Sōdeska, who were left in town. The rain was blowing into his kennel; and I crept down in the grey of the morning to comfort him, and found the faithful D—— there before me. It seems he had been very cross with the noisy puppy till the nature of the trouble was made clear; and all day long he was reproaching himself and making excuses for poor baby Gordon, whom he treats exactly as if he was a two-legged baby instead of a four-footed one.

Another faithful person is once more with us, to my great joy, and that is Furihata, the good policeman. We have not been without news of this hero since we parted; for at the New Year H—— sent him a little present, which was acknowledged in English as follows:

"To Hon. Fraser.

"Dear Sir,—Accept my best Thanks for Your very kind present as it New Year's compliment. That is valuable in itself; but I shall doubly esteem it as a gift from You.

"Yours very truly,
"F. Furihata.

"416, Nagano Streets, Nagano Ken."

On reading this, I felt sure that Furihata had made great progress in English; and as we must have an escort in these solitudes, asked before leaving town to have him awarded to us again. I was rather disappointed to be told that, much to the regret of the Foreign Office, my request could not be granted, as the man had left the service. On inquiring what had become of him, we learnt that he had got tired of wielding the strong arm of the law, and had taken a place as railway porter at Shin Karuizawa Station, about half an hour from here. Then I thought no more about the matter until the day I came here. Our journey was, as usual, extremely sensational. Train, jinriksha, sedan-chair, and "shanks's mare"—as our old nurse used to call going on foot—were all tried by different members of the party, not to mention the jumping matchbox called a tram-car, which nothing would induce me to enter, although I consented to let it carry my precious luggage. There was so much of this that it filled the whole car, the only one to be had, leaving just room for one "boy," an inexperienced creature, who jumped in with the courage born of ignorance. He was left in town last year, and knew not the horrors of that winding, precipitous mountain road, about three feet deep in black mud. The servants who had tried it last year turned from it like one man, preferring a four-hours' walk up the steepest paths of the mountains to a repetition of their previous sufferings.

It was early in the afternoon when we finally started from Yokukawa to make the ascent. Only three jinrikshas could be found in the whole town; my own chair had been brought from Tokyo; and after great efforts a *kago*, or basket-litter, was got from another village with two coolies for my little *amah*. It was about as big as a good-sized workbox; but she packed herself into it with great ingenuity, and smiled, as she always does at everything, from presents to scoldings. Most of the dogs had gone on already with Mr. G——; so we had only Tip, the Brown Ambassador, and the elephantine Gordon, who had cried aloud all the way from Tokyo. Even the experienced Tip had been very unhappy in the train; and now they both trotted delightedly through the mud and wet grass for two or three miles, and then politely but firmly asked to be taken up. We had not yet parted company with the jinrikshas; so Gordon was solemnly installed with the Chief, and Tip got on the little footboard of my chair, standing well over the edge, as dogs always will do, and sniffing excitedly at the wet mountain breeze, which doubtless brought him news of pheasants and rabbits. Once he lurched, flopped hopelessly over the edge, and hung in his leash for a second, till I pulled him up again, a sadder and a wiser dog.

As we mounted higher and higher among the lonely hills, a fine wet mist came down, wrapping us round like a veil, and making the figures at the head of the procession look huge and indistinct to those at the end. The mountain shrubs and all the nameless flowers gave out their bitter-sweet perfume; and many a wet branch shook its rain of cold drops on my neck, as I passed rustling through the leaves, borne high on the shoulders of the men. At last the point came where things on wheels must part from things on feet; the Chief took the *riksha* road, and I and the *kago* and the walkers began to climb the other. The walkers included, of course, Rinzo, O'Matsu's husband, who considers himself entitled to go with me on all the expeditions; "Small Cook San," an absurd fat boy, very proud of his European clothes (his commander, "Big Cook San," who is about half his size, had gone on before); and, bringing up the rear, Kané, the artistic pantry-boy, who spends his time in worshipping my English housekeeper, Mrs. D——, for whose benefit he makes the most wonderful Japanese landscapes in washtubs or old boxes, with bridges and waterfalls, and little men and women, miniature lanterns and goldfish, and pine trees three inches high — perfect curiosities of imagination and dainty handiwork. His bit of a room is always a study of art-arrangement, his hanging pictures and ornaments all in exactly the right places. He is quite the tallest man in the servants' quarters, and had caused me nearly to choke with laughter that morning when he appeared at the station got up in a military suit of dazzling white, frogs and buttons complete, and crowned by an enormous pith helmet. The whole costume was so carefully copied from that of our Government official, Inspector Peter Peacock, that I thought for a moment it was he as I saw him pass in the distance.

Kané looked quite as neat and dazzling, after his long tramp up the wet mountain paths; every time that I turned my head to see how my poor retainers were getting on, a succession of beaming smiles met my gaze, one behind the other, fading away into the enwrapping mist, like that of the immortal Cheshire cat. The top of the pass was nearly reached, and I, looking before me, had forgotten my companions, and had been enjoying the divine misty solitudes for two hours or more, when, a few yards higher up the steep path, a sudden frantic commotion of wagging tails became visible, followed by an outline in the grey haze that soon resolved itself into Mr. G——, surrounded by all the dogs. In two seconds more the columns were, as war correspondents say, involved in inextricable confusion. Three dachses, two setters, and the old pointer Bess were jumping over me and each other in the wildest transports of joy. When the dogs subsided a little, I had a chance to notice another spectre in the mist, an official spectre, standing at attention in a policeman's uniform. "Furihata?" "Not yet," said Mr. G——. "This is the inspector of the district; but you will find Furihata at the house. On hearing of your wish to see him again, a paternal Government ordered him to give up portering and return to the service of his country. Of course he obeyed, and you will have him all summer!"

And so it was. When I came within sight of the cottage, Furihata, gorgeous in white and gold, came towards me accompanied by his sergeant, and exclaimed, with a melodramatic gesture and a voice of triumph, "My Furihata!" I said, of course, that I was very glad to see him, and to know that he was to be attached to us during the summer. He escorted us solemnly over the threshold of Peace Cottage, and then, on the steps, gathered himself up for a grand effort, and exclaimed with a gasp, "*My* — protection — British Legation — Karuizawa!" He was so pleased with this phrase that he came back twice that evening to say it again, and has, I hear, repeated it to several of our friends who have taken houses here for the summer; only for them the wily creature substitutes "foreigners" for British Legation.

I wrote you so many letters from Karuizawa last year that I fear there are few new things left to tell you of now, except two expeditions which had not taken place then: one to the Iriyama Toge; and one to Komoro, a Buddhist monastery in the hills. I will begin with Iriyama Toge, the Cathedral Rocks, as foreigners have named the place. You remember that our home here is on the northern edge of a plain made by a wide sweep between two parallel lines of mountains, all at such a height that, as a prosaic British friend of ours puts it, "one has left all that bamboo tropical rubbish behind." No bamboo grows here, no camellia trees or palms, only pine and oak and chestnut clothe the hillsides; but the *Lilium auratum* blooms in profusion, and our cottage is like a hothouse just now with the masses of splendid flowers, lilies, white and scarlet and golden, bluebells, hydrangea, and a most superb white blossom like gardenia growing on trees twenty feet high. These and many others the gardener brings in every day from the woods, and our few tame garden flowers look poor and weak beside them. As I was saying, we have our home among the foothills of Asama Yama, the never-sleeping volcano, which is the background of our view. From us the land drops for a little way, and then one finds oneself on the level flowery

ASAMA YAMA

floor of the valley, about four miles wide, and extending some six or seven miles towards the south before it begins to drop in sheer terraces down to Nagano, Naoetsu, and the sea-coast. The Iriyama Toge is the fence of hills which rise softly on the southern boundary of our upland valley; softly on our side indeed, but between them and the distant plain below comes one of those amazing successions of crags and peaks, gorges and ravines, grey rock and green woodland and mossy slope, which look — as if some Titan had been sampling creation in the smallest possible space. If ever there were Titans, this country must have been one of their homes. Asama Yama is active enough now; but we have seen, thank Heaven! no such play as she used to indulge in — play which covered her southern slopes with boulders, some of them a hundred feet in diameter; which in 1783, during the most frightful eruption the world has ever seen, continued for six weeks to shake the empire of Japan to its very foundations, while, as the writers of the time tell us, "the mountain was on fire from the crown to the base," and never ceased to pour out lava, mud, rocks, and ashes (these fell two inches thick eighty miles away), while the roar and smoke seemed to go up to heaven itself. Over fifty villages were then destroyed; valleys were filled up to the brim with stones; our upland plain, which had been a rich rice-bearing district, was covered with something like four feet of solid scoria, while the streams which watered it were turned aside; the loss of life could not be counted; the lava stream ran thirty miles in sixteen hours down the northern slope, and lies there a black scar to this day. No wonder that the country is deserted, that the two or three hamlets are poor and miserable! Who would build good houses near such a devouring monster? who that could help it would come within reach of its devastating breath? I never realised until we came here that it was our beautiful Asama Yama that had done all this mischief, or I doubt whether I should have had the courage to settle so close to its sides. They tell me that the height at which we have built, and the intervening foothills, would make us quite safe in case of a new eruption; but I am inclined to pray for peace in our time, all the same. As we go across the plain towards Iriyama Toge, the layers of scoria are clearly shown in the cuttings made here and there in a fruitless attempt to find an arable surface. For all time the lovely plain can be nothing but the mountain's outer court, as it were, Asama's garden, rich in wild flowers and in nothing else.

Through these we went, knee deep in "aster and in golden-rod," across the plain, to where our horizon-line rises in grassy slopes that look as if they had been shaped and smoothed by a gentle hand; but here and there a stern rock stands out, like an ascetic in the world, protesting against the ease and softness with which he sees himself surrounded. One of these rocks, high up near the crest of the hills, stands out huge and four square in natural granite, with a place for the preacher in the centre; and this the foreigners have called Pulpit Rock. But we pass round its base and over another crest; and then we are on the ridge of the Wami Toge, and can look down over the weird and beautiful valley of rocks, through which a deep-cut path winds off towards Takasaki and the distant plain. The surprise of this sight is perhaps its especial characteristic: at one moment you are strolling leisurely, after something of a climb, up a slope which seems to end in a grassy ridge a few yards farther on; you have left great rocks and hills behind, the turf is soft under your feet, and you say to yourself, "We will just rest a little on the knoll, and then we will be getting home; for there is no more to see now. This is like the Asama foothills."

And in a minute you stand on the green ridge, and a new and magic world — a world of bower and castle, keep and buttress, soaring minster and deep-cut fosse — lies spread beneath your astonished eyes. King Arthur's Court might come riding out in golden array from that grey portcullis; King Arthur's Queen might lean over that skyey parapet, waiting for one upward glance from her hero-traitor knight. What deeps are in that ravine, where some laidly worm might coil its dragon scales! What heights in those distant

CROWS IN JAPAN

spires, melting in golden haze, where a wandering King might dream the hours away with Morgan Le Fay and her airy sisterhood! The turf creeps in green velvet folds to the castle's foot; the drawbridge lies for ever across the empty moat; the sunset floods with squandered gold the unpeopled bastions of the fort; only the wood-pigeons whirl round the eaves of the Queen's high bower; no step or cry is heard, save that of a poor man in blue coat and straw sandals who urges a heavily laden pack-horse up the dark road which winds, so deep-cut that we can hardly see it, round the castle's base. We are in the heart of the central mountains of Japan; the great castle is a nameless rock; King Arthur's fortress a bit of nature's forgotten play; and I, a dreamer, who sit here for hours, weaving the worlds together in my dreams, East with West, Past with Present, Legend with Truth, till my comrades gather round me, telling strange stories of hair-breadth climbs among the rocks, calling high and long for two who seem to have lost themselves in the labyrinths of this granite city. At last we see them far down, looking weirdly small, waving their hands to us from a point which they have scaled. They are two who often get lost in company; so we turn, smiling, and leave them to linger as they like, while we make our way home across the plain, clinging to the skirts of the daylight as they sweep all too swiftly from us. Sweet is the slow walk home across the evening fields; the grass is all in twilight at the root, but the last light lingers softly on the billowy surface, where pale-purple asters, and white stars of Bethlehem float as on a cloud. Hundreds of sunset lilies are turning their pale-gold faces to the west, as a signal that day is done. In the hot hours they sleep, and as we passed at noon every cup was closed in the sunshine;

THE RUNNING POSTMAN

but now that the twilight cools the air, they open wide, and stand in starry multitudes along the plain; behind them the misty mountains and the hushed empurpled sky; at their feet a tangle of low grasses steeped in dew; and "God's peace over all, my dear, God's peace over all."

Far away, where the plain turns sharply to the south, stands a little town called Komoro — a town of eager industries and uninteresting surroundings, far less picturesque than our shabby village where every house is decaying, every screen is torn, where the children and the cats scatter into wretched-looking homes as we and the dogs pass by. Poor old Karuizawa was a grand place once, a stage on the long Nakasendo road, where every Daimyo must pass on his way from Kyoto to Yedo. Now only mountain pilgrims and crazy foreigners like ourselves ever go near it; the railway has turned two miles aside, and the place has become so poor that it has not even a public bath! Since our coming this year our butcher, our rice-dealer, and our own laundry man have all set up their signs in the village, proclaiming that they are specially appointed to attend the British Legation. The place is a favourite one with the populous Canadian missionaries; and I hope their patronage, combined with our own and that of our friends, will bring a little prosperity back to the town. But Komoro is quite a different thing; it lies right on the line of railway, has good inns, and thrives on making saddles, tools, and carts for the whole province.

When we went to Komoro the other day, it was not to stay there, but to make an expedition to a strange Buddhist convent far back in the hills that overhang a river, whose name, I am ashamed to say, I have forgotten to ask. The road, after leaving Komoro, goes for some way between rice-fields, over the very hottest country I have yet traversed in Japan. The fields are separated by little dykes just wide enough to walk on; and these are intersected

again and again by temporary canals of the most
minute kind, patted into being with the back of a
spade so as to conduct the water from one level down
to the next, and so on. For all rice-fields must be laid
out in terraces, so that as soon as the water has thoroughly overflowed one field it may drop a foot or so to
do its work in the next, and so on through field after
field till every plant is fed. Between the fields the
dykes are green now, and here and there a lonely
blood-red lily waves like a signal in the air. The
colour is an intense scarlet, and partakes in some way
of the nature of flame, since it can be seen at distances
where all other tints, including white, would pass unnoticed. I had brought my chair, and was, as usual,
far in advance of the rest of the party, who had chosen
to walk — a great mistake on such a burning day.
Soon my men turned from the dusty road between
the evil-smelling rice-fields (alas! agriculture, to be successful here, must — excuse the word — stink), and took
to a path which, after crossing a fairly full river, penetrated into a rocky range of hills on its northern side.
How welcome was the shade and coolness of the groves!
I think the men walked faster than they do on cooler
days; and while my companions were still struggling
up the sides of the slope, we were racing along the
crest of the ridge, all our troubles over. It was just
midday when the path dropped again, in the direction
of the river's noise (the stream itself was invisible), and
the dull-red gate of some sacred building showed at the
end of a short alley thick-set with oak trees. A still

farther descent, and we were inside a grey stone court, with very old buildings round three sides of it, while in front a terrace spread between two walls of rock which rose straight on either side. The place was set in a very cleft of the rock, like a sea-swallow's nest. No sun came here, although above and behind us high noon lay on the land. Before us the rocky walls ran a long way out, and between them, far away, bathed in noontide glory, the country beyond the river seemed to swim in the blazing heat.

I have at home a picture of the gentle lady Murasaki Shikibu, who eight hundred years ago retired to just such a spot as this to meditate on the romance which, by command of the Empress, she was to write. It was in August, by the light of the full moon, that she sat all night on the balcony of a temple between the rocks, far uplifted from earth, and gazing down on Lake Biwa as we here gaze on the distant river. If her temple was like this one, I do not wonder at the power of inspiration which, overflowing her mind, caused her to write the chief incidents of her story on the back of a roll of Buddhist Scriptures, till all the space was covered. Next day, when the sacred frenzy was over, she discovered what she had done, and in time copied out the whole book anew to make reparation.

Here, in the rocky monastery of Komoro, all was still, and the light was not light, but clarified shadow, an even dusk, in which all objects were perfectly to be apprehended, but none smote the weary eyeballs more strongly than another. I cannot give you the sense of remoteness, of isolation, of tempered peace which the atmosphere inspired. Coming from the sun-stricken world outside, it was like turning from some wild passion of love, that scorches and kills, to the impersonal tenderness of a mother-heart, to pre-natal dawns ere individual suffering had stamped the soul with the individual immortality which it must carry, for better, for worse, through eternity. Peace was in the brown earth, where the dust fell softly from one's feet, as if knowing how tired they were; peace in the hermit trees, which had chosen to grow in small hard clefts, far above the noises of river and plain;

A BROWN-WINGED FALCON

peace on the grey-faced rock, and all along the patient steps and ledges by which a path had been wrested, inch by inch, from the butting crag, so sharp in its dizzy drop to the river's bed that the eye hardly dared to follow where a brown-winged falcon, whirring out from its eyrie, fell like a falling stone on its unseen quarry below; and peace, in armfuls, heartfuls, where at last, after passing by bell and shrine, by gateways cut in the edge of the cliff against an empty sky, by narrow steps round the brinks of chasms that sank out of sight in the darkness, the path came out on the bare crag's top against a rock that shadowed it still, and watched, like a sentinel, over — a dying man.

Lying on the scant grass, his face to the sky, his limbs doubled under him, was a poor Japanese, a man of about eight-and-twenty, dressed in thin cotton, and gazing out with eyes where suffering was not yet subdued in unconsciousness. He groaned pitifully, but shook his head in refusal of the help that all were longing to give. The bonze, who was acting as guide, explained. The man was doing a voluntary penance, fulfilling a vow. Eight days and nights he had passed here, without touching food or drink. He had still two days more to suffer, but would probably die first. It was his own wish; there was nothing to be done; it was better to leave him — in peace.

And surely you are at peace now, poor brave martyr to the only good you knew? God is not one who will reproach you for giving more than He asked.

CHAPTER XXXVII

DEATH OF FATHER TESTEVUIDE. — HOLY POVERTY. — UNSUS-
PECTED PHILANTHROPISTS. — THE LEPER HOSPITAL AGAIN.
— A LEPER'S DEATH. — MÈRE SAINTE-MATHILDE

August, 1891.

FATHER TESTEVUIDE is dead. Father Vigroux takes his place.

Such is our news from Tokyo; and ever since it came, somewhat late, to our solitudes, I have been thinking very sorrowfully of the little Hospital in the hills, where profound grief will be felt for the loss of the dear missionary who has been father and mother to the poor sick people there. Thank God, I cannot help saying — thank God that he went before the disease had fastened on him! His death was for his people, nevertheless. For months at a time, when funds were low, he used to starve himself, in order to spend on his sick the money which should have gone for his own food. Besides the lepers, he had many poor, and was sometimes the only priest in a very wide district; so that the hardest work constantly fell to his share — as, indeed, it does fall to all our priests here, where the demand far exceeds the supply.

Do you know what our priests have to live on in Japan? Fifteen yen (thirty shillings) a month. Out of this they must pay house rent if there is no dwelling-house attached to the chapel, food, clothing, the expenses of getting from one part of their parish to another, and (do not laugh) their charities! I cannot make out that any one of them has any private income; if they had, it has all been given *pour les œuvres*, and thirty shillings a month is what they receive — and live, or die, upon!

"Why — why?" I cried in indignation, when I first learnt all this. Because there is no more to give; the Church is in the straits of holy poverty. The class who, especially in France, used to contribute so generously to mission work has been obliged to devote those moneys to voluntary schools since the name of God has been eradicated from all the public ones; and missionary work would be paralysed if the priests could not live — like paupers: dear, kind, clean, holy paupers, but just that. I have heard it said that the sum spent by different sects of Protestants in Japan equals that which the Holy Father has at his disposal for mission work throughout the world. I do not know how true this may be; but, watching the two systems at work, close beside me, I have come to the conclusion that in these matters money is of secondary value, of next to no value, as compared with prayer, self-sacrifice, and the Heaven-taught discipline of a holy life. It is impossible for the most hardened scoffer to make the acquaintance of one of our priests or sisters of charity here without feeling that he is in the presence of a power for good. As I heard one man say, "Well, people don't do this kind of thing to amuse themselves! 'Pon my soul, the poor chaps deserve to succeed!"

And here let me render a tribute to the scoffer, as I have known him in the East, the British or foreign bachelor, popularly supposed to be so immersed in his own comforts and pleasures, in his club and his whist and his billiards and — other things, that it would be in vain to turn to him for assistance where the poor are concerned. Well, after a long experience of charitable work, I must say that the jolly foreign bachelor is the only creature (barring the Empress of Japan and some ladies of her Court) to whom I have never once turned in vain. Generally a hopeless pagan himself, and often living on very small pay, the moment one speaks of orphans or lepers or earth-

A BLIND MASSEUR

quake victims, his hand goes into his pocket, and out comes all (and sometimes a good deal more than all) he can possibly afford. Never was there a more kind-hearted and generous creature; and many a time, where I had asked for a real necessity with regret and hesitation, the regret and hesitation have been transferred to the acceptance of a sum which must have made a large difference in the giver's banking account. Once the dear Tsukiji nuns had their house so full of sick and poor that it was absolutely necessary to start an infirmary at once, and a relatively large sum was wanted to do it. We had a charity ball, or something of the kind, coming off for another object, and I could not compromise its success by appealing to my usual public for this new need. Five gentlemen, quite unsuspected by the world of philanthropic tendencies, made up the sum for us between them, and the infirmary has been full from that day to this; numberless cures, baptisms, and conversions have taken place there, which must surely, in great part, be put down to the credit of my five friends. And the kindness of the bachelor to the little children and the sick! The toys and cakes smuggled down to the nuns for the little ones, the sums of money sent "just to give the poor little beggars a bit of a treat," the touching way in which my beloved sœur Sainte-Domitille will say, when everything else has failed, "Eh bien, il faudra écrire à Monsieur un tel," with the certainty of not being refused! It is all very instructive, and makes one think even better of human nature than one did before.

And now, as I was saying, dear Père Testevuide has gone home, after very great suffering. He had been sent away to a little Sanatorium which the missionaries have in Hong Kong, in the hope that the change of air would restore his strength. The attempt only succeeded, as the Archbishop says in his letter, in laying another cross on his kind heart—that of dying away from his own *chère mission.*

His place has, of course, been filled at once, by a Father whom I have known well in Tokyo, Père Vigroux, who is the Apostolic Pro-vicar, and whose hands have always been as full as they could hold of work. It will be impossible for him to drop his other tasks at once; but God only knows how he is going to accomplish them and look after the lepers as well. The Archbishop wrote to him, asking him to undertake the Gotemba business, and he accepted promptly. But Gotemba is just now a problem of a very anxious kind. There is next to no money to keep it going; there are thirty in-patients there, and others are asking for admission all the time; poor creatures to whom the treatment would be of inestimable benefit, whether as arresting the still curable symptoms of the disease, or as palliating and softening the horrible sufferings of its more advanced stages. But how can they be received if there is no money to pay for their medicines or their food? The original Hospital, built with such pathetic economy by Père Testevuide, was already far too small for those whom he received; and before his death he managed to throw two wings out from the main building, and with these it could now accommodate eighty patients. But the founder just managed to feed thirty by going about and begging food for them himself. He knew the district, and was greatly beloved; and yet he could never quite carry out the desires of his heart. No wonder that good Père Vigroux felt, even while undertaking it, that it was an enormous task.

"Votre grandeur," he writes to Monseigneur Osouf, "veut bien me confier la direction de l'hôpital des lépreux . . . j'en remercie Dieu, et si j'ai lieu de craindre de n'être pas à la hauteur de la tâche, je ne l'accepte pas moins avec la plus grande confiance."

He then goes on to give a short report of the work; and any one who reads it must, I think, feel as I do, that of all works of charity this is perhaps the one where the good done is most direct, the need most pressing. The new director's first grief was that of being unable to receive all the patients who had implored to be admitted. However, he took ten of the most suffering, and hopes soon to collect funds to allow of his undertaking a few more. His description of his new parishioners is too sad and terrible to be repeated. He says that the forms of the disease are varied, and most awful; but that at any rate the poor patients know that henceforth they will never be abandoned to their fate; that shelter and food and clothing, medicines for their sick bodies and kindness to cheer their sad hearts, will never be wanting. Eleven of the number are Christians; and he says that although all are resigned and patient — no Japanese is otherwise, even in great suffering — these are positively happy. The certainty that if they bear their misfortunes patiently they will enter into happiness supreme and undying when this short life is over makes them perfectly serene and even gay. More than one seems even thankful for the misfortune of a sickness to his body which has brought his far more sick soul to the Great Physician. And these, little by little, will convert the others, who seem ready even now, in their poverty and suffering, to accept and cling lovingly to the merciful faith which would perhaps have appealed to them in vain in health and prosperity.

It has been found impossible to keep one patient on less than ten pounds a year; and the good Father beseeches charitable persons to contemplate the possibility of endowing a bed. From time to time charitable entertainments are given at Tokyo especially for the Hospital; but a few regular subscriptions help more than spasmodic giving, and, alas! the want is very great. From reasons which I think I told you before, scarcely any provision is made for lepers here; and every now and then some tragedy occurs which just tears at one's heart-strings for pity.

I must tell you a story; please forgive the horror of the beginning, for the sake of the end. A month ago, up here in the hills, where of course our papers come a day late, I was horrified to read in the *Mail* an account of a poor leper who had been found (and left) dying by the roadside in a suburb of Yokohama. The indignant Britisher who wrote said that in the course of a walk his attention was attracted by the cries of some one in great pain. Coming near the spot, he found, to his horror, that a crowd of Japanese boys were pelting with stones a poor creature who was rolling on the ground, naked, in agony, in the very last stages of leprosy. The Englishman, I am sure, dispersed the boys, and probably gave the poor wretch some money, but in his letter mentioned nothing but the pitiable condition of the man, which he described as such that it required the greatest courage to come near him. Of course one would have given worlds to help; but Yokohama is far indeed from Karuizawa, it was already evening, and all that night I was made miserable by the thought of the leper's suffering, which I could do nothing to alleviate. In the morning the thought came to me to write to the nuns of the Convent in Yokohama, and get them to look into the case; there would be no need to ask them to help, when once they knew of it. The answer came on the next day but one from the Superior, Mère Sainte-Mathilde; she is over seventy, and has more than fifty years of "vocation" behind her. I must give you her letter just as it came, except that I translate it into English:

"DEAR MRS. FRASER,—I have heard it said that souls speak to one another; and, indeed, I believe it. Last night I saw you come to me with such ardour, such precipitation, that it woke me several times from my sleep; my mind was full of you this morning, when your letter was put into my hands. Be comforted. He for whom to-morrow is as to-day, and who sees the desires of our hearts, accomplished yours for the unfortunate leper before you had formed it. The leper was baptised by one of our Sisters, and died soon after in perfect peace, and with the most lively gratitude for the grace he had received. . . . The poor man was discovered by a charitable gentleman, who at once went home, procured a carpenter, and with him brought nails and wood to build a kind of shed over the poor creature, whom it was quite impossible to move. He gave him wine and food, and then hastened to call us to see if it were still possible to instruct and baptise this dying man, who was literally at the last gasp. The Sister sat beside him for three hours before she could make him grasp the necessary truths. He became unconscious again and again, and even when conscious would not listen, appeared not to hear what she was saying. At last she sent the jinriksha coolie back to the Convent to ask for some water of Lourdes, and prevailed upon the sick man to swallow a few drops. The moment he had done so a change came over him, and he gave the most rapt attention to all that she was saying. Whereas before not a word had gone to his heart, now, by the protection of our Blessed Mother, light flooded his soul, and he eagerly asked for the baptism which would open for him the gates of eternal peace and joy. His gratitude was touching, and he did all that he could to express it."

As I read her letter some old lines that a friend used to repeat came back to me:

"O power to do, O baffled will,
O prayer and action, ye are one,
* * * * *
And good but wished with God is done."

CHAPTER XXXVIII

THE DEFINITION OF A *SAMURAI*. — *SAMURAI* MEN AND WOMEN. — *SAMURAI* IDEALS. — THE RED CROSS SOCIETY. — SWORD-DAMASCENING. — CLAN GOVERNMENT. — SAYONARA, TOKI!

TOKYO, October, 1891.

YOU have, I fear, a right to be puzzled at my apparently indiscriminate use of the title of *samurai*. You say that I describe a prince, an interpreter, and a waiting-maid all by the same term, and that such carelessness is misleading. But it is not carelessness, and the appellation is appropriate to them all; so it is not misleading. It simply applies to the whole of the class who had a right to carry arms, and their descendants; and it is the fault of Japanese ideals if it has come to express everything that is heroic and dignified and honourable. The first *samurai*, recognised as such, were the descendants of the fighting men of Yoritomo, the first of the Shoguns (1186–1199). He had found it necessary to put the provinces under a kind of military prefecture, each commander having a large body of troops at his disposal. As time went on, the soldiers came to consider themselves immeasurably superior to the peaceful part of the population, and Iyeyasu, who loved fighters, increased their privileges, and laid down laws which made them everywhere feared and respected. They were as a rule clansmen of great chiefs, and in more ways than one resembled their prototypes in the Highlands at home. Very few possessed property, but all were entitled to rations of food from the lord whom they served; they lived in a kind of barracks round his house; they never married out of their class, and the noble ladies had as a rule only *samurai* women and girls to wait on them. Some were *rônins* (chiefless men), who had lost their lord, and wandered through the country at will. Those who had a chief were bound to attend him on all State occasions, fight his battles, and revenge his wrongs. They were reckless, idle, overbearing, and constituted a dangerous class in the country; but all agree in admitting that, owing to the dignified retirement into which the great nobles mostly withdrew after the reconstitution of the empire, and to the want of enterprise and the intense conservatism of the lower classes, it is to the *samurai* that the great advance of Japan in our day must be ascribed. Almost all the distinguished men of modern Japan, the thinkers, the educators, the pioneers, have been drawn from their ranks; they were the first to make their own the modes of thought, the education, of foreign countries; and while worshipping the sword as the god of *samurai* honour, they have not disdained the means by which other nations have reached greatness. Agriculture was always considered by them as a gentleman's occupation, and no *samurai* lost caste by entering the service of a nobly born master. He could not enter the service of any one who was not a noble, and he could not engage in trade or become an artisan. The people were divided into four classes — *samurai*, farmers, merchants, and artisans. Iyeyasu constituted the *samurai* the masters of the other classes, and enacted regulations by which the mastership was made a reality.

A *samurai* was supposed to have but one law, that of honour; loyalty to his lord came first of all, and on that altar even father and mother must be sacrificed. Wife and child were hardly counted; being a part of himself, their service must be as complete as his. No *samurai* could take joy in life while an insult to his chief remained unavenged; and he often refused to survive his master. That master himself could have no higher code of honour than a simple *samurai*, and the name gradually became applied in the sense in which we use "gentleman." The duty of a *samurai*, the honour or the valour of a *samurai*, are current expressions; an action not worthy of a *samurai* means something base and churlish. There were many degrees among the different members of the class as far as social status was concerned — some being heads of families, and having retainers of their own; some merely private soldiers as it were, with no property beyond the precious sword: but, as I have said, the principles of honour were the same for all; and the *samurai* were the framers of the extraordinarily elaborate and punctilious code of Japanese honour, by the side of which the maxims of European mediæval chivalry seem rough and rude. A terrible blow was dealt to the class when the Daimyos laid down their power, when the *samurai* were disbanded, and the whole intricate and ancient edifice of Japanese feudalism crashed down at the Emperor's feet. But the race was too good to perish; translating its ancient code of honour into a more modern tongue, it rallied round the throne, and has done so much for progress and good administration (in spite of such accidents as the *soshi* or the fanatics) that I think I am right in calling the Japan of to-day, with its working Parliament, its growing press, its army and navy, its just codes and admirable schools, its vigorous loyalty and its real good sense, the Japan of the *samurai*.

In no country in the world more than in Japan does the woman faithfully reflect the opinions and codes of the man of her own class; and the *samurai* woman is as brave, as self-controlled, as calmly self-sacrificing as her father or her husband. As far as self-sacrifice goes, she has more to give. His honour will always remain to him; hers may be asked for, and must not then be withheld. The *samurai's* wife must be chaste as Lucrece, faithful as Penelope; but she has deliberately sacrificed herself, again and again in Japanese history, for the good of her family or her husband's lord. More than one story have I heard of a *samurai* wife selling her liberty away for years to procure the price of weapons and armour where these were needed to vindicate the family honour. Such a woman, on her return from bondage, would not have been regarded as a fallen thing; on the contrary, all honour and gratitude would be hers for what would be considered an act of unmixed heroism.

Had she been asked to sell her soul for an honourable object, it would have been considered base in her to withhold it.

But dishonour as dishonour would only be wiped out with death, and the *samurai* women knew from childhood the use of the fine short sword whose baptism of blood could wash away any disgrace. They were trained and drilled to use spear and bow and arrow in the defence of the castle, which, as so often happened in the bloody annals of the Highlands, was exposed to attack in the absence of the chief and his fighting men. Then the women would put on their war dress, a distinctive costume never worn at other times; and many a good defence they made, holding out till help could come. Were they overcome, there was always a short road to honour and peace — nine inches of the delicate blade which each of them wore from earliest childhood in times of danger. When one reads of *samurai* women being taken prisoners, one may be fairly sure that there was a child to be protected, a husband to be saved; then they could throw themselves at the conqueror's feet, and win by their beauty, as Tokiwa won from Kiyomori, the pity which would have been refused to their misfortunes.

No *samurai* woman could live with the weight of an unavenged insult upon her. In the stories and plays which turn on the life of feudal times, we are shown women who call each other out to single combat in punishment of such a wrong, and no reproach of unwomanliness seems ever to have attached itself to them. I often wonder how the Japanese man really regards his womankind; how he did regard her in the old fighting days, when she was so constantly his second sword, as it were. The Japanese saying is, that a woman's spirit is her mirror, as the sword is the soul of a man. They have made a mirror the chief symbol of the State religion of Japan; and here, as elsewhere, every true woman must be something of a soldier at heart. Could a woman without warrior blood in her veins rouse her little boy in the black chill of a winter night, saying, "Yone, my son, the fencing has begun in the square! Join thy comrades, or they will outdo thee in the day of battle"? Not once, but again and again did the mother of one of my friends thus send him forth, shivering indeed with cold, but warm with emulation, to fight with his young comrades sham battles in the dark nights, and come home, bruised and sore perhaps, but with the generous blood coursing through his veins, and the sense of victory warming every nerve.

"A WOMAN'S SPIRIT IS HER MIRROR"

Ah! the sword is a great teacher, and strength is not earned in ease. The boys in all the schools of Japan are taught drill and musketry and sword practice as regularly and persistently as they are taught reading and writing. But, then, schools here are not prisons, not penal settlements; boys lose neither their morality, their courage, nor their self-respect by attending them. With us the schoolboy must be unmade before there is room for the gentleman or the soldier to appear. In Japan, education avowedly goes to the production of both, and from the time the child knows his own name clean ideals are set before him. Happy Japanese mothers! How quiet they must sleep of nights! The ideals of the race have not changed, and I hope they never will.

All courage, all calmness, all indifference to self — these were and are what *samurai* men and women have a right to expect of each other; and should the nation ever again be plunged in war, I fancy the *samurai* spirit will have much to do with carrying it through and over its difficulties. This spirit was curiously shown the other day. A very great friend of ours, Mr. Sannomiya,[1] of whom I have so often spoken to you, met with a serious accident. He and several others were posted along the sides of artificial canals, up which the Japanese beaters drive the wild duck for the guns. These canals are deep and narrow, having high green

"THE FENCING HAS BEGUN!"

[1] Now Baron Sannomiya.

banks on either side, with a bamboo fencing at the top, pierced here and there for the guns to pass through. The place will look utterly deserted, and yet be bristling with guns rendered quite invisible by these screens. Well, by some mistake poor Mr. Sannomiya received the whole of a charge of duckshot at precisely the distance when the charge had expanded enough to cover his whole per-

A SAMURAI LADY IMPLORING HER SON NOT TO COMMIT SUICIDE

son. He was very much hurt. The unwilling assailant was ready to commit suicide from despair; but this would not have helped poor Mr. Sannomiya, who was taken to the Red Cross Hospital in a very critical condition. His wife told me afterwards that the surgeons were anxious to administer chloroform before extracting the shots. They warned the patient that the operation would be painful in the extreme; but Mr. Sannomiya scoffed at the idea. "Who ever heard of a *samurai* taking chloroform?" he asked, and lay still while thirty-six pellets were cut out from his head alone. Very high fever and six weeks of painful convalescence in the Hospital followed — weeks during which he never uttered one complaint; and when I saw him at last, he looked like the ghost of his old cheerful self. With my usual brilliant tact, I managed to invite him and Marquis K——, his assailant, to dinner on the same day not very long afterwards. I only remembered the unfortunate combination too late to alter it, and I think that the *samurai* spirit was shown quite as much by the urbane kindness and gentleness of both the men that evening as it had been by poor Mr. Sannomiya's silent stoicism in the Hospital.

Madame Sannomiya is one of the ladies who have done most for the Red Cross Society here, of which the Empress is the President and the ruling spirit. We all belong to it, and have beautiful little medals, which we wear at the functions connected with the Hospital. Anybody who likes may become a member, and the meetings are crowded by a very representative gathering of the population. The first one to which I went was quite a revelation to me of the way in which the Empress has managed to draw the people to her. An immense enclosed hall in Uyeno is set aside for these meetings. For the avoidance of crushing, it is divided into sections, which run down both sides of its whole length, leaving a path up the middle. A high platform at one end is reserved for the Empress and the Imperial Princes and Princesses, and we have our places on benches at the side. The great space was so thickly packed with people that it seemed as if there would not be standing room for another pair of feet, and every class except the very poorest seemed to have furnished members. But I do not think it was entirely interest in the Hospital which had induced them to pay their little or big subscriptions; I think the crowd came (and only subscribers are admitted) in order to see the Empress stand on the daïs, and to hear her read the report of the year. The Empress, amidst a silence of intense excitement and respect, stepped forward with a paper in her hand, and in a clear voice read the report it contained. This was what was so truly amazing — the most modern thing I have yet seen in Japan!

After she had finished, those who were to be newly enrolled went up the steps of the daïs, and received their medals and diplomas from Prince Komatsu, who said a few words about the Empress's gratitude to all who helped this charitable scheme so dear to her. There was a great deal of bowing and band-playing, and then the Empress retired; and we went off to look at some sword-forging, or rather sword-damascening, which had been got up for one of the Princes in another building. I am afraid I do not know anything about blades; but I was immensely interested in the old sword-smith and his work. He and his two assistants were dressed in white ceremonious-looking costumes; a kind of white square tent had been erected over his ovens and bellows; and he kept up a running fire of orders to his assistants in a low voice during the whole process. The blades were handed to him one by one, when he drew on them a lovely design, apparently without forethought, in a black substance; the blade was heated white hot; and then, with tools which to me were nameless, it was welded and hardened, and fused in the fire and welded again, polished, cooled, and then handed up to the Prince's aide-de-camp, who showed it to his master. The result was most beautiful, and purely Japanese; but the Prince seemed indifferent, and barely glanced at the blade. The old man looked profoundly discouraged, and started on another at once, as if hoping to please him better the next time. I was very sorry for his disappointment. It was nothing to the descendant of a hundred generations of sword-smiths that we, ignorant foreigners, should admire his work; but that his own Imperial Prince, in his gorgeous military uniform, with a foreign sword at his side, should not care for the weapon of honour, "the soul of the *samurai*," that evidently cut very deep indeed.

I was speaking of service a little while ago, and of how the servant shares in the honour accorded to his master. All our servants belong to one clan; and I was warned on first coming to live here that it would be a mistake to introduce strangers, as they would be very badly received. I cannot quite make out who governs the politics of the clan; but I see that my *amah* and her husband are extremely powerful in it. Once or twice, when necessity has induced me to take some highly recommended servant from a friend, the experiment has always ended in the new servant's coming to me with extreme regret to announce that a grandmother in a distant province had been taken dangerously ill, and required the presence of all her relatives at once. Sympathy was received with silent respect, a small present of money, although perhaps much needed, somewhat unwillingly, because at that time I did not know that to give money not properly wrapped up in paper is all but an insult. Then the new servant would disappear, to return no more. Only one have I lost in a different way, and then I confess that my wrath was extreme; but it was a question of the internal government of the clan, and my poor little housemaid had to go — to Honolulu.

Her name was Toki, and she was a widow, with one little boy, about ten years old. She was very small and delicate-looking, with a fine oval face, high-bred features, and a beseeching gentle expression, as if life might be softened into treating her more kindly in the future than in the past. The women's work in the house is so very light that there was no hardship in the service. I found that even O'Matsu did not insist upon the attentions she usually claimed from Toki's predecessor, having set up a servant of her own, a nice little girl of twelve or thirteen, whom she bullied gloriously. Toki had been several months with us, and I had got quite accustomed to seeing the slight graceful figure shadowing my path, when one day Mrs. D—— came up to say that there was terrible trouble in the servants' quarters;

Toki was weeping bitterly, and said she must go away. Rinzo and O'Matsu had decided that she was to go away.

I bounded on my chair, and then Rinzo and O'Matsu were called and interrogated. They send Toki away? Never! They loved her as a daughter, and it was breaking their hearts that the dear girl insisted in the most headstrong manner on going to Honolulu, to marry a member of the clan who had lost his wife since he emigrated. But he was a good man, rich, chief cook to a foreign gentleman; doubtless Toki would be happy. Still, they would miss her very much, and were *so sorry* that she was going!

There is an omnivorous emigration agent for Hawaii here, who is, they say, highly paid for all the Japanese he can send across. I had never come into collision with him before; but if I could have laid my hand on him that day, he would have heard what the tracts call "a few plain words." I was certain that the most dreadful pressure was being brought to bear on my gentle little Toki, who was devoted to her son, and, in a minor way, to us. The next interview I had was with her. I told her that no power on earth should take her away if she wanted to stay; and that I was sure it was her duty to remain with her son. She cried bitterly, poor soul; but said that her kind relations had apprenticed her boy to a jeweller on the *Ginza* (the street of shops), who would certainly make his fortune; that it was her own unprompted wish to go to Honolulu to marry the rich man's cook whom she had never seen;

that Okusama was too kind, too much kind (oh dear! oh dear! and more floods of tears), but she would sail on the 17th.

And so she did. O'Matsu took her down to Yokohama, and was in black disgrace for a month afterwards, during which she too wept copiously over the missing of the headstrong Toki and Okusama's unkind suspicions. At last she had to be forgiven on account of her charming manners and her general usefulness. Then, with surprising regularity, I was told that Toki had written to say that she was very happy, to say that her husband gave her five meals a day all of the best rice, to say (by the next mail this) that she had a kind Japanese doctor and three large gold rings, to say, by the next mail again (O'Matsu forgot to state who wrote this letter), that — she was dead.

Sayonara, little Toki.

CHAPTER XXXIX

A TERRIBLE EARTHQUAKE. — THE DESTRUCTION OF A PROVINCE. — *KAKKE*, A STRANGE DISEASE. — JAPANESE TRAINED NURSES

November, 1891.

ON October 28th, early in the morning, we were roused by the most terrifying shock of earthquake that I have yet experienced. The disturbance took the dangerous form of violent vertical movement, accompanied by fearful rumblings and the crashing of stones. We were all asleep; but even in sleep that apprehension never leaves one, and before I was awake I had reached the door, and was trying to get out into the gallery. Sometimes the door gets jammed during an earthquake, and in any case it is not easy to open it when the floor is tossing like a ship at sea, and the roar and crash are so awful that you cannot hear the voice of a person standing at your elbow! As a rule the shock has a duration of from thirty to sixty seconds, and that feels like hours in the horror of dismay that it inspires; this first one of October 28th went on for seven minutes, and was followed by lesser ones for many hours. For all its terrors, it did only minor damage here; but in the south it has practically wiped out a large and thriving district, one which had always been considered exceptionally free from such visitations, and as yet the loss of life and property cannot even be estimated.

It had another most unusual quality of earthquake shocks: it had been predicted. On what grounds precisely it is impossible to say, but with confident certainty, at any rate. The last really severe earthquake (I am not speaking, of course, of volcanic eruptions, which are generally accompanied by shocks of more or less violence) took place in 1854; and it was prophesied that there would be another in thirty-seven years — a prophecy which has just been fulfilled. As, for twelve hundred years, there is no record of precisely that interval between one earthquake and another, it sounds like an arbitrary prediction. Thirty-seven is one of the Japanese mystic numbers; when that period after a death has elapsed, the survivors perform certain rites for the benefit of the dead — ornament their shrines and make offerings to them. And doubtless many of those who perished in that earthquake are being so remembered now. But this catastrophe has, I think, surpassed in horror all those remembered by living people. The centre of the disturbance was at Gifu and Nagoya. At this last place seven hundred shocks of earthquake were registered between October 28th and November 3rd. Professor Milne's beautiful seismographs were quite incompetent to register the strength of the shocks, which far surpassed anything that had been contemplated when the machines were invented. The description of the visitation at its centre is awful past belief.

Two towns and many villages are completely destroyed; railway lines are twisted like wire; huge bridges tossed into the air and snapped like matchwood, the stone pillars on which they stood being sliced smoothly through their whole diameter. Mountains have slipped from their foundations; a new lake has been formed; three hundred and fifty miles of river dykes injured — one half of this totally destroyed; a grove of bamboos was taken up and flung sixty feet from where it stood; the earth has opened in frightful fissures, and in some cases closed again over the houses and bodies it had swallowed. The lowest estimation puts the houses totally destroyed at 42,345, those partially ruined at 18,106. As for loss of life, that will never be known, I fear; every turn of the spade brings dead and dying to light, and many of the wounded were so frightfully hurt that it was impossible to save them. As all the telegraph communication and railway traffic was interrupted, it was not easy to bring assistance immediately to the sufferers, and the first doctors and nurses who got to them were on their feet for days and nights, and did more than seemed humanly possible to help the poor creatures. At Ogaki Hospital, two surgeons dressed the wounds of six hundred patients in forty-eight hours.

The misery and destruction were as usual enormously increased by the fires which at once broke out. What the earthquake left the fire devoured; and now, with the winter coming on, at least one hundred thousand people are without houses, without food, having

RESULTS OF THE EARTHQUAKE

lost their means of gaining a livelihood, and everything else in the world. Of course every kind of assistance is being given by the Emperor and the Empress, by the Government, by public subscriptions, and private individuals; nurses and doctors have flocked to the afflicted districts, and relief camps have been started, where allowances of food are dealt out; but with all that, the suffering is awful, the want all but impossible to satisfy. Here we do nothing but collect money and clothes, bandages and blankets; and the railway companies carry it all free of charge down to the scene of the trouble. I am glad to say the English trained nurse from St. Hilda's was sent down at once, with two Japanese nurses and a doctor, at the mission's expense, and have been doing good work among the sufferers, who are, every one says, perfectly patient and resigned. There has been no murmuring even at the misfortunes, and their patience and gentleness make it easy to organise and carry out the plans for their help. The excellent organisation of the Red Cross Society has shown itself now; and the indefatigable efforts of doctors and nurses have certainly allayed much suffering and saved many lives.

I hardly know Dr. Hashimoto, the director of the Red Cross Hospital. He is utterly devoted to his work, and never goes out; neither does his colleague, Dr. Takagi, of the Charity Hospital; but I have been brought more often into contact with him. He took me over the wards the first time I went there, and explained to me the evolution of that extraordinary

A RELIEF CAMP

disease *kakke*, which seems to be a purely Japanese ailment. The muscles of the legs become useless, without any symptoms of paralysis, and gradually waste away, leaving the limb cold and shrivelled. The disease attacks men, and hard-working men more than any other class of the community, and is frequent in districts where the people live on rice alone as their staple food. My *amah* tells me that in her province, where a kind of rough oatmeal is mixed with the food, the disease is almost unknown. The soldiers suffer from it a good deal; but it is hoped that the meat diet lately introduced in alternation with the native rice and fish food will do much to overcome the weakness. In the navy the men are generously fed on meat, rather to their own distaste, but very much to their physical well-being. I think I told you that Count Saigo, the Minister of Marine, is a firm believer in European food methods, and carries them out in his own family.

At Karuizawa, or rather about a mile away from the village, in a pretty gorge, is a little spring of warm mineral water which is supposed to be very beneficial to *kakke* patients; and numbers of soldiers from some military hospital used to be sent up to bathe there. They were lodged in the inn, and seemed to be under no especial control; but a milder, gentler set of fellows it would be impossible to find. They made friends with every child in the village; and as soon as they grew a little stronger would generally carry a baby friend about with them. They used to go off in bands of nine or ten at a time to the little tumble-down bath-house in the gorge; they were all dressed in a dark-blue *yucata*, with the number of their regiment worked on it in red, straw *waraji* on their feet, and nothing by any chance on their heads except the shock of bristling black hair which is induced by the constant practice of shaving the head in childhood. How often in our queer journeys I have seen the careful mother shaving her baby's head while he was asleep! The little one never stirred; and when the process was over, the mother would reach out for the small green mosquito net, supported on split bamboos, and put it down over the baby in a safe square, and then creep away to her household work. This shaving is very irritating to the poor infant's skin, and induces forms of eczema the most distressing and obstinate. The nuns have no end of trouble in this way with the children brought to them.

In going over the Charity Hospital, the University Hospital, or that of the Red Cross (chiefly devoted to accidents and surgical cases), one sees none of the anomalies that I have noticed in some of those conducted on more elementary lines. No infectious or contagious diseases are received in the wards devoted to ordinary patients; the nurses are admirably trained, and if wanting in initiative to meet a sudden responsibility, are at any rate religiously obedient to the doctors, and invariably kind to the patients. I have had many sieges of illness since I came (the climate is anything but favourable to the highly nervous organisation of the European woman); but I have been partly repaid for these by the delight and amusement of making the acquaintance of one who is now a real friend — my first Japanese trained nurse. I shall never forget the day when she first loomed on my astonished vision.

She was barely four feet high, her complexion was dark in the extreme, her feet were incased in white linen socks with divided toes, and shod with dainty straw sandals with green velvet straps. Her figure, the shape of a very soft feather pillow which has been hung up by one end for days, was draped in a tight-fitting white apron with a large bib, and she was kept inside her buttonless and stringless clothes by a cruelly tight and wide leather belt put on over apron and all. Into this belt, holding her breath for a long time first, she could, with a great effort, push her fat silver watch, her clinical thermometer, two or three yards of a Japanese letter (which she would read, a foot at a time, when she thought I was asleep), her carefully folded paper pocket-handkerchief, and the relentless little register in which she noted down, from right to left, strange cabalistic signs, with which she and the doctor conjured every morning till they knew all the sins my pulse and temperature had been committing for the last twenty-four hours. Her name was O'Tora San (Honourable Tiger Miss), but her ways were those of the softest and most harmless pussy that ever purred on a domestic hearthrug, and oh, what a nurse she was! So gentle, so smiling, so very delightfully sorry for one! It was quite worth being ill to revel in such seas of sympathy. I have often caught the tears running down her little brown nose when the poor Okusama was extra bad; and through long nights of pain has she stood by my bed, or sat on her heels on a corner of it, fanning me ceaselessly with the all but imperceptible flutter of the fan's edge — a movement only possible for those wonderfully sensitive Japanese fingers, but most refreshing to the fanned one.

When it was time for her to have her meals, my chief maid, O'Matsu, a dainty-looking princess of nature herself, would creep into the room, having shed her sandals at the door, and, after inquiring about my health, would make a deep and graceful obeisance to the Honourable Tiger Miss, and inform her in a respectful whisper that her honourable dinner was ready. The polite little Tiger would jump up, return the bow, ask my leave to depart, and slip out to feed on fish, pickles (such dreadfully strong-smelling pickles!), and rice, washed down, as they say in the Waverley Novels, by thimblefuls of green tea or fish soup. After about fifteen minutes of solid feeding she would return, come to my bedside, and express her gratitude for the meal supplied to her. Then she would drop down on her cushion in the corner, and with the calm unconventionality peculiar to her race let out a couple of holes in the leather belt. Another polite summons would be brought to her with more bows at about eight o'clock every evening, when the Japanese bath in the back yard had been heated to boiling-point. O'Tora San was always invited to take "first wash," before even No. 1 boy, *amah*, or chief cook. This was a great compliment, for the hierarchy downstairs took its bath according to rank with as much exactness and punctilio as if its members had been ambassadors being received at Court.

O'Tora San had the real nurse's gift for feeling the time, and waking at the right hour; and for eight days and nights I think she never failed to come to my bedside every two hours to replenish the ice-bags in which I lay. Once she had to go away for two days for some family reason, and was replaced by a dreadful person, who had never nursed in a European house before, who did not know a warming-pan from a smelling-bottle, and who further irritated me by reading endless Japanese newspapers printed backwards on pink paper. How glad I was when on the afternoon of the second day my little Tiger returned, smiling sweetly as usual, with an enormous sheaf of Japanese pinks in her hand, and looking so nice in her own soft grey silk *kimono* and sash, instead of the hideous hospital apron and leather belt.

A TRAINED NURSE

Many of the Japanese trained nurses have come under the influence of Canadian Methodist missionaries, and their phraseology is sometimes startling in the extreme. A colleague of my little Tiger was nursing a friend of mine, the wife of an American clergyman. O'Take San (Honourable Bamboo Miss) was rather pretty, and on being questioned admitted that she had been married — once. My friend became all sympathy, expecting to hear of early widowhood and a broken heart. She asked timidly what had become of the husband. She was electrified by the answer. "Wal" (O'Take San had an aggressive twang, acquired with much care), "I guessed he didn't love his Saviour 'nough, so I sent him right away. See?"

I will add here two little letters which I received from O'Tora San and a friend of hers, written to bid me farewell in the summer of the next year. The first is from O'Tora herself, and wonderfully well-spelt and written:

"TOKYO CHARITY HOSPITAL.

"MY HONOURABLE MADAM, — I have a great honour to get an opportunity to write you. I am very sorry that I could not meet you before you leave Japan. Indeed, I was always thinking to visit you; but as my body is not free as a nurse, I could not succeed my purpose. Once I had been at Yokohama as a nurse, my engagement was finished, and I returned Tokyo. Alas! you were not in Tokyo. Will there be no time to meet you again? If my thought goes so far as this point, I always burst into tears. Madam, permit my negligency. If I may have an honour to receive your letter, I shall be very much obliged of you, and will keep it as long as my life as the memory of yours."

O'Tora's friend, to whom I had been able to show some trifling kindness, wrote more than once to thank me. Indeed, one often feels very small at accepting the lasting and effusive gratitude with which little services or gifts are received. Her letter runs thus, and shows that she had come under missionary influence:

"MY HONOURABLE MADAM, — I have great honour to write you. . . . Miss Matsui (O'Tora San) told me that you were ill, so I was quite astonished, and tried to visit you; but, alas! you were then for Europe. I therefore have nothing for you but only to welcome you, again in Japan. I am sure that you will be again in our country. I am, madam, working at hospital, and for me nurse is suitable. For the glory of Almighty Father I am eagerly studying nursing. . . . Indeed, our hospital is just like some Christian school; Rev. Wada, pastor of Shiba Church, gives us important sermons every Saturday evening, and we are to attend Church every Sunday morning, and in the evening there are Bible lessons constructed for us. . . . My heart is filled with joy and thanks. . . . By God's mercy I am quite healthy and strong in spirit and body. Some day when I get leisure, if you return, I shall have an honour to visit and thank your kindness orally.

"I remain, dear Madam, always
"Your faithful servant,
"Sawa Tanaka."

CHAPTER XL

THE MARRIAGE OF PRINCE KANIN AND PRINCESS CHIYE SANJO. — THE WEDDING DINNER AND THE WEDDING CAKE. — THE STORY OF THE SUN-GODDESS. — BUDDHIST AND SHINTO NUNS. — AN IMPERIAL ABBESS

January, 1892.

THE end of the year was marked by the marriage of young Princess Sanjo (her name is Chiye) to Prince Kotohito Kanin, one of the Imperial Princes, who has spent some years in France studying naval matters. The wedding itself was conducted in private; but a great dinner was given in the evening at the Aoyama Palace, to which we all went. There were most of the Imperial Princes and Princesses, crowds of officials and colleagues, and the whole thing was rather brilliant. It was so funny to be solemnly presented anew to the little bride, and to make her the profound curtseys which the royalties here expect. I am afraid we both laughed; and when the ceremony was over, she made room for me on the sofa, and we had a good talk. She looked quite charming in her first white brocade, her first diamonds; and the little new airs of dignity sat very prettily on her, I thought. She never went to these solemn evening parties before, the Japanese not expecting girls to appear at them; and I should think it must have been rather an ordeal to have to receive such a number of people at once. All through the long dinner, the first she had ever attended, she was as gay and composed as if she had been doing nothing else all her life, and some of us remembered her wonderful fortitude and courage after the death of her father last year. Her mother has never quite recovered her strength since the blow; and Princess Chiye tells me that she has had a great deal to do for her four little sisters, who look to her for guidance as well as companionship, and who will miss her sorely now that she has been carried off to a palace of her own.

The young Prince, the bridegroom, might be taken as a typical representative of the old Japanese aristocracy. His slight figure, delicate and beautiful features, his tiny hands and feet, all make him one's ideal of the mediæval boy Emperor, kept from all contact with the rough realities of life, served, worshipped, and — irrevocably enslaved. But Prince Kanin is a free man, and his erect bearing, clear voice, and flashing eye show that there is nothing of weakness below the slight and boyish exterior. He is immensely interested in his own profession, and ambitious to see the Japanese navy put on the most efficient and splendid footing. His French is fluent and clear; and through the long wedding dinner, where I had the honour of being his neighbour, he talked well of many things, and thanked me for what he chose to call the kindness I had shown to the

PRINCE KOTOHITO KANIN

Princess in these past years. The dinner was long, but admirably well done, and the flowers, all carefully chosen as the lucky and joyous ones, most exquisite. In all the decorations the beloved pine branches, with little cranes and tortoises perched on them, were freely used; the wedding cake was an artistic presentment of Fuji San, pure white, with little pine trees and the lucky animals climbing round its base. After a great reception which followed the dinner was over, and the royalties had retired, I told the Prince's *grand maître* that in England a wedding cake was always cut up and distributed

THE PRINCE'S AUTOGRAPH

among the guests. This was evidently a new idea;
but it was at once adopted with enthusiasm. The *grand
maître* made the first incision, and then handed the
knife to me, as if uncertain whether I wanted half or
a quarter of the enormous thing to take home with me.
However, he was not long in doubt; and the moment I
had cut a tiny wedge, all the other women present came
and begged for a piece. Sheets of the pretty Court paper
were produced, and when I went away I carried off
a little pine tree, a white crane, and a green tortoise,
as well as the flowers and bonbon-box which I had
found at my place. The tortoise is a most enchanting
creation, with a great flat back, a beseeching waggly
head, and a long tail of pure green silk, which distinguishes him from all other tortoises as the only one
symbolic of riches. The pine is for happiness, the crane
for long life. I hope dear little Princess Chiye will
have both!

And now, in these winter days, what can I tell
you that you have not heard already? For this is
my third winter in Yedo, and I begin to fear that I
have related enough to weary you of all its ways and
customs. On the principle which used to make you
read the accounts of Arctic expeditions in our Roman
Junes, shall I tell you the story of the sun-goddess,

THE PRINCESS'S AUTOGRAPH

the mother of all Japan, to whom even our Emperor Mutsuhito in this year of grace 1892 traces his descent?

Do you remember the story of Izanami and Izanagi, in which the precedence of man was established for ever? The conditions seem to have been too hard for poor goddess Izanagi; for she soon afterwards died, and went down into Hades like any other woman. Izanami was heart-broken, and made up his mind to win her back; and he descended, shuddering, into the place of death. The presence of corruption was intolerable to the young god, who, unlike our Orpheus, turned and fled from the shadow-land without having found his wife; and when he reached the light again, sought but for one thing—water wherewith he could purify himself from the contaminations of the pit. So he ran gladly to a beautiful stream on a fair island, and quickly he stripped himself of his clothes and plunged into the water. But so great was his power and virtue, that even from his clothes and his staff, as he threw them on the ground, were born comely gods and goddesses; full-grown they came, and stood smiling and making reverence to their august father who was still sporting in the water like a heavenly fish. And from the water that washed his right eye was born the moon, the Lord of Night, and Izanami could hardly look at him for his white brightness, and he dashed the water over his left eye as he covered his face with his hands; and then suddenly the flood which had been cool against his bare limbs became warm, and he tried to open his eyes, and dared not, feeling that there was that without which would blind them. But at last he grew more courageous, and as he felt warmer and warmer he looked up, and saw a wonder: that which had been born from the washing of his left eye was the Fair Shining of Day, the sun-goddess Amaterasu. She was so beautiful, that, from her, beauty spread in waves on the world around. On the water she stood, with golden feet that pressed but sank not through the waves; her stature was very great, and her hands were shedding living gold-dust on the river and the sea and the mountains; and her hair stood out round her in a wheel of flame, whose points reached to heaven above, and to the edge of the world around her; and her breath was like fire of fragrant incense, so that wherever she turned her face flowers grew up in the land of the gods. But Izanami feared to be burnt, and once more plunged his face in the water in which he stood; and when he raised his face, drops fell from his nostrils, and became another god, the god of wind and tempest, of gentle breezes and of fearful storms, and his name is the Impetuous Susanōō. And he cooled the air with his breath, so that Izanami could look on the

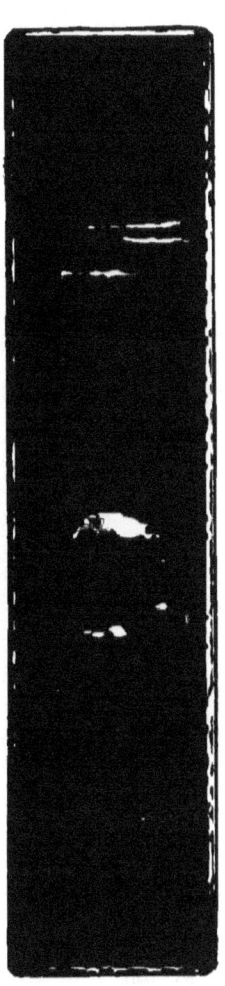

MOON PANEL (IN GOLD LACQUER)

sun-goddess unhurt; and Izanami cried, "Happy am I, with three such beautiful children — the Possessor of Night, the Impetuous Man, and Amaterasu, the goddess of the sun!"

But the Impetuous Man, Susanōō, liked it not that his sister Amaterasu should be greater and fairer than he; and he complained to his father Izanami, saying, "Thou for thine august self didst establish precedence over my august mother. How is it, then, that my sister, who is but a woman, should have all this glory?" And Izanami, who had forgotten the days of his youth, was very angry, and bade him depart from his presence for ever. And Susanōō departed, exceeding sore and angry; and went to pick a quarrel with his sister Amaterasu, not being minded to leave home without also leaving trouble behind him.

MOON AND MIST (GOLD LACQUER)

Amaterasu came out proudly to meet him, and they had a trial of strength, one standing on each bank of the river of milk. Amaterasu took Susanōō's sword, and bit it in three pieces, and ground the fragments with her teeth; and thereafter opened her mouth, and out came three beautiful women, with the sun on their faces, and cold, cold steel for their hearts. And Amaterasu said, "Behold the women of whom thou needest have no jealousy! Thou who art not worthy of sisters, I give thee slaves!"

And Susanōō the Impetuous said, "Better than that can I do! The sun-goddess can make slaves, but I, the storm-wind, make warriors!" And he tore the jewels from her neck and arms, and the jewels from her hair; and he ground them to dust in his sharp teeth, and then blew the dust out on the air; and it floated across the River of Peace, and fell on the farther shore at the feet of the sun-goddess, and rose up — five tall warrior-gods, great men of valour, fully armed with heavenly armour. And Amaterasu laughed, and said, "Well hast thou done, my brother! Slaves to thee, warriors to me!" And she car-

PRAYER BEADS, AMONG THE SACRED TREASURES OF ISÉ

ried away the five war-gods to her home; and Susanōō planned another revenge, seeing that she had shamed him again.

Now Amaterasu was in truth a wise goddess; and although she could battle valiantly if need be, yet she loved her woman's work best, and, after her quarrel with Susanōō, came home, and dropped her shining war garments, and crept into the great hall clad only in a trail of mist, and sat down meekly at her loom among her maidens, who were weaving silently long garments of rosy gold for the next day's dawn. And Amaterasu sat at her loom above the rest; its beams were pillars of stars, its shuttle a shooting star; and the warp she wove was blue and the woof was gold.

Then suddenly a great rending noise was heard, and Susanōō tore open the roof of the house; and before Amaterasu could spring from her place, he flung over her and her weaving a grisly covering, black and white and dropping gouts of blood, the skin of a piebald horse which he had flayed from tail to head. Wildly the maidens screamed, and ran from their places. Amaterasu fled from her weaving more swiftly than the shuttle threads the loom, and she ran and hid herself in a cave, and pulled a stone before the door. Then was the world in darkness, and reed-growing Japan became a kingdom of the night.

Terrible was the confusion that followed. All the powers of evil were let loose; and in the noise they made in their fancied triumph it was hard for the righteous gods to speak. But these gathered together in the bed of the River of Tranquillity, which runs through the plains of Heaven; and they talked long and earnestly, trying to discover a plan by which they could induce the sun-goddess to return and rescue the universe from the darkness in which it was plunged.

"Will she not come out, if we show her beautiful garments," said they, "and gems to take the place of those which Susanōō ground to powder?" So they planted mulberry trees, and made shining garments of their bark and hemp, and made inner garments for the goddess from the fibre; gems, too, they found, green and blue and white, and these they polished and made into necklaces and bracelets: but the goddess remained hidden, and would not come out. Then they built her a palace of heavenly architecture, and filled it with beautiful adornments, and called to her to come forth and behold it; but she would not. And the gods were in despair; for the world was still dark.

Then there came a god, small and old, but wondrous wise, and he is called the Thinker, for all thoughts that ever were in the world are in his heart first; and he laughed softly in his white beard at all the plans of the young gods. "Clumsy and halt are all your efforts," he said to them. "You say to her, 'Behold, here are jewels, and here is a palace; look, O Amaterasu!' Not so will the goddess heed you; little she cares for that she knows of. 'Tis that she knoweth not of, that she longs to know, which will draw her from her cave! I will teach you the ways of the August Female Deity!"

So the Thinker called Amatsumori, the blacksmith of the gods, and he caused him to hammer out a mirror; and this was the first mirror that was ever fashioned.

THE GOD WHO IS CALLED THE THINKER

Amatsumori made it out of iron that had fallen from Heaven; and he hammered and smelted and polished, and hammered and polished again, till he had made the mirror worthy to reflect the unbearable beauty of the sun-goddess.

And then the gods took all the gifts that they had made, and they hung the garments and jewels on a tree like a standard; and they carried the mirror also, and came to the door of the cave. Far to the north it lay, in a land of ice and darkness; and the door was closed with a huge grey stone. When they reached it, they made a great fire to warm themselves — for Amaterasu's going had left them cold — and then they began to sing and make merry, even as the Thinker commanded.

Music came from the strings of bows; a bamboo

grew up hollow to make a flute; and a little goddess called Uzumé, young and light of foot, began a joyous dance on a hollow drum, which gave back a note for every beat of her little feet. And as she danced she sang, a strange song with many meanings; and the fire crackled, and the bow-harp and the flute made music, and the gods burst into roars of laughter at Uzumé's wild song; and in the darkness of the cave Amaterasu was angry first, saying to herself, " Ah! they are glad now who grieved at my going. Who has taken my place, I wonder?" And she came very near to the door and listened, and could make nothing out of the uproar; and her woman's heart said, "I must know what it means — if I die for it!"

So, very gently, she pushed back the stone a little way, and immediately a beam from her face ran athwart half the heavens, and she saw that the gods were rejoicing greatly. Then she pushed the stone a little farther, and cried angrily, "How is it that you rejoice when I have left you? How can Uzumé dance and sing when darkness lies on Japan, and none can see his fellow in the land of reeds?"

"No darkness more," said Uzumé; "we have found a fairer goddess than thou! Behold!" And she held up the great mirror, wherein was reflected the beautiful face of Amaterasu herself, with her eyes like the midday, and her hair a wheel of white flame. And Amaterasu crept nearer, and came out of her cave to gaze on her own reflection; and as she did so the strong gods hung a straw rope before the entrance, the rope that none may pass.

So they persuaded her to remain among them, and to live in the palace they had prepared. And although she looks longingly at her cave sometimes, and even goes near the entrance for a few short days, when she sees the straw rope she remembers all her brother- and sister-gods who loved her so much, she remembers all the generations of her children in the land of reeds, and she turns back and smiles on them once more, unwilling to leave them comfortless.

And in time Amaterasu came to love reed-growing Japan more than all the plains of Heaven. And when there was a question as to which of the heavenly deities should go down to rule its people, Amaterasu would have sent her own son; but he said, "Nay, I will abide with thee; let us send my son, Ninigi, thy august grandchild." And to Ninigi Amaterasu gave the three sacred things — the mirror of the heavenly reflection which had lured her from the cave, the holy sword, and the sacred jewel, telling him to keep them for ever; and as to the mirror, she said, "Hold this sacred, for it is my spirit. In thy house and close to thee let it dwell; worship it as thou wouldst worship me."

Ninigi obeyed; and so did his grandson, the great Jimmu Tenno, the founder of the present dynasty, which has reigned, according to Japanese chronology, for over two thousand years. But one of the Emperors in the year 92 B.C. thought that the time had come to house the sacred treasures in a palace of their own, and he built the first of the shrines of Yamada in Isé, where they have been kept ever since. The sanctuaries of Isé (it is the name of the province) are built in the purest Shinto style, of plain woods, with the fewest possible adornments; they are not allowed to stand more than twenty years, and are always renewed after exactly the same pattern in every detail. One set of buildings is prepared just before the expiration of the period, and the sacred emblems in their centuple coverings are removed with tremendous pomp from the old to the new temple, the old then being broken up and sold or given away in minute particles as charms. The Government have been bringing out a work on Isé, with most perfect coloured engravings of the relics kept there.[1] The mirror is considered too sacred to be looked at, and has, it is said, not been beheld by mortal eyes for many centuries; a new cover of rich silk is always put over the old one when this begins to wear out. The Government publication has superb engravings of ancient swords, musical instruments, prayer-beads, and stuffs; the "jewels"[2] so constantly spoken of are fragments of polished stone of great brilliancy, shaped very like a human ear, and pierced with a hole as if to hang on a string. The shape is constantly reproduced in ornamental designs, and to my mind resembles one of the "eight fairies" or sacred signs of China. The resemblance is probably fortuitous, as Shinto, the Way of the Gods, is not supposed to have borrowed its

[1] I have all that has appeared of the work; but it has now been stopped, having proved fearfully costly.

[2] A good example of these jewels is given in the smaller pendants of the necklace shown in the illustration on p. 347.

emblems thence, and has had many a fight to preserve and recover its own from the encroachments of Buddhism. In many places the two faiths have been welded into one, so dear and familiar to the people that no "purification" can dissociate them in the popular mind. But the Isé shrines are devoted to the pure Shinto worship; and are, according to their own priests' account, precisely the same in their simple form and short ceremonial as they were two thousand years ago.

For many centuries, I believe, a Princess of the Imperial family was always the High-priestess of Isé living as a nun, and devoting herself to the care of the sacred regalia and the worship of the sun-goddess.

This brings me to the subject of nuns, both Buddhist and Shinto, who have interested me greatly, when from time to time I have come across dear old ladies with shining shaven heads going in and out of the temples. These are, I fancy, merely widows, who have vowed not to marry again, and who spend most of their time in praying for their dead. There are two kinds of Buddhist nuns, called the Professional and the Unprofessional. The Unprofessional nuns are (and were always) the widows of men of a certain position and standing. They do not, as a rule, leave their homes; but having vowed not to marry again, they remain faithful to the vow, and devote all that is left of life to prayer before the family shrine, or *butsudan*. Here the mortuary tablet of the dead man is set up, and before it the widow makes the daily offerings of food in the small and severely plain vessels set apart for such a use. Flowers may be placed there too, and incense-sticks alight, whose fragrance will be a solace to the spirit, which in a true yet unexplained manner is believed to be in the Meido, the land of shadows, and yet in the home at the same time. The worshipper calls to it by ringing a little bell, just as in the temples those who would pray first clap their hands, to ask the god to look and listen, as my poor Ogita used to say. In the old feudal days of Japan the wife and concubines of the Shogun or any other Daimyo were obliged to become nuns after their husband's death; the wife would keep her old place in the house, but the concubines lived in another building together, all their needs being supplied from the chief house. Both wife and concubines were expected to spend most of their time in praying for the dead. You remember that that masterful lady Masako became a nun after the death of Yoritomo.

The Professional nuns live very strict lives. Besides the vow of chastity, they promise lifelong abstinence from flesh meat of any kind; and they are obliged to assist in serving in the temple both morning and evening. Great misfortunes and reverses would often send the daughters of the family into the convent in past times; where leprosy was hereditary the daughters always became nuns; and sometimes the death of a betrothed lover would drive a heart-broken girl to the refuge of the kindly convent, where she would never be troubled by the addresses of any other suitor.

There are now, I am told, very few temples which have nunneries attached to them. One of these, however, is at Zenkoji, not far from our summer house in Karuizawa. It was established in very early times, and the present abbess is a beautiful woman belonging to a noble family in Kyoto. She is always gorgeously robed in royal purple. Very different are the poorer Professional nuns, whom one sometimes sees about the streets, dressed in long black gowns, their faces completely hidden by their enormous hats, and ringing a little bell, which is an appeal for alms.

But for the bell they are extraordinarily like the poor Franciscans who have an orphanage at Sorrento, and whom I have so often seen going round in their great straw hats and dark robes, generally with two or three small girls carrying the bundles of food which had been bestowed on them. Dear old things! I could have embraced the Japanese recluses for their sake!

CHAPTER XLI

A VISIT TO THE MUSEUM. — AN ANCIENT CAR. — MY GUIDE.
— CHRISTIAN RELICS. — PERSECUTORS AND PERSECUTED.
— AN HOUR IN THE ART SCHOOL AMONG THE LACQUER-
WORKERS

April, 1892.

SPRING is, after all, Japan's loveliest season, when the country smiles and weeps, pales and flushes, like a maid decked for her bridal. I have seen it three times now, and yet it comes as a long-expected joy, eagerly watched and waited for. Everything seems lovelier than usual this year; and though my heart has made a thousand journeys over the westward water, and Europe is drawing me with irresistible compulsion, yet it saddens me to think that I shall not see the cherries bloom next year, nor the wistaria arbour flush from grey to purple, sink back from purple to green. I shall not write many letters after this, and I am wondering which, of all sights and scenes yet undescribed, you would rather hear of on this soft spring day.

Did I ever tell you of my delightful visit to the Uyeno Museum and the School of Art, under the guidance of the director, Mr. Okakura? It always seems to me that, if I see things at all, I have the good fortune to see them in the most charming way. The Uyeno Museum is a store-house of art treasures and historical memories, and to have the delightful and learned director for my companion there was a great joy. It was one morning in the beginning of April that I drove up through the flowery avenues to the great building where he was waiting for me. From

CHERRY TREES ON THE SUMIDA RIVER

the brilliant sunshine and the waves of cherry blossom that seemed breaking like foam through the dark branches of the pines, we passed to the twilight dignities of the great halls, where all the legacies of the past — weapons of war and robes of gold, lutes and fans, swords and drinking-cups, embroideries and lacquer and enamel, all the discarded pomps of a splendour-loving people — are gathered and set, line by line, case by case, as if for burial. There is something strangely like death in the still untroubled air of such places — air so separate, in its irrevocable calm, from all the joyous pulsing of the live world in the sunshine without, so sealed and set apart from the vibrating existence of to-day, that I almost doubt if the ghosts (Japan is full of ghosts) of those who made these things, and who doubtless hang round them still, would acknowledge a descendant, a compatriot, in the modern Japanese, the man of science, who took me past them, and told me in quiet, somewhat scornful tones of their histories and values.

My guide, who is perhaps the greatest existing authority on these subjects, was dressed in his own dignified costume, and seemed outwardly in harmony with the Japan of the past. He has large brilliant eyes, and a low clear voice; his English is fluent and complete. He rather laughed at my delight over the first object that met my view, a magnificent bullock-cart, which used to be the Imperial travelling carriage. It is as large as a small room, with heavy wheels, that must have turned with august slowness over the august roads; time could have been of no value to the august travellers then. Heavy beams of the most splendid black-and-gold lacquer support a four-square tent of lacquer and carving, with jealous curtains, heavily tasselled with silk, closing the openings of the front and sides. Very long poles run out, also in lacquer; and these were attached to stout white bullocks, who advanced, step by step, their hoofs weighted with the pride of drawing the Son of Heaven, who, sitting in his gilded shrine, and passing through his fair domains, must have found it very easy to believe that he had the makings of a deity in him, at all events.

Not always was it an Emperor. Sometimes the car was surmounted by a golden phœnix, and then the brown men and women in the rice-fields of "reed-growing Japan" knew that their Empress was passing by. I have a print, a Japanese print of the last century, full of figures in trails of purple and rose, and pale carmine and primrose gold. The colouring is that of the iris gardens of Hori Kiri, when the sun is setting softly behind the translucent, silky-bannered ranks, shining here purple, there white, there gold or copper, as the flowers grow. And in the crowd of lovely figures there are movements and swayings so like the iris shapes that in my mind I call it the iris picture. Now the central thing in my picture is the Imperial bullock-cart, exactly as I found it in the Museum. The beautiful shape, graceful for all its square strength and roominess, is hung with curtains of delicate blinds, each held in place by a great tie of silk; its poles have that splendid curve of strength as if of themselves they had leapt forward in the royal service. In my picture the phœnix does not crown the roof; and there are no bullocks, but a crowd of lovely maidens, gathering close round their Empress, who has descended to the ground. So many are they, so eager to serve her, that I think they must have been trying to draw the cart themselves; but if so, it had been too much for their slender strength, so now the Empress stands in the midst of them, still between the

"THE EMPRESS . . . STANDS IN THE MIDST OF THEM"

shafts, her wonderful drapery blown a little about by
a rebel wind, her beautiful face with a sad little smile
bent down on her breast, where her two hands are
trying to hold her splendid robes together. You can
see her figure swaying to the wind. And the girls,
in draperies scarcely less splendid, have taken each
some part of her princely baggage: one a crown on a
cushion, one a *jui*, or fairy sceptre, one her bow, one
her arrows; others carry musical instruments, some hold
the shafts; and past them all the rebel wind is sweeping,
playing with streamer and gown, and causing the heads
to bend for fear that the wonderful wings and coils of
hair should be set straying by its force; and to it they
all oppose the yielding strength of the iris. Their faces
are far paler than their robes, and in my picture even
these are fading now, so I know that they are long
dead; doubtless the wind had its way in the iris garden.

And my guide wondered that I cared to stand so
long looking at the old bullock-cart!

Well, at last we went on, and he led me through
hall after hall of strange things: prehistoric were many
of them, arrow-heads and knives, and spear-heads in
stone — the things on which humanity seems to have,
so to speak, cut its teeth simultaneously all over the
world; strings of those strange "jewels" the *maga-
tama*,. stones curved like an ear, and the *kuda-tama*,
like straight tubes, worn as ornaments once, and then
coming to be regarded as talismans and holy things.
Only in one part of the Emperor's dominions does their
use still survive — in the Loo-Choo Islands, where many

a grim old custom is carried on to this day. Of all living races that I know of, the Loo-Chooans are the only people who have the courage to face the worst horrors of corruption in their care of the dead. These are laid away in caves, and for five dreadful years it is considered the duty of the living once a year to take them from the kindly shroud of the darkness, bring them to the light and wash the poor remains, then wrap them again in their coverings, and lay them by. After five years the body is supposed to be sufficiently reduced to be put in boxes and placed in the household shrines. The Japanese Government have repeatedly forbidden the practice, but find that it is still carried out by stealth, to the great danger of the population after any epidemic. I had a curious glimpse of some Loo-Choo people last year, which I will record here, as I think I did not tell you of it at the time.

I had taken a huge party of children and young people to — switchback in Uyeno Park! Yes, a splendid switchback was set up under Iyeyasu's pines, and was much patronised by the Japanese. Well, just as my English boys and girls tumbled out on the platform after their third ride, a grave party of Loo-Chooans came and paid their fee. They were (as we found out) well-to-do merchants, who had made up their minds to see the wonders of the capital. The party consisted of two middle-aged men, one youth, and a most reverend senior, an old man with a beautiful white beard, erect head, and piercing dark eyes. All the men had larger eyes and smoother, darker skins than the true Japanese, and much of the gentle look of the Malayans. In their dress a dark-purple colour predominated, and there were some slight variations from the ordinary Japanese cos-

A DAIMYO'S MEDICINE-BOX
IN LACQUER (BACK)

A MEDICINE-BOX (FRONT)

tume, but not enough to attract attention. All my gay young people stood aside to let the strangers have their turn, and these took their places with a solemnity evidently mingled with awe. The old man sat down on a front seat, and spread his robes in geometrical lines over his knees, joined his hands as if in prayer, and looked straight before him. The younger men got in, and off they went at a breakneck pace. The youth clutched the seat, and screamed; the middle-aged men clutched the seat, and were silent. The old man came back precisely as he had gone; his beard was nearly blown off his face, and his garments were all over the place, but he had never turned his head or ceased to look solemnly before him, and his hands were folded as if in prayer. My young people made an entreaty through our interpreter that he would go again. The sight was entrancing to their young imaginations. No, thank you. It was all doubtless most clever and beautiful; but the gods had been kind. Let us not presume on their favours. Good-bye.

I left you in the Uyeno Museum, you say? Did I? Well, the switchback is only just outside!

> "C'est bien de moi! Quand je chevauche
> L'hyppogriffe au pays du bleu,
> Mon âme sans corps se débauche,
> Et s'en va comme il plaît à Dieu!"

You must take my stories as they come, or not at all!

Yes, I saw many things that day. Are not the lists of them in the helpful pages of Murray, written by two of my great friends? The director asked me if we cultivate the nose in Europe. I turned my profile to him with just pride; but that was not what he meant. The art of smell has been brought to its perfection here; and I was shown little bronze burners in which one, two, three — a dozen different kinds of aromatic stuff can be burnt at once, the puzzled guests being required to name every ingredient used. At one time these perfume parties were very popular, and Mr. Okakura told me that he knew people who could detect each and every perfume of any combination, there being over fifty kinds of incense in all.

A GOLD LACQUERED CASKET OF THE EARLIEST PERIOD

Then I stood for long by the relics of the Japanese embassy to Rome, when the great Daimyo of Sendai, Date Masamune, sent one of his nobles with a huge train of followers to acknowledge the supremacy of the Pope, and to ask for his prayers and assistance. There is an oil-painting of the ambassador, in early seventeenth-century costume, praying with folded hands before a crucifix; in a case are various objects of devotion — rosaries, crucifixes, and so on; and close by are the horrible blocks of metal, generally stamped with a crucifix, which in the persecutions were laid down before the feet of those suspected to be Christians — they must walk over these or die. How many thousands refused, how many pure souls left their martyred bodies to their enemies, how many delicate women and little children kept their faith and lost their lives, we can hardly tell. Christianity was stamped out as a national religion; but I think the martyrs prayed for their beloved country, cruel as it had been to them. And a little germ was kept alive. Nearly thirty years ago, some missionaries landing near Nagasaki found whole villages hidden away in the hills by the sea, where the old prayers were still said just as they had been learnt two centuries before, where baptism was administered and marriages and burials prayed over faithfully, although never a priest had set foot there since their first pastors had been killed. The poor people's joy was overwhelming; but even at such a recent date persecution found them out again. They were exiled, and dispersed for a time. But only for a time. Universal toleration was proclaimed in 1873, and on the twenty-fifth anniversary of their discovery, after my arrival in Japan, the Catholic Bishops and their priests went in state to celebrate a great religious festival among these faithful people. A friend of mine who accompanied them told me that nothing could be more entire or beautiful than the faith then shown. The people came flocking on foot over the hills, whole fleets of boats covered the sea, and the good souls wept for joy, crowding round the Bishop to touch his hands, his robes, his feet.

Let us forget the persecutors: has not every nation numbered such at some moment of her history? I like to remember that all those faithful martyrs were Japanese; that in their sweetness and constancy "le Bon Dieu a fait des siennes," as an old nun said to me one day; and that everywhere in the island empire we may feel that we are surrounded by true hearts and brave spirits, loyal to the best that has been revealed to them. As far as Christianity is concerned, the revelation goes, step by step, with the lives led by Christians here; and when I hear of hatreds and jealousies and pitiful scandals, I do mourn almost more for the good retarded than for the evil done. Evil in its nature is passing, and the insult to the majesty of God will find its reparation in the sacred heart of His Son; but the good retarded? Ah! that is a different matter! So many lovely actions and humble prayers and glad thanksgivings robbed from the heavenly treasury, just because — Christian men and women, with grace to draw on and truth to look at, and God's right hand to lead them in the sight of men and angels in this poor old nineteenth century, will *not* lead Christian lives!

Ah! I am preaching again! Let us get back to business.

We finished the morning in Mr. Okakura's especial domain, the Art School, situated in the same grounds,

A HAPPY FAMILY

and not very far from the Museum. Here students were carving, painting, drawing; and many a bright face was turned upon us as we passed from room to room. That which interested me most was the making of lacquer — a long and complicated process, which I had never beheld before. In little rooms the men sat one or at most two working together, in just the silent, patient way which seems fitting for the production of that marvellous material. From the first handling of a thin bit of wood to the point where decoration pure and simple may begin, thirty-seven separate processes must be gone through. A very fine and thoroughly seasoned wood is used for the foundation; the first applications of lacquer are rubbed away again and again; a fine textile substance is spread on the surface, layer on layer, as one by one absorbs the rare varnish; then these are polished again, each drying being effected slowly in moist darkness; then, in fine red lacquer, comes a layer of gold-dust, laid on thick and moist, and entirely covered again by that gorgeous scarlet, its only use being to make the red richer and deeper; and at last, after weeks and months of preparation, the decorative work comes, a marvel of richness, bird and beast and flower in raised gold, where every modelling is clear and effective, yet the whole smooth to the touch as the inner walls of a sea-worn shell. It is almost indestructible: you can fill your bowl with boiling spirits, you can drown it for years in the salt sea (I have seen beautiful old specimens of lacquer recovered from wrecks), and it will always return to you, whole and smooth and golden as on the day it first saw the light.

When it became necessary for me to tear myself away from the lacquer studios, the chief artist, Fukumatsu, who, Mr. Okakura told me, is considered the greatest living worker in lacquer, had a long conversation with the director, and I was told that he wished me to have a little specimen of his work, which he would make for me from the very beginning, allowing no one else to touch it even in the preparatory stages. It should be something with my *mon*, or crest, upon it, and he came down to the carriage to have a look at the "stag's head proper erased" on the panel. That, however, did not strike him as artistic, and I was asked whether some other presentment of a stag would do as well. Any other animal would do as well, I thought, in Mr. Fukumatsu's inspired fingers; and after thanking him for his kind thought, I said farewell to the director and his lacquer magicians. Life was very full just then; and though I did not forget my visit to the school, Mr. Fukumatsu's benevolent intentions went clean out of my head.

Six weeks later a packet was brought me, wrapped in covering after covering of soft yellow silk. When these were shed away, a tiny black box lay in my hand, decorated with a golden stag — a thing so fine and perfect that it might be worn as a gem. The inner surface (the whole thing is barely an inch and a half across) is a tangle of golden weeds on a powdered goldstone ground, and the two halves fit together so that you can hardly see where they close. A letter from Mr. Okakura accompanied the charming gift, asking me to keep it in remembrance of my visit, and saying that Fukumatsu had begun it on that day and had just finished it now. It will be one of my pet treasures, the materialisation of a most pleasant memory.

CHAPTER XLII

THE EMPEROR'S SILVER WEDDING. — A TYPICAL GATHERING.
— NŌ DANCING. — THE CURTAIN FALLS

Tokyo, *April*, 1894.

TWO years have passed since I wrote my last letter from home to home — years in which all the old threads have been taken up and strengthened and renewed; and now I am once more in this half-way house of the world, whence a step to east or west brings me nearer to Europe. I do not think I have really been so far from Japan that I did not sometimes see the cherry blossoms drifting on the wind, did not sometimes hear the scream of the wild goose through the winter sky and the long roll of the surf thundering up on the Atami beaches. Whatever life brings or takes away — and I came with a heavy heart to this other home of my love, as if life or death, I knew not which, were chanting some final dirge in my ears with every break of the sea against the ship's side — whatever comes, Japan will always be my second home. One cannot explain these things. I have lived in many countries, north and south and east and west, and, except in the Rome of our childhood, in none have I found the spirit of beauty, the spirit of peace, the skirts of Nature's robe ever at hand to cling to, as I have here, "east of the sun, west of the moon," in the land of the gods, reed-growing Japan.

Fuji smiled on me as of old beyond my bower of cherry blossom to-day; the garden has gone mad with some jubilee of growth, throwing out thousands of gorgeous roses even so early as this, before the azaleas have done flaming over their fairy hillocks; every palm tree in house and garden is going to flower this year; the bamboos are all a-feather with new shoots; the great wistaria arbour is a dream; and I have a crimson carpet spread under the translucent green and purple, and sit there whole days just watching things grow, and seeming to hear the sap bubbling up to intoxicate the world with beauty.

There have been some splendid Court functions to celebrate the silver wedding of the Emperor and the Empress. The anniversary fell on March 9th, just after our arrival, and for many days we lived in a kind of pageant of pomp and colour. I shall never forget the *nō* dancing at the Palace; but I had better tell you the story from the beginning, if I can.

On the morning of the 9th there was a great reception at the Palace, which, from entrance to audience-chamber, was full of the most beautiful flowers. We mustered in force; and when it was our turn to go in and congratulate the sovereigns, H—— and I led quite an imposing staff up to the steps where they stood. Of late I have been the only woman in the party, and it was delightful to have dear Mrs. L—— with me this time, looking quite charming in her mauve-and-silver Court gown. I had found a brocade all over strawberries, and in spite of H——'s sarcastic quotation, "Ce n'est plus la mode de s'asseoir sur son blason" wore it bravely. We were received in a small drawing-room, as we usually are for a private audience.

The Empress was wearing such a mass of diamonds that you could hardly see what her dress was made of. Everything was white, and in the brilliant sunshine that glowed on white jewels, white satin, white flowers, I remembered my first real sight of Fuji, with the blaze of the winter midday lying white on its dazzling snows. The Empress's fine little face was as white as all the rest; but her dark eyes shone very happily under her diamond crown, and there was quite a ring in her voice as she answered all our pretty speeches; indeed, she talked more gaily than I have ever heard her do before. The Queen's message arrived just an hour before we started for the Palace, and we were profoundly thankful that it came in time for H—— to deliver it

THE GRAND MASTER OF CEREMONIES

at the audience. The Emperor looked like a piece of the sun himself in his brilliant uniform and splendid decorations; and he, too, had for once laid aside the cold calmness of his usual manner, and laughed and talked as if he were in the best of spirits. After the stock phrases had been exchanged, he told me that he heard I had brought a wonderful dog from England (a new Dachs, who took command of Tip and all the rest the day he arrived); and I felt cold for a minute, fearing that politeness would require me to place Tôney Bones at his Majesty's disposal. But — I did not!

There was a review in the afternoon; but I did not go to that, preferring to reserve my strength for the evening, which promised to be long and interesting. The Emperor and Empress, by the way, began their day with a religious service in their private chapel two hours before they received us. The Emperor's taste in religion, as in other things, is for extreme simplicity; and the chapel, which I regret not to have seen, is of course pure Shinto, containing the *ihai*, or mortuary tablets, of his Majesty's ancestors. All the Imperial family and the chief dignitaries of the empire assisted this morning at the service, prayers being offered in turn, and incense burnt before the *ihai*. All the day had gone in giving audiences and reviewing troops, and I thought their Majesties had a right to be very tired, when the time came for the evening's entertainment to begin.

It consisted first of a dinner, given to eight hundred people in different banqueting-halls of the Palace, the

Imperial Princes acting as hosts for the Emperor, who presided at the table in the great dining-room, where two hundred guests were accommodated. I had been through the room again and again, and had often wondered how it would look filled with people and lights and flowers. So I saw it now, lighted from end to end with soft shining candles (no electric light has been used in the Palace since the burning of the Houses of Parliament), lined with flowers, the long table which ran round three sides of the room just one line of light and silver and hothouse blooms. The seats for the Emperor and Empress were tall gilt armchairs, and behind them the wall ran back in an alcove, a reminiscence of the *tokonoma*, the alcove of honour in the chief room of a Japanese house. This was a bower of flowers, and in the midst of them were set two quaint little figures of a very old man and a very old woman, the Darby and Joan of Japanese legend, who, though humble (they are always represented in poor clothes, and carrying implements of work — the old man a spade, the old woman a broom), lived in the greatest contentment and happiness to extreme old age, never having quarrelled in

COUNT INOUYE

MARQUIS SAIGO

their lives. I have often seen the quaint figures, with their smiling, wrinkled faces and snow-white hair, at lowly festivals and in poor people's homes. There was something rather touching about finding them here, put up as the types and patrons of married happiness, in the midst of all the pomp and magnificence of the Imperial feast.

Just opposite the sovereigns' places, the silver ornaments took the shape of sculptured cranes, each over four feet high, with silver pine trees beside them, and great silver tortoises at their feet. These were presents to the Emperor from some of the Princes of the Imperial family. The work was lovely, and they made a beautiful effect, rising out of the sea of flowers and silver and gleaming glass. Beside the plate of every guest stood a miniature crane, with a tortoise at his feet, exquisitely worked in silver and enamel, forming the cover to a casket of bonbons. These were the Emperor's gifts to his guests, and certainly mine is a curio that I should be sorry to part with. The dinner was admirably served — no small triumph when you remember that European methods, with all that they entail of utensils, glass, porcelain, silver, and linen, do not enter into the daily life of the Palace at all. The service was perfect — a footman to every two guests; and all this crowd of men did not get in each other's way, attended quietly to one's wants, and made, in their dark liveries of crimson and black and gold, an effective background to the long rows of guests, where the women were almost all in white, relieved with gold or silver and covered with jewels, the men with hardly an exception in all the glory of smart uniforms. Only the chiefs of missions and their wives had been asked to the dinner, and there were but four of the latter, so my place was very near the Emperor and Empress; and I had quite enough to keep me good and amused while the feast lasted. There

SILVER WEDDING MEDAL

were people present that night who rarely show themselves in public: old pretenders to the throne; old leaders of rebellions; fierce fighters, the story of whose feats would make one's blood run cold but for the hot white fire of heroism that lights them up. How strange it was to sit opposite to these men here in the Palace; to watch the calm dark faces veiled by that mantle of cold suavity

SILVER WEDDING MEDAL

more impenetrable than an iron mask; to listen to the quiet small talk of an official feast; to watch the decorations rise and fall on breasts that were heaving to madness with the lust of war or the pride of race or the desire of revenge only a few years ago! Tokugawa, Mori, Iwakura, Kido, Saigo, the brother of the Satsuma leader, Kawamura, who so tenderly washed the beloved

COUNT OKUMA

rebel's head while the brother wept over it — name after name down the long table spoke of that recent history of the country which to-day's Japan has left a thousand years behind. Here are some of their portraits; for these typical countenances will bring the guests more clearly before you than any words of mine. All the heads bowed one way, all the glasses were lifted with a gesture of devout, passionate loyalty, when the Emperor's health was drunk; and the Emperor, sitting there, not talking much, but smiling kindly on all within his vision, must, I think, have felt warm at heart with the conviction that at last he has prevailed; he has carried out the dream which worked in his restless brain in the many splendours of Kyoto, in the long fight against bonds which had grown with the growth of centuries, which burnt into his spirit all through his boyhood, till he risked all to snap them, and — prevailed. He rules alone to-day, in spite, perhaps because, of all that he has granted in reforms, in public freedom, in representative government, and individual liberty. I do not believe there is a man of any party in Japan who would not be glad and proud to lay down his life for his Emperor. If a war should come, Japan's armies will gather of themselves from every home in the empire.

But I must not talk of war now, for the silver wedding was a festival of peace. When dinner was over, the Emperor and Empress held a kind of *cercle* in one of the drawing-rooms, where all the vases and wreaths of flowers had swarms of silver butterflies hanging over them. There was a little pleasant talk, and then we all went to the throne-room, where the *nō*, the ceremonious dance, was to be performed.

Here we found a crowd of people, all the other guests indeed, waiting for the sovereigns' arrival. The room itself had been a good deal altered, and I hardly recognised the five hundred square yards of polished parquet over which I have had to skate with slow dignity on various occasions. The throne, which is usually here, had been removed, and a high daïs had been erected, where two *fauteuils* were placed for the Emperor and Empress, with seats below on either side for the Cabinet Ministers and for the Foreign Representatives, running a little way down the two sides of the room; but close to the throne

BARON ITO

behind were seats for the Imperial Princes and Princesses and for the Empress's ladies. They looked charming, all massed together in their shining dresses and jewels under the lights. The Empress was wearing a still more gorgeous gown than she had on in the morning — a cloth of silver with a design of phœnix plumes in the brocade, I think. She looked very white and fragile against the dark silk hangings behind her chair, a little wraith of royalty, wrapped in trails of misty silver, the long gleams breaking from the diamond stars in her crown as from the edge of a sword whirled in the sun.

The place was already crowded, and the moment we had found our seats some curtains which hung over the glass screen at the farther end were drawn back, musicians came in, made a low obeisance to the sovereigns, and crept to their places at the back of a low square platform, which, covered with green cloth, occupied the centre of the room. It was only slightly raised above the floor, and was well below the daïs on which the Emperor and Empress sat.

And then the *nō* began. Here is a translation of my programme card:

"THE 9TH DAY OF THE 3RD MONTH OF THE 27TH YEAR OF MEIJI

BANZAÏRAKU

Music composed, 1300 years ago, by the Emperor Yomei. It represents the joyous flight of a Bird of Paradise in the Golden Age.

Enguiraku

Music composed, 987 years ago, by Fujiwara Tadafusa, General of the Life Guards. The accompanying dance was composed by Prince Atsumi.

Taïheiraku

Music rearranged, from the Chinese original, 1037 years ago. It represents the idea of the establishment of peace by the regulation of every disorder or discrepancy.

Baïro

Music from India, transmitted to Japan, 1160 years ago, in the reign of the Emperor Shiomu. It is also called Baïro-Hajinraku, and represents the idea of the submission of enemies."

Such is the programme, indeed; but how can I describe to you the extraordinary scenes and sounds to which these few bald sentences and unintelligible names introduced us? The first effect of the low, grinding music, with its threatening drum effects and stormy cries, was painful; a feeling of tension, anxiety, unnaturalness, took possession of me, and I wanted to get up and move about, to do anything that was absolutely impossible; but when the Bird of Paradise came floating over the floor, with golden wings and flowing draperies and outspread arms, as if seeking for its mate, the sense within me had found its air, and breathed with a gasp of joy. For the Bird of Paradise seemed to be a beautiful girl, very slender, and so light that she rose and fell, as it were, on the wings of the music, which followed and wafted her on, backwards and forwards, floating and sinking, just as the spring wind carries the birds that have flown too low in my garden. There was nothing sudden or unexpected about the dance at first. The Bird of Paradise sunned itself in the light; then another, its mate, came gliding towards it, and there were two of them, darting, swaying, whirling hither and thither across the dark stretch which in some way gave the impression of being empty air; faster and faster the quick, darting movements came; more rapidly the draperies' soft floating reds and golds were blown in ever-recurring twists and folds round the slight figures; then the music died, and the dancers knelt with their heads low on the ground in homage to the Emperor, who smiled, and said a word of precious praise, sure to be treasured for a lifetime.

There was a pause, and I awoke from the kind of trance that had fallen on me, and looked round slowly, trying to remember where I was. A Japanese friend leaned forward from behind me, and began to tell me some more of the fairy tale. These were not girls, but boys; all the nō at Court are performed by men alone. Yes, doubtless they were not bad; indeed, there should be none better, since for eight hundred years the same family had always provided the Emperor's dancers, and were trained to these exercises from father to son, father to son. But see, the new dance is beginning, a martial measure. Those men are dressed in armour; the music is harsh and loud; they wheel and turn, they retreat and advance; the light strikes on cold pale faces and gleaming eyes, on helmets towering with some dragon crest, on gloved hands grasping a spear, on mystic fell of fox or badger wrapped for a charm round the up-curved sword-sheath. And my obedient spirit follows on, to dreamland, fairyland — to a new and yet old country of my thoughts, where these strange rhythms, the triumphant measures, have meant more to me than I can remember to-day. I cannot understand the little buzz of talk which breaks out after each performance, as if those around me were glad to warp back, like a spent bowstring, to the common lines of life. I can sympathise with the Emperor, whose face lights up, whose eyes dilate, as he watches the mysterious *nō*, he has ceased to talk, and sits in silence, waiting for the next lifting of that curtain of the dreamland of history.

MY SILVER CRANE

Ah! this is the Indian music — a strong, many-throated strain, with tender intervals and pauses and swelling notes of sober joy. Who knows what voices gave it birth four thousand generations back in the country over the sea? Strange, indeed, are the dresses of the dancers now, six tall men, straight as palms, lithe as the spear cut from the young bamboo, with close-shod feet, and close-wrapped sleeves that show every turn of the fine wrist as it darts or draws back the spear that compels the submission of enemies. Are the men six, or one, I wonder? Faultlessly matched in height and figure, they go through their rapid evolutions with such precision that every streamer and end of drapery makes the same curl on the air at the same moment. Their dress seems like a close-clinging tunic and under-robe of some soft silk tissue, in which threads of red and gold are closely intermingled, so that the folds which seemed red in the shadow break in dusky gold where the light falls on them. But the whole costume is composed of ribbonlike bands of material, which hang close when the wearer is in repose, but shake and part and float on the wind of his motion; and as the movement swings on in a triumphant step, these bands fly aside, all at the same instant, at the same angle, and reveal gleams of splendid armour beneath — breastplates where the light twinkles on gold and lacquer, arms where a sleeve of mail clings to the supple muscles — show the sword-hilt on the hip, and a long straight blade hanging by the swift straight limbs. Six great spears dart upright, cross their points, are laid out in a square on the cloth while the dancers thread quick steps across and across them; and at last, as the music screams for victory, the men fall back, each in his place, stretched almost on the ground, his head by the spear's head, his feet at the spear's foot; they hang for an instant, as if in the act of falling still, and at a sudden note spring to their feet with their draperies whirling behind them, they drop the spear-points in low obeisance towards the Emperor, their heads touch the ground in uniform homage, and they are gone; the screens have closed behind them. See, the royalties are moving; they pass down the lines, smiling a kind good-night to all. The ninth day of the third month of the twenty-seventh year of Meiji, the Period of Enlightened Peace, is over, and the curtain of To-day has fallen, grey and tangible, over the dreamy splendours of the Past.

BY THE SAME AUTHOR

PALLADIA

A NOVEL

12mo.   Cloth. $1.25

"A novel of the good old-time size, such as always gives the genuine story-reader a sense of having a full meal set before his mental appetite. . . . There is nothing like plagiarism or inspiration at second-hand about the story, and yet something in the atmosphere reminds the reader of the breezy regions in which Mr. Hope loves to revel." — *Boston Transcript.*

"This story is a most complicated (and be it said fascinating) mixture of orient and occident. Corinthian craft and German court etiquette, hearts veined with wild gypsy blood beating in tune with the self-repressed, calm blood of British propriety." — *Milwaukee Sentinel.*

"A very ingenious and exciting story of adventure, incident, and romance."
— *The Outlook.*

THE BROWN AMBASSADOR
A Story of the Three Days' Moon

12mo.   Cloth. $1.25

"The story is told with a sprightliness that is likely to insure for it, and for its winning characters, a warm place in the hearts of youthful readers."
— *Bookman.*

"This story is well told, and the interest is sustained in a way which will prove entertaining to the young reader." — *Chicago Evening Post.*

"A book of no small fascination. . . . Those who, their curiosity roused by the title, dip into the book, may be sure, if they are the right kind of people, of reading it through with pleasure and finishing it with regret." — *Critic.*

"The threads of fairy fable and ordinary child life are very skilfully entwined, and the result is a most amusing and entertaining fiction."
— *Churchman.*

THE MACMILLAN COMPANY
66 FIFTH AVENUE, NEW YORK

www.ingramcontent.com/pod-product-compliance
Lightning Source LLC
Chambersburg PA
CBHW030424300426
44112CB00009B/844

www.ingramcontent.com/pod-product-compliance
Lightning Source LLC
Chambersburg PA
CBHW030424300426
44112CB00009B/844